IRON EYES

My Life as a Hollywood Indian

IRON EYES

My Life as a Hollywood Indian

by

IRON EYES CODY

as told to

COLLIN PERRY

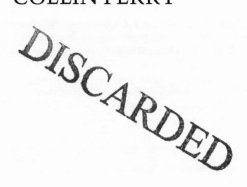

NEW YORK   EVEREST HOUSE   PUBLISHERS

LIBRARY OF CONRESS CATALOGING IN PUBLICATION DATA:

Cody, Iron Eyes, 1907–
   Iron Eyes, my life as a Hollywood Indian.

   Includes index.
   1. Cody, Iron Eyes, 1907– . 2. Moving-picture
actors and actressess—United States—Biography.
3. Indians of North America—Biography.   I. Perry,
Collin.   II. Title.
PN2287.C555A34   1982   791.43'028'0924   B   81-19632
ISBN 0-89696-111-7   AACR2

TO BIRDIE

&

to my grandson

IRON CHEBON CODY

VVVVVVVVVVVVVVVVVVVVVVVVVVVVVVVV

PROLOGUE

THE HOUSE IS an ordinary one by Los Angeles standards. A modest, one-story white stucco is surrounded by the obligatory little lawn and cyclone fence, all nestled on a hill along Griffith Park Boulevard in northern Hollywood. It is a simple house, the only extravagance being the custom-made late-model white Cadillac parked in the drive.

I am greeted at the aluminum storm door by a tall man wearing long, black braids, a loud shirt, and hand-beaded moccasins made from what looks like an old pair of Hush Puppies. His sad, dignified face, deeply etched with age-lines, is instantly recognizable as the haunting one with a single tear in those famous ads for the environment. I shake hands with Iron Eyes Cody, the lines in his face almost disappearing as he breaks into a boyish grin. "I'm amazed you found this place. You must have an Indian's sense of direction."

I don't tell him I had gotten lost a good five times trying to thread my way through the maze of winding Hollywood roads.

I'm led into a huge room with beautifully woven Indian blankets hung over the windows for drapes. It is dark and cool. The few pieces of furniture are old, somewhat tattered, resting near the walls as if in retirement and making way for real buffalo skin rugs scattered in the open space. An enormous color TV stands in the middle of the room. Every square inch of wall space is taken up with paintings by famous Western artists, movie stills, antique guns actually used by warriors of the Great Plains over 100 years ago, hand-made bows and arrows, headdresses, horns and antlers of various animals, and dozens of plaques and trophies. On the floor along the walls is stack after stack of movie stills, dog-eared scripts, books, magazines, and fan mail. There are piles of fan mail.

We sit drinking beer in a corner of the room after some dusty

[9]

papers are removed from two creaking lounge chairs, and talk. Or rather Iron Eyes talks and I listen. He says it's been a long day, that he'd run around from one charity concern to another before making it to the studio. It began with an old friend who'd become a drunk stopping by and hitting him up for thirty dollars to "buy a new shirt."

"I knew he wouldn't buy no shirt if I let him loose with that money, so I went with him and bought a shirt and a pair of shoes. Then I gave him money for whiskey."

Iron Eyes then tells a story about how Errol Flynn one day accidentally shot him in the back while fooling around on the set drunk. "Some people just get mean and careless when they're drinking. I don't know why, but it seems especially true with Indians. Myself, I get meaner than hell." We laugh when, after he takes a big slug of beer, I ask if he thinks I'll be getting out of his place with my hair intact.

It grows late too quickly. As he drinks more beer, Iron Eyes confines his "meanness" to merely becoming more talkative and interesting. I am offered a place to sleep, which I happily accept. He leaves the room and reappears with what looks like an oversized Halloween gorilla costume and a pillow.

"Here," he says with cheerful hospitality, indicating where I'm to sleep by waving the huge buffalo robe coat towards the buffalo rugs on the floor. "This should keep you warm enough." He dumps what must be forty pounds of three-inch-thick hide in my lap. "Feel free to watch television," he says before closing his bedroom door.

I silently thank God for the four or five beers in my veins and, with a shrug, take off my clothes, sit on the floor, and slide into my primitive bed. It smells a little gamey but is comfortable, somehow reassuring. The faint moonlight wedging itself between the cracks in the blankets hanging on the windows gives an eerie, lifelike luminescence to the ancient ornaments on the walls. Before falling asleep I hear the sound of Indian chanting coming from Iron Eyes' room. *Hey*-yeh-yeh-yeh, *Hey*-yeh-yeh. Must be a prayer, I think, and drift off into boyhood dreams filled with adventures unknown to my conscious life.

I wake to the whistle of water boiling in the kitchen. It is still dark and my watch says 5:30 A.M. In troops Iron Eyes with a cup of foamy Nescafé and a sweet roll.

"Good morning!" he booms, placing my breakfast on the floor beside me. He's wearing Adidas running shoes, khakis, and another incredibly loud shirt. His face is flushed with exercise. "I just ran a few miles up in the hills. Have some coffee and let's get started," he says, rubbing his hands together. "I'm giving a speech before the county supervisors at eleven."

Groping for my pants I mutter to myself that this man can't be over seventy years old. But he must be at least that old. I gulp coffee and, between mouthfuls of roll, ask if he always gets up this late, mentioning that I've been wide awake for an hour waiting patiently for him to drag himself out of bed. He smiles, saying he'll make a good Injun out of me yet. We seat ourselves in our chairs, I flick on a tape recorder and pull out my notebook.

"Okay, Iron Eyes, let's begin at the beginning. Tell it in your own words."

COLLIN PERRY
May 1981

IRON EYES

My Life as a Hollywood Indian

1

OH JEE-E-E-SUS it's cold," groaned the tall, skinny young man dressed in nothing but a loincloth. With his thin arms outstretched, he resembled the top part of a totem pole.

Make-up time on location, 7 A.M., about sixty degrees. It was 1925, I was eighteen years old and under contract to Paramount as "technical advisor." This semi-naked young man's temperature was being dropped with a kind of reddish-brown paint I was spraying on him called *bole armenia*. The studios used it to make white actors look like Indians. It was also used to make light-skinned Indians look more like "real" Indians. He was hopping from foot to foot, slapping his long arms around his thin chest trying to keep warm. With his angular frame and bright blue eyes, I thought he cut the silliest figure of a redskin I'd ever seen. Well, maybe next to some of the *over*weight white guys we used to dress up as Indians. Cecil B. DeMille used to call them "Red Beer Bellies."

"You're supposed to be the technical advisor for this here picture, aren't you?" he managed between shivers. "How about finding me a buffalo robe coat or something. I'm colder than hell."

"Sorry," I said, not too successfully holding back a giggle. "You know Mr. Sykes wants all of you to play it stripped."

"Well," he mumbled, head down and glancing up with his eyelids fluttering—nervous gestures which were to later endear him to half the world. "Well, seems as though a fellow ought to be kept from freezing to death."

Everybody on the set got a good laugh out of him in that getup, I can tell you. But then, after this shy, twenty-four-year-old named Frank James Cooper got through stunt-falling off a fifteen-foot cliff into a rope net for an action scene with 500 other "Indians," and after a few months of riding, shooting, falling, and similar stunts playing both good guys and bad guys, he went on to become Gary

Cooper. Nobody snickered again. More about Coop later on in the book.

Coop became my good friend and I knew him for the thirty-five years he reigned with his fellow kings out here in Tinsel Land. In fact, I've been personally close to many of the Hollywood greats. For some reason people who at the snap of their fingers could make or break careers often confided in me all their problems, desires, (often acting out the latter) and fears (in Hollywood, that's with a capital "F"). A real insider's life, you might think. An enviable one. The Great Spirit was beaming down his benevolence full blast on this Injun.

Well, okay. I've been lucky. Just wandered off the reservation into fame and fortune (don't I wish!). But looking back over it all I feel I didn't live so much the insider's life as one who spent his time looking at it from a particular vantage point on the outside. I've lived this double life, somewhere between white civilization and my Indian heritage. Never felt completely comfortable with one or the other, to be honest. And since my "role" has never been clearly defined, I've also spent a good deal of time just looking at myself, trying to figure out who I am. No better way of getting to know yourself and others, this being on the outside.

I don't think my father, Thomas Longplume Cody, ever really knew himself. Actually, his name was "Codey," accent on the second syllable. It was changed, or transformed, when he toured with his brother throughout America and Europe with "the greatest one-man tableau that ever lived," Buffalo Bill Cody. Guess they figured one Cody wasn't enough, and that shouldn't come as any surprise as Buffalo Bill made claim to being an expert Indian fighter, guide, lover, and all around American hero. What he was, of course, was a dandified egomaniac blowhard and genius showman. My father told me Buffalo Bill could tell the damnedest stories you ever heard, entertaining his troups of performers for hours with Old West blood and guts make-believe. He was admired by all, including the hundreds of Indians he took along on tour. Indians love a man who can tell good stories and every tribe has its favorite yarn spinners.

You may know that Chief Sitting Bull toured with Buffalo Bill for a few seasons. My father got to know the old chief pretty well, as

I came to know his son, John Sitting Bull. Buffalo Bill claimed he tried to save Chief Sitting Bull's life when it was rumored the chief had been stirring up trouble among the Sioux with the "Ghost Dance." The "dance" was just a sad, harmless religion, started up after the Indians' defeat, that promised one day the white man would disappear and the buffalo return. Devotees also thought that if they wore a special Ghost Dance shirt, it would protect them from white men's bullets. The army didn't like this religion too much, not feeling comfortable with the notion of the white folks disappearing. They sent the Indian police around to gather up Sitting Bull and bring him in. Buffalo Bill supposedly tried beating them to the chief to give warning, but was somehow tricked and "took the wrong road." The Indian police, wearing uniforms and badges, made it to Bull's cabin first. A scuffle ensued. One of the police shot Sitting Bull, and the great medicine man who led the Sioux nation at Little Big Horn against Custer fell dead.

My father was an expert horseman and used to trick ride for Buffalo Bill. Alongside him were about 650 other Indians, Cossacks, Bengal Lancers, gypsies, and other colorful "Wild West" types. The real genius behind Buffalo Bill, though, was his public relations man, Sherm Canfield. He's the one who spread around all the stories about what an incredible shot Bill was and how many Indians he'd scalped single-handedly. Once, on tour in London, he slipped up, though. As Bill rode into the arena all decked out in his spangled, glittering Wild West outfit, his long, elegant, silver hair brushed back, and sitting astride a magnificent white stallion, old Sherm intoned: "Ladies and Gentlemen, boys and girls, Colonel William F. Cody—Buffalo Bill Cody—will now shoot the glass balls off his horse."

The Victorian ladies and gentlemen of old London Town were not amused.

To get a better idea who my father was, we should go back a few generations. I have a great-great-grandfather who was among the Cherokees herded up out of the Southeast and driven like cattle to Indian territory in western Arkansas. This "distasteful" work was given to General Winfield Scott, as he stated in his memoirs. He knew that many of these Cherokees were more civilized than the whites moving in to replace them. But, what the hell, duty was

[17]

duty, and he had his marching orders from President Andrew Jackson himself. With the soldiers using bayonets to prod along the stragglers—some of them pregnant women—they eventually made the journey. It's estimated some 4,000 of the 15,000 Indians perished along route.

Some of the Indians, including my relatives, pushed further West, on into Oklahoma territory. Then my grandfather, Randolf Abshire Cody, was born. It's important to understand that these Eastern Indians were already well assimilated into European civilization, mixing their own culture with that of the white man. Some Cherokees were prominent businessmen and farmers, living in two-story, cantilevered Georgia mansions, complete with black slaves. When the Civil War broke out, Randolf joined up with the Confederates. He became a guerrilla fighter, intending to terrify the North through acts of sheer brutality and ruthlessness. They called themselves the Quantrill Raiders. Organized by William Quantrill, they charged back and forth through Kansas and Missouri, burning whole towns and killing everything that moved.

I don't imagine this sort of life—the life of a professional killer—was easy to give up. When the fighting stopped, Randolf turned his now hardened soul to the business of crime. He became a first-rate highwayman, holding up stagecoaches, banks—any place where there was loot. He also stole horses whenever he got the chance. Like every outlaw, he had his vanity. Part of the allure of a life of crime was the attention you were bound to get in the papers—in fact, I came to know a few famous outlaws myself, as I'll tell you later, and each one without exception was a headline hunter. Anyway, Randolf had a problem. According to my father, he and his gang had no great ambitions. They used to take only enough money from each bank to get along for a while. And, miraculously, they never killed anybody. No other self-respecting bandit charged out of a bank without leaving a few tellers on the floor riddled with bullet holes, right? They had big competition for space in the papers with the likes of Jesse James and Charlie Pierce and Tom Horn, killers all. And while Randolf came up with a nice, catchy name for himself, "Valentine," he didn't do too well for the gang as a whole, which he called "The Riders." "Valentine and the Riders." Sounds more like a rock'n'roll group than a bunch of desperadoes. There were colorful characters in the group: four other Indians who wore black Mexican felt sombreros with silver trim and cartridge bandaleeros crisscrossed on their chests, plus a Black man named "Two Bits" who acquired his title playing piano for that sum in bars and whorehouses. But as a group, they just didn't make it. They got caught a lot, and Randolf spent two years in jail till he gave up outlawing altogether. He went back to Oklahoma and, with some of those horses he had stolen, set himself up in the horse ranching business. He passed this business on to my father.

Impatient, ruthless, and intelligent, my old man wasn't about to settle into horse raising in any ordinary fashion. Like his father, Randolf, he also became a horse thief. And he wasn't going to be just your usual kind of horse thief, winding up dangling at the end of a noose. Like I say, he was smart and without scruples. What he did was become a phoney veterinarian.

The way it worked was this. People would bring him their sick horses—maybe a shoulder rubbed raw and infected from pulling the plow all day. He'd proceed to cut the sore section open and bleed it to drain any infection. Then in two or three days he'd take a piece of ordinary bluestone (a kind of sandstone often used in roadbuilding) and stick it in the wound. Bluestone applied like that is an antiseptic, all right, but it burns and eats away everything—germs, flesh, even bone. He'd leave it in till it created a good size hole, then take out the bluestone and sew the wound back up again.

The unsuspecting farmer would come back for his animal and see the infection gone but, feeling the stitches, would ask about the hollow space under the hide.

"Oh, he's cured all right," my father'd say, "but had to do a lot a cuttin'. 'Fraid he'll never pull a plow again."

"Iszat so?" The farmer would look thoughtful. "You interested in maybe takin' her off my hands?"

"Mmmm, maybe, maybe."

"How much you give me for her?"

Now this horse would still be worth seventy-five or eighty dollars because, although it was true you'd never pull a plow with it again, it would still make a decent saddle mount—if, that is, you knew—as my father did—how to graft skin.

"Tell you what. Give you ten dollars. Cash."

"But Dad, that horse is—," I would interrupt.

"Shut up! Yeah, she ain't worth much except what the glue factory'll pay. The hair won't grow back and you can't even ride her now. Give you ten," and he'd start taking ten dollars out of his wallet. The farmers usually felt they had no choice.

So my father would then proceed to open up the now almost "healed" hole, graft skin in there, and within a couple of weeks when the coat would begin growing back he'd be riding around in town on that horse drunk as hell. My mother would often have to come and get him. It embarrassed me deeply to have to help drag my own father off his horse and carry him into the house.

I think he started drinking when he was about twenty-seven or twenty-eight, about the time he got into the "vet" business. He'd say to me, over and over, "Oskie [I got my name Iron Eyes later], don't *ever* drink. Now here's a dollar. Run out and get me a bottle of whiskey."

Guess he was using himself as a sort of living example of what can happen to you if you stray too far off Sober Road. Because you never quite knew what to expect from him when he was drinking, he scared the hell out of me. Maybe he scared a lot of people for much the same reason, because he managed to command a good deal of respect in the community. When he wasn't hitting the sauce, he was even charming in a beast-calmed-by-music sort of way. Being an acknowledged expert on Indian culture—and lacing his native history with juicy stories about Buffalo Bill or the Plains Wars—he was often invited to community functions to give lectures. While he was touring with Bill Cody, he collected Indian artifacts, bought them up by the truck load. He had, in fact, the largest private collection of Indian cultural objects in the world— at that time it may have been the biggest in the world, public or private. It included that buffalo horn headdress worn by Sitting Bull, the complete white buckskin outfit of Chief Joseph of the Nez Percé, a sixteen-shot Winchester rifle used by an Arapahoe warrior in the Little Big Horn Battle, and thousands of other fine things. He would often take some of this stuff along when he made his presentations, giving dramatic illustration to his stories. Folks seemed to warm up to the story about the Winchester in particular. My father often showed up at these gatherings half crocked, but he wasn't the type to get sloppy drunk and slur his words or stagger about. In fact, no matter how much he managed to put away before, the excitement of the crowd always stimulated him, making his voice firm and resolute, his eyes glittery:

". . . and that's how the Sioux and Cheyenne whipped Custer's behind at the Little Big Horn. And this, ladies and gents, is an actual rifle used by an Arapahoe in that great fight. You'll notice the stains on the rifle butt. This is blood, no doubt, smeared on during hand-to-hand fighting just before the end, when all Custer and his men had left was rocks and such. Five years after the battle, this gun was passed into the hands of a Navaho feller I met in jail, who used it to kill an Indian agent who was raping his wife . . ."

That sort of thing. He could really keep 'em hanging with stories like that, including me. Each time he told it, it was different, so he never was boring to himself. But when he wasn't lecturing and he was drunk, he was usually mean—and even dangerous. Once he even almost tried to kill me.

My older brother, J. W. Silvermoon Cody, and I were out by the corral one day and there was this cow jumping around and acting crazy, so my father told me to rope and bring her in. Then he went somewhere to lie down and sleep off the afternoon drinking.

I must have been less than ten at this time and couldn't handle a rope like my brother, so I just grabbed the damned animal by the head and my brother roped her. Then he said, "Hey, let's have some fun with this cow."

"Wha'dya mean 'fun?'"

His eyes were gleaming with mischief. "I mean let's play cowboy! I'll hold her and you get on and ride."

I was game, and dumb enough. Climbing aboard, the cow immediately started bucking, mooing, kicking, and running around, my brother laughing till I thought he'd burst. Suddenly the cow turned mean, threw me off with one violent lurch, and, as I grabbed on the rope with my brother, began dragging us both all over the place. Finally we slowed her up enough to tie her to a tree, but by this time the dumb beast was so hysterical she went round and round, round and round with us just standing there watching helplessly. She ended up choking herself to death.

By this time my father had awakened, came over to the scene of the crime and in a cold, flat voice asked what had happened.

"Well," began my brother nervously, "see, we were just having a little fun with the, uh, cow there and suddenly she got crazy and ran around the tree and we couldn't do nothing 'cause she'd a taken both our arms off and—"

That was all the old man had to hear before taking up a piece of that rope and whipping the hell out of both of us right there on the spot. I've got a pretty short fuse myself, though. When he was through taking my hide off I choked back the tears and blurted something like, "You ever lay a hand on me again I'll kill you!"

He just looked at me with a face blank and inexpressive as a lizard, his eyes yellow and snake-like. He told me to step into the barn for a minute, that he wanted to "talk." I followed him, so scared my crotch itched fiercly but my pride kept me from backing down.

We got into the barn and he pulled out this huge pistol he always kept strapped in his belt. He pointed it right at my gut. His voice had not the slightest trace of emotion when he snarled in slow, deliberate tones, "I've shot men for less than what you just said to me. You know what I think? You must be lookin' to get yourself killed, boy."

"Okay, so go ahead and shoot," I managed, but a tear edged its way out and trickled down my cheek.

For a minute I was sure he'd actually pull the trigger. My knees almost buckled. But his eyes blinked as though he were coming out of some kind of trance and his face became human again, like it was when he wasn't drinking. His hand shaking, he lowered the gun. He just continued standing there, looking down and shaking his head, as I slipped past him and ran out the door.

I was the only "real" child of my parents—the other eight brothers and sisters being either adopted or from some "previous engagement." My mother's name was Frances. She was short, round-faced, always cheerful, and very strong—typical Cree Indian. She was strict with us in the sense of observing customs and propriety while my father didn't give a damn. She was rock steady and a firm disciplinarian. She was the foundation of the family with a heart as big as the prairie—which is why I suppose she would take in practically any kid without a regular home. She was our comfort, our refuge from the old man when he was in one of his drunken, Jekyll-and-Hyde-like rages.

But as you might expect, there were times when she couldn't take it anymore and would grab up us all and just take off, hiding from him for a while. We must have slipped around to half a dozen towns in Oklahoma and Texas for months before he'd catch up with us and promise to stop drinking. He would be his sweet and charming self when he wanted something desperate enough. They'd be together for a while before he'd take to the bottle again and start the whole cycle over.

When we weren't hiding bottles of cheap whiskey from my father—or hiding ourselves from him—we had a pretty good time of it, though. Our house was big enough for the ten of us, including my now-tamed grandfather. It was furnished in what I guess you'd characterize as "Western" style with a lot of rough but comfortable furniture and antlers and guns on the wall, things like that. We had a big fireplace and would all sit around it at night singing Indian songs and telling scary stories. There's nobody that likes his scary stories more than an Indian. After we'd get through raising each other's hair a few inches and all the older folks had gone to bed, somebody would always dare one of us to go down the basement stairs with all the lights off. And if you were brave enough, of course, there'd be that same somebody there waiting for you, making groaning noises of an evil Indian spirit, the Wicheebooboo. We had some wonderful times, scaring each other like that.

When my father wasn't drinking, he truly enjoyed spending time with his children. He really knew horses, of course, and taught me to ride well as well as to hunt and fish. Going with him on his lectures, I learned a lot about Indian culture, and no matter what we were doing he'd always take a moment to explain how a particular tribe would go about doing this or that. He taught me Indian sign language and to speak enough words of five different dialects to get by on: Cherokee, Navaho, Seneca, Delaware, Sioux. I even learned how to sing and dance from my father.

But when he was drunk, that was another story. I'm sure he'd have just as soon dropped me off a cliff somewhere. I've never understood it, but he hated himself. And since I was his only real child, when he was drunk there must have been too much in me that reminded him of himself.

The year when I was about twelve, I was working on my father's ranch. One day two men dressed like they were about to take an African safari pulled up to our front door in a shiny new sedan. I stood by my father as they explained they were in the motion picture business, an outfit called Famous Players Lasky. They were location people, or second unit directors, scouting around our area in Oklahoma looking for a good-sized cornfield to stage a scene for a picture called *Back to God's Country*. My father, suspicious as usual, asked them how in the hell out of the entire state of Oklahoma they stumbled across his little ranch. He had a cornfield, sure, but his main concern was horses. I think he thought they were some kind of police. They said they needed horses, too—and Indians. People in town told them Tom Cody was an expert on Indian culture and had many friends. He'd fit the bill perfectly, and if he was interested he'd be paid one hundred dollars, in advance, above any expenses. I'm sure my father at this point thought these guys were crazy to offer that kind of money to "borrow" his ranch, but he took an interest.

"What kind of expenses?" he asked. One of the men tipped back his sporty-looking hat, smiled, and put his hands in his pockets.

"Well, for starters, we'd like to buy up all the corn in your cornfield."

"My own price?"

"Whatever you say—within reason, of course."

My father looked at me and allowed himself a little snicker.

"Of course," he said. "Within reason."

That's how I first came into contact with movie people. My father looked upon this whole thing as a business arrangement—he couldn't have cared less who was borrowing his ranch for a few days, at least at the outset. Me? I thought it was great! If the two exotic-looking characters that handed over a crisp one-hundred-dollar bill to my father after shaking hands on the deal were any example, why, there was no telling what adventures were in store for us. The day the crew was to arrive, I was right there at the train station in town eager to greet them.

Famous Players Lasky had given over an entire train to this production. This movie wasn't to be any cheap, two-reel quickie. Behind the passenger cars was one boxcar after another filled with the most fantastic junk I'd ever seen. There were huge lights and miles of cable wound on giant spools, black boxes filled with mysterious contrivances, trunks, boxes, carts. Cars were packed with antique-looking furniture and other props. Enough stuff to fill an entire house was being systematically stacked beside the tracks. A perfect replica of a covered wagon was wheeled out of the side of another car. Everywhere, workers and technicians scurried about, yelling orders at each other and carrying things. One of them had a clipboard. Soon, everything was piled onto horse-drawn wagons rented from local farmers, and, with three personnel cars leading the way, they were off! I rode happily on the tail of one of the wagons, waving to a crowd of at least half of the people in town that started following us along the twenty-mile dirt road to our ranch.

Back to God's Country was a silent film, of course, this being long before talking pictures. It was directed by Irvin Willit, a dapper, extremely good-looking man with a commanding presence, and it starred Richard Barthelmess, a star of the post-war years and early twenties. It was a Civil War epic, and the scenes they were shooting on our ranch had to do with escaped war prisoners hiding out in a cornfield. They were captured (I'm not sure which side—the North or the South—was doing the hiding) and held in a stockade. There were also a lot of interior shots done inside our house, but as I never saw the movie in its completed form I can't remember what they were.

As soon as the crew arrived, they began the work of transforming our ranch into a movie set. Out went our furniture, in went the antique chairs, tables, pictures, and rugs. The facade of a stockade was erected in a few hours, together with a couple of other buildings. They ran wires all over, put these pipes up overhead at various points (a sprinkling system to simulate rain). Director Willit walked about, sighting up and down the field of corn through a window-like frame he made with his hands. He had his cap on backwards, and wore a nicely tailored tweed jacket, an open-collared shirt, and baggy, casual slacks. My father thought he was crazy, too.

[25]

"We need some trees, here," said Willit. "Have to get some trees."

My father took a sip from the pint bottle he carried in his hip pocket.

"Now wait a minute, Mr. Willert. First, I thought you folks were just gonna come here and use a cornfield for a few days. Then you start taking my house apart and building all these foolish things. Now you say you're gonna bring in some trees? This don't seem right to me somehow."

Willit regarded my father with the thin smile of one used to dealing with men of unstable temperament. He put his hand on his shoulder.

"Mr. Cody," he said soothingly, "I promise you, personally, that everything will be back to normal when we're through, everything perfect, just as it was. I can also assure you there's a reason for all we are doing here, although it may seem a bit strange. So, what did you say you wanted to charge for the corn?"

"The corn? Oh, yeah. Oh, say, fifty dollars should do her."

"Fifty dollars. Right. By the way," he said, winking, "it's Willit, not Willert."

Quite a smoothie. I was to meet a lot of them in Hollywood.

Willit did bring in some trees. Had them cut in a nearby forest, hauled up to the set, and planted right where he wanted to lend more composition to his scenes. When the leaves on the trees started browning, he had them spray-painted with green paint, believe it or not. Even I could see something screwy here.

"Mr. Willit, why do you have to paint the trees green in a movie without any color?"

"Because, son," he offered, "they have to *look* as if they were green. Brown doesn't look like green in black and white." I pondered this and decided that Hollywood people could do anything.

With the set ready, they started shooting. The cameraman had his cap on backwards, too, and now I knew why—it was for sighting through the camera. But the biggest difference in the way a film was directed in those days was that there was a lot of noise going on around the filming. With no sound, the director walked about yelling orders and giving encouragement, refereeing fights, mimicking facial expressions or a gesture he might want, all with the camera humming away, oblivious to the racket of the crew hauling things around, people talking, laughing, whatever. There wasn't any need for, "Okay, quiet on the set!"

Willit used the cornfield for a number of scenes. The only trouble was that at the end of each day, it was trampled down by the horses galloping back and forth. What to do? Obviously it would have to be re-planted each morning with fresh corn stalks. The entire field. There were on any given day about a hundred people from at least fifty miles in all directions from the ranch, standing around watching the movie makers. They were corralled and cordoned off to keep them out of the way. Willit picked up his megaphone and said he'd offer anyone fifty dollars who would let the film crew tear up their corn, bring it up to our place, and re-plant it each morning. He had about one hundred volunteers. So that's what he did, re-planted the whole goddamned cornfield each day so it could be realistically trampled anew.

In one scene they needed a few Indian kids sitting by a stockade while soldiers on horseback jumped it. I was one of them. There was some risk, of course, and after a take (they rarely took more than one in those days) Willit said to my father, "Hey, you know that kid's pretty brave. Let's see what else he can do." He used me in various bits for about ten days—talking to the prisoners when they were caught, running under fences when horses rode by, that sort of thing. My big scene came when he needed some dancing Indian kids. I taught them some fast-stepping, Oklahoma-style stuff that apparently impressed him. We got to play a pretty decent-sized part.

I suppose everybody even remotely connected with the entertainment business—and this was fairly remote, I know—has something happen, some big part in a high school play or maybe making his friends laugh with his own jokes, something that injects the damned occupation directly into the bloodstream, hooking you for life. Maybe there's something of the exhibitionist in all of us, from superstars to cost accountants. Anyway, I was now thoroughly hooked and fancied myself in show business. I was going to be a big shot film star for the major studios. In *Hollywood!*

And my father? Shooting was completed in two weeks, and after putting the ranch back together—save for one of the painted trees left standing as a memento—Willit paid my father. He no longer thought the film industry was crazy. And Willit, since his specialty was Westerns, saw in Tom Cody a valuable asset.

"Why don't you come to Hollywood, Tom? I could use a man like you. Hell, you could earn a hundred dollars a day. And if you come, bring those two boys along. Plenty of work for them, too."

Actually the real deciding factor came during the following year. My father was arrested five times. The "horse vet" business was catching up with him. Each time he was acquitted for lack of evidence, but it appeared likely they'd nab him eventually. Besides, as word got around, business fell off. Moreover, my mother threatened to tell the judge of his abuses and have him thrown out, rather than she leave him. All considered, it was a good time to go into the movie business. Not long after my twelfth birthday, I found myself on the train sitting next to my father and brother, headed West for Hollywood.

VVVVVVVVVVVVVVVVVVVVVVVVVVVVV

2

Hey, what the hell you doing up there?" A bicycle cop was glaring at me from thirty feet below my perch in a palm tree.

"I never saw a tree like this before," I said. "Just wanted to see what it was like climbing one without any branches."

"Well, now see what it's like getting down from one without any branches before you fall and kill yourself!"

That was one of the first things I did when we came out here—climb up one of the palms on Hollywood Boulevard. We had ourselves settled into a big house with a huge, barn-like garage at 6500 Sunset Boulevard. It was right next to the Hollywood Athletic Club, where we would go and work out. Later, we ran laps and shot basketballs with the likes of Clark Gable, Cary Grant, Buster Crabbe, and Johnny Weissmuller, but this was before their time. My father looked up Irvin Willit, and the director kept his word, but only after a considerable amount of haggling over salary. The first movie in Hollywood we all worked on together was called *North of 36*—meaning, for mysterious reasons, somewhere in Kansas. My father was what they call the "technical advisor," responsible for properly outfitting the Indians, having them use the right dances, sign language, smoke signals, and so on. My brother went out and hired the Indians—including making trips to local reservations. (It was much later that we started dressing up whites to play minor Indian roles.) I went to school when I could and played kid-Indian bit parts in films. About the only thing I can remember about *North of 36* was this terrific cattle stampede which destroyed a whole town. Of course the town was all a facade and, true to form for the early Westerns, one entire structure fell down completely as the cattle came charging by. People watching the movie may have known they built those old frontier towns a little on the flimsy side, but the whole building? Whoosh, just like that? The scene wasn't about to be shot over, as the cattle were on loan for only a day from a local rancher. And the set was now half destroyed, so that was that.

We converted our barn to start housing our growing collection of Indian artifacts and outfits. At this time it came to about 100 hand-stitched buckskins, 250 breech cloths, another 250 moccasins, and about fifty-five genuine eagle feather war bonnets. We had hundreds of bows and arrows, enough to outfit an entire army. We had tons of beadwork and pottery, baskets, artwork, drawings, and over 100 tepees. We were in business. Much of this stuff is still being loaned out to the major studios today, and when I die I'm donating it to various Indian museums. Needless to say, it's priceless.

It was still long before they replaced most of those beautiful Hollywood Boulevard palm trees with neon light poles, before the police bicycles were exchanged for patrol cars. D. W. Griffith had already filmed his controversial masterpiece, *Birth of a Nation*, some scenes of which were shot right up the street from where I now live, along Griffith Park. I did, in fact, appear in a couple of early Griffith two-reelers that did a lot to upgrade the Indian image: *The Massacre* and *Fighting Blood*.

These are creaking antiques, primitive by today's standards, of course. Yet they were made years after the first Western was filmed. Nobody's too sure when that was, exactly, but back before the turn of the century people stood around in "mustoscope parlors," peering into peepholes at the flickering image of stagecoach robberies or Indians scalping settlers. Some claim the first movie ever to have a beginning-to-end story line, a plot, was Edwin S. Porter's *The Great Train Robbery*, done in 1903. In fact, there are film makers who think this picture is the bible of American movies. Personally, I think it's a little overrated. It was shot mostly in New Jersey, and in one scene that was supposed to be taking place out in the Wild West of a hundred years ago, you can see a telltale section of a sewage drainage pipe. What you probably couldn't make out was one bit player named G. M. Anderson. Anderson had first convinced director Edwin S. Porter that he could ride horses like a Texas Ranger, and was hired to play one of the bandits in *The Great Train Robbery*. Actually he'd never been on a horse in his life, and after being tossed into the New Jersey "sagebrush" a few times, was demoted to the role of an extra. But as *The Great Train Robbery* went on to tremendous success, Anderson decided the movie business was for him. He moved to the then film capital of the world, Chicago, and found work directing for a man named Colonel William Selig. The movies he made for Selig's outfit didn't do too well—probably too imitative of *The Great Train Robbery*—so Anderson looked up an old friend named George Spool, and the two of them headed out to Niles, California in 1908. They started their own company, "Essanay," using the initials "S" and "A" of the two founders.

Now this was a big move for American Western movie making. Realistic location shooting had only been tried sporadically—by Anderson, in fact—but now the film makers were out in the real West where the sun shone all the time and there was seldom a discouraging cloud. Unfortunately, there weren't any actors, either. Thinking about it, Anderson had decided that what was lacking from earlier Western efforts was a central character. A "star." But after looking all around California for an actor, *any* actor, to be his leading man, he gave up and settled on himself. He was overweight and not too good lookin', but G. M. Anderson became our first Western movie hero. He called himself "Broncho Billy."

His first movie was *Broncho Billy and the Baby*, all about a good guy/bad buy who turns all good and hangs up his guns on account of his falling in love. It was a smash, and Anderson went on to make 500 Broncho Billy Westerns in the next few years. By 1909, in fact, there were at least a dozen companies cranking out little Westerns, hundreds of them whose negatives have long since crumbled to dust. A handful of Anderson films, plus a few by Edison, Selig, and Bison, are all that remain for us to see.

Broncho Billy had set the stage. It was now up to people like D. W. Griffith and Thomas Ince to carry on the momentum. It was Griffith who pioneered certain techniques that we think are elementary to basic melodrama nowadays. He was the first to use "cross-cutting" of action scenes, jumping from one sequence to the next—cavalry chasing Indians, Indians about to converge on the settlers, settlers tending their families, unaware of the danger—

and mixing in long and short shots. There's great art to this technique, and we take it all for granted now. Griffith went on to do other kinds of movies, including adaptations of literary classics and propaganda stuff like *Birth of a Nation*. But he never abandoned the Western, and routinely took his acting troupe out to California in the winter (he summered in New York) to do his sagebrush operas.

Indians during this period of the early teens were usually portrayed in one of two ways: bloodthirsty savages or noble, but childish, first Americans who had received a bad shake by the white settlers. The first Indian "tragedy" was introduced. In *The Heart of an Indian*, Thomas Ince showed some tender exchanges between a white woman and an Indian maiden on the theme of motherhood. The movie ends with a massacre of the Indians after a series of mishaps with the soldiers, and introduced the first Indian actor-star, William Eagleshirt.

In the meantime, there was a starving playwright named DeMille in New York who collaborated on a few minor musicals with a producer and former vaudevillian named Jesse Lasky. They had a mutual friend in one Samuel Goldfish, a glove salesman. The three men met often for lunch, and one day DeMille said he was off for Mexico to earn money writing about the conflicts going on there. Lasky said, "Why not make movies, instead?" DeMille, brimming with excitement, grabbed Lasky's hand and said, "Let's!" The three formed a company, calling it "Famous Players Lasky." In a short while DeMille was off for Arizona to film his first Western, *The Squaw Man*. When he got to Arizona, it snowed. He pushed on to California and, in a little sleepy town for retirees, he bought a big, green barn and set up his film studio. The barn came complete with a horse. The town's name was Hollywood. In 1913, after the success of *The Squaw Man*, DeMille started grinding out a movie every month. Samuel Goldfish changed his name to Goldwyn, quit Famous Players Lasky, and teamed with Louis B. Mayer to form Metro-Goldwyn-Mayer. Famous Players eventually became Paramount and Hollywood hasn't been the same since.

But since Broncho Billy, the Western movie was still without a star, Hollywood or no Hollywood. As it happens, *The Squaw Man* had originally been a Broadway play, and a former Shakespearean actor named William S. Hart had the lead role. Hart decided he liked Westerns more than the Bard and took off for Hollywood in 1914. He looked up his old roommate from New York—also once an actor—Thomas Ince. Ince directed Hart in *The Bargain* and Hart's career as the first *realistic* Western star took off. His dress was right—usually just a dime-store shirt and scarf and a Mexican sash beneath his gun belt (most real cowboys actually wore these sashes, using them to tie the hooves of a roped steer). The settings for Hart's movies were right for the West, namely dusty and drab. The plots, while routinely melodramatic, stressed the plight of individuals against great odds. They didn't necessarily end happily. Hart invented Western realism.

At just about the same time—in fact a couple years before Hart got his start—another dude offered a vision of the Old West exactly opposite to that of Hart. His name was Tom Mix and he was the first showman cowboy hero, complete with fantastic trick riding, fancy costumes (including a diamond-studded, horsehair belt!), and plots that emphasized cheerful entertainment. Tom Mix was sheer fun, and he brought with him a reputation that almost equaled Buffalo Bill for sheer bull. Among the various careers he was supposed to have sampled before bounding in front of the camera was a soldier in the Spanish-American war, the Philippine insurrection, and the Boxer Rebellion in China, and horse-breaker for the British in the war against the Boers. He was a champion rodeo performer, cowpuncher for the Miller Brothers' 101 Ranch Wild West Show, a Texas Ranger, Deputy U. S. Marshal, and close friend of Will Rogers. Amazingly, meticulous research hasn't been able to turn up any evidence against his claims. But I knew him personally, and I still say he stretched it.

Our little family came into Hollywood about the time Mix was entrenching himself into Western myth, around the late teens. As I mentioned, there were some movies during the silent era which avoided stereotyping Indians, although most fell into the two opposite-extreme types of nobility or savagery. I like to think we at least had something to do with keeping Indians accurate in terms of costume, manners, and the like. But I should explain here that this was the *entertainment* business, not historical documentation. There had been bloody wars fought out on the plains, at this time just forty years ago. The people wanted blood and sentiment, and nobody in the movie business was about to deprive them of it for the sake of some higher truth. That certainly included my father, who would have promptly found himself out of work had he felt otherwise, and business, while good, was a bit spotty as it was.

Then came a big break.

By 1922, Famous Players Lasky was about to start filming the biggest Western of the silent era, the first Western epic, and the first epic of any kind not directed by Griffith. Jesse Lasky tried to get his ace director, C. B. DeMille, to direct *The Covered Wagon*, but DeMille was off trying his hand at "art," something at which he would fail miserably. (You'll visit with old C. B. DeMille a lot in these pages.) Anyway, the man they turned to with their $500,000 budget—an unheard-of sum for a movie in those days—was James Cruze, mostly noted for his Shakespearean background. And what Lasky and Adolph Zukor (who had by now replaced Sam Goldwyn) wanted for this production wasn't your run-of-the-mill Indians living in and around Los Angeles. They insisted on genuine, honest-to-God wild Injuns for the battle scenes. No Filipinos or unemployed Italian bricklayers wearing wigs. They turned to Tim McCoy, who was generally regarded as an expert on Indians after having served as adjutant general for the state of Wyoming, and after having helped historians trace out the actual routes of Custer's men and the Sioux and Arapahoe in the Little Big Horn battle. Before that, he had been a cowboy and a U. S. Cavalry officer. With the help of my brother, Tim hired five hundred Sioux and Arapahoe and took them by train to Milford, Utah, where *The Covered Wagon* was to be shot. Then, Tim and my father served as technical advisors, while I came along to play one of the Indians.

This really was a big picture. Before the Indians even arrived, there were three thousand extras camped out in drafty, army-style tents, hundreds of horses and tons of equipment, including several dozen Conestoga wagons. Cruze was a short, nervous guy who was losing his hair with worry over the movie business. He had his hands full enough. Then the Indians arrived, along with their wives, children, horses, tepees, the works. They camped themselves in the surrounding hills, protected from the wind whistling about the flimsy army tents. Since they were promised to be fed, they began helping themselves to entire sides of beef in the mess tent. The cooks, understandably, stood idly by and watched as these "wild" men carted off their best hunks of meat. My father watched, too, roaring with laughter.

"Wha . . . what's *this!*" stammered Cruze. "What the hell do they think they're doing with my meat?"

"Well, sir, you said you'd feed 'em, didn't you? They'll cut that meat up in strips and hang it in front of their tepees to dry. It'll last 'em the rest of the shooting, I should think."

"Last them, hell," mumbled Cruze. "They're just stealing." And he stomped away.

We weren't in Milford long when a blizzard came howling down from the north, so my father, brother, and I immediately moved into the tepees of Sioux and Arapahoe we had befriended. We knew those army tents would be unbearably cold. Tim McCoy, who not only knew how warm tepees were with a nice little fire going in the center, but also knew army tents, did the same. In fact, he settled in with an old man named Goes In Lodge, one of the half dozen actual veterans of the Little Big Horn battle he had befriended and brought along on this trip. Goes In Lodge got his name when, as a young warrior, he singlehandedly walked into the male lodge of an enemy tribe and wiped them all out with his tomahawk. Tim asked Cruze to join him.

"Are you crazy? Sleep in a greasy tepee with that . . . *savage!* Chrissake, he might kill you in the middle of the night."

Cruze politely declined.

We were pleasantly surprised to find the Indians had been distilling a mean thousand-proof booze from the sugar they were taking from the mess tents. Or at least my father was happy about it. We spent our nights comfortably enough. But the poor bastards in the army tents practically froze to death. Spring location shooting was rough work, and I would get snowed in many a time in the years to come. Much to his credit, though, Cruze pushed his people on, trudging through the snow and yelling orders through a cracking voice. Some of the best scenes of *The Covered Wagon* were produced in these snowbound conditions. Most other directors—all I've known, except maybe C. B. DeMille—would have cancelled till the weather broke.

[35]

Then it came time to do a scene where all the Indian tepees are placed in a circle, but with the entrances facing each other, as you undoubtedly see in many Hollywood movies. Cruze consulted Tim and my father.

"Look, you guys. I want to shoot a scene tomorrow, I want the tepees in a circle and the entrances facing each other, just like in the old days."

"That's not the way it was in the old days," said my father. "The tepee entrances always face east, not each other."

"So? So we face them different this time."

"Can't do that, Jim," said Tim. "They're supposed to greet the rising sun."

Cruze was getting to the boiling point.

"The rising *what?* What is this, a movie set or a resort hotel? You tell the goddamn Indians to take their goddamn tepees, turn 'em around a bit, and—"

"Nope."

"Why not," he screamed. "What's the harm?"

"Look, Jim, there's something you don't understand," said Tim calmly. "Indians don't like changing habits. They've been facing their tepees towards the east for thousands of years, and they aren't about to change on account of some movie."

"Izat *so!*" spat Cruze. "Well, we'll see about that, you Irish red-faced sonnavabitch. *Cody!*"

My father snapped to mock attention. "Sir!"

"Come with me!"

He saluted, and marched off with Cruze. After getting into the middle of the Indian encampment, Cruze started shouting, cursing, and flailing his arms about till he had a crowd of curious Indians gathered around him.

"Alright, now tell them that tomorrow morning I want them to have their tepees in a circle, except this time the entrances are to be facing each other. Okay?"

My father shrugged. "Sure."

He told them in signs what Cruze had asked, and the elders of the tribes nodded politely and smiled.

Cruze turned to Tim. "See?" he snorted in disgust. "All you gotta do is ask 'em right!"

The next day we were up at dawn. Cameras, lights, props, generators, actors, and actresses all surrounded the tepees. The tepees were all still facing east. Cruze sat slumped in his director's chair, a defeated man.

"Don't they understand?" he said, waving at the Indians with a listless hand. "Don't they realize this is an epic?"

By the end of eight weeks in Milford, we had most of *The Covered Wagon* in the can. After reviewing the rushes, Lasky realized he had a winner on his hands and added more scenes to be shot. This time we needed some buffalo for long shots, so Tim and my father were ordered to bring some in from Yellowstone National Park, where there was still a few roaming around. Fortunately, Tim knew Horace Albright, then the equivalent of U. S. Interior Secretary, and we managed to round up fifteen buffalo and have them shipped down to Nevada by boxcar. (Old Horace became a good friend of mine, incidentally, and is still alive at this writing—a spry ninety-four years old.) Now, the Indians were delighted with these buffalo and practically lived with them on a day-to-day basis. They became so tame that I even got to ride around on one. But, when it came time to send them back, we all realized they were no longer suited to life in the wilderness. Tim opted for sending them to Catalina Island, off the coast just south of Los Angeles, where the elements would be kinder to them. And that's how the buffalo found their way to Catalina, after having served as extras in *The Covered Wagon*.

Lasky decided on opening his picture at Grauman's Chinese Theater, then the grandest piece of architecture in California (I still think it is). The only movie shown there prior to *The Covered Wagon* was Douglas Fairbanks' *Robin Hood*. Lasky struck on the idea of having a live prologue of Indians used in the movie— singing, dancing, and telling stories in signs while Tim McCoy narrated. I was to be one of the Indians on stage, joining fifty others. Tim brought his Indians right into Hollywood and had them camp in the Cahenga Pass in the hills. Opening night was fantastic. This was the first time I'd ever seen Grauman's Chinese and I must say it was impressive. Outside, the usual searchlights used for big openings blazed their paths through the night sky, crisscrossing the turbaned Egyptian who strode back and forth on the roof, guarding over the place with a flintlock (only in Hollywood could you find something as weird as *that*). Inside were pillars like those from a Greek temple, everything glittering in gold. It was so unreal to me, and I can't imagine the impression it made on the other Indians. In addition to Goes In Lodge and other Little Big Horn survivors, the prologue act included a white woman with flaming red hair named Mrs. Broken Hand. She had been captured by the Indians as a girl and refused to return to civilization. *The Covered Wagon* and its prologue were a great success, eventually netting almost $4 million for Famous Players Lasky. No wonder. Admission at Grauman's was an incredible $1.50 (the average movie ticket in those long-lost days was a thin dime).

With *The Covered Wagon's* success came the Western movie assembly line. The public was mad about Westerns and couldn't get enough of them. A little, dusty corner of Hollywood, called "Gower Gulch," became the hangout for people hoping to get into the once-every-week cheapies being cranked out. The trail was now blazed for more cowboy stars. With Tom Mix in the lead (in terms of earning power, he was in the five-figure bracket per week, along with Mary Pickford and Charlie Chaplin), other characters soon followed: Tim McCoy (of course), Buck Jones, Hoot Gibson, and Ken Maynard. They all came to be known as the "Big Five." There were others, to be sure, but these five had the most staying power and audience draw. Some lasted well up through the thirties, into the sound era. Others didn't fair so well. Art Accord, for instance, was one of the many Hollywood figures of the twenties who found his voice a bit too squeaky for sound equipment. He dropped out of the movie business, started rum-running during prohibition, served time, and then committed suicide in some fleabag hotel in Mexico. Tim McCoy and I went to his funeral. We've buried a lot of cowboys in our time, Tim and I.

Actually, there should be another name added to the top drawer of Western stars in the early days, making it the "Big Six." He was the only star of major importance who maintained top billing up through his entire natural life. His name was Rin Tin Tin. He was a dog. For those who remember only the Rinty of TV fare, and only with much effort, let me tell you this was one of the truly remarkable talents ever to race across the silver-screened open prairie. In fact, when he's compared to the competition by film critics and directors, Rinty usually comes out on top. In Jon Tuska's book *The Filming of the West*, my old friend Nat Levene, Rinty's director for his last two pictures, had this to say:

". . . when I worked with [Rinty] we needed very few retakes and almost no extensive rehearsing. That dog knew just what was expected of him. He would watch Duncan [his trainer] for a signal, if movement was required. . . . as for emoting, or playing a scene right, he didn't need any coaching. That's the unusual thing about that dog. He actually seemed to *understand* the storyline well enough to bring off his role better than most of the other actors in the picture. I had more trouble with Tim McCoy and Buck Jones later at Columbia than I ever had with Rinty. . . . one of the truly professional actors we had in Hollywood at that time . . ."

I say "old friend" of Nat Levene. Actually the old coot cheated me out of overtime on countless occasions and, as you might suspect, was something of a misanthrope. But everything he said about Rin Tin Tin was true, for sure. The dog actually had close to a human range of emotions — and with complete command of them in front of the camera. He also could read your mind, something familiar to people who know and love animals. In one scene, I was to come charging around a bend on horseback, see Rinty up in a tree, and shoot him with an arrow. Before he got older, Rinty would do just about all his own stunts — jumping off cliffs, off moving trains, off rooftops, onto the backs of villains escaping by horseback. His timing was perfect. But in this case, he took one look at me mount my horse and merely adjust my quiver of arrows, and he jumped out of that tree like hornets were under his tail. We had the damnedest time getting him to hold still while I "shot" him. Rinty and I became good friends after that incident, though — provided I didn't reach for my bow in his presence. This particular serial, *The Lightning Warrior*, was Rinty's last and best. It had some great stunting, and was something of a forerunner in the cliffhanger department; the end of each hour-long sequence left the hero dangling off the edge of a handy precipice. I was playing a "bad" white man dressed as an Indian and having them blamed for various mischief. In the end I "take off" my Indian disguise and reveal my true identity. It was tricky makeup work pulling that one off, I'll tell you. A year later, Rin Tin Tin jumped into the arms of his owner after having acted out a scene and just quietly died. He was fifteen.

Tim McCoy went on to stardom at MGM. He needed his own technical advisors and turned to my father at first. But the old man's drinking was becoming worse, his attitude more belligerent. Tim came to rely on me to "fill in" for my father, and it wasn't long before I was being introduced all around Hollywood. I met other producers and directors—Cecil B. DeMille, John Ford, King Vidor to name just a few. I worked on another landmark epic of the silent era with Ford, *The Iron Horse.* Ford was twenty-nine in 1924, and he'd already directed fifty films, thirty-nine of them Westerns. He obviously loved the genre. *The Iron Horse* was as lavishly funded (by Fox Studios) as *The Covered Wagon.* It, too, was shot almost entirely on location, this time in Nevada. We all lived exactly like real railroad tracklaying crews did fifty years earlier, this being the first filmed story of the Union Pacific. We slept in tents and ate out of tins and had a wonderful, miserable time of it. I did some assistant directing of some of the action sequences involving Indian attacks in this one, and I'm happy to say they are judged by some to be the best Indian fighting scenes ever. But first prize for oddball achievements has to go to the publicity people at Fox. *The Iron Horse*'s star was George O'Brien, and of him they said on billboards: HE'S NOT A SHEIK OR A CAVEMAN OR A LOUNGE LIZARD—HE IS A MAN'S MAN AND AN IDOL OF WOMEN.

Wonder how that would go over with today's audiences?

In between filming I squeezed myself into the schools out here till about age eighteen when I dropped out for good to go on a world tour with Tim McCoy (although much later I attended college). I had a fairly normal time of it in school, distinguishing myself in sports more than book learning. I joined the cross-country track team and got up to eighteen miles a day. I usually got along with my teammates, but there were a few dopes who you would think made a living out of picking on kids a little different. One was this hulking moron named Frankie who must have been close to twenty years old. He had a full-grown beard and the kind of bulky muscles you get working every day on a farm, and he used to call me "blackie" or "dumb Injun." Once he tried taking my horse or pretended he was taking it. This character could have flattened me with one swipe of his stubby paw, so he got away with it for a while. Then one day I stood up to him. Got myself flattened, but redeemed in the eyes of my schoolmates. Frankie let me alone after that.

It was during this time, shortly after filming *The Iron Horse* and while still in high school, that I met my wife, Birdie. It was 1924, and I was on the set of MGM's *The Scarlet Letter* with Lillian Gish. I was technical advisor and playing a bit part as an Indian carrying Chillingworth's bundle of clothes as he came into town to witness Hester Prynne's trial. They shaved my head Mohawk style for that one. And I look pretty mean when I'm bald, not the sort women warm up to. Anyway, Birdie was an extra in this picture, one of the proverbial Indian women sitting along the road weaving baskets and gossiping. She had looks that grabbed you right away, not so much sexy but bright and glowing. Her shining black eyes were almost spiritual, yet lively and enthusiastic. Happy eyes. Her figure was lovely, managing to show some nice womanly curves through her buckskin dress. Her long, black braids framed a pretty face with regular features and a full mouth.

My father was on the set of this film for some reason I can't remember—probably nursing a hangover. I asked him if he knew her.

"Who?" he said with a tired sigh, not bothering to look where I was indicating.

"That one, over there on the end, the one doing all the talking."

"The fat one or the skinny one?"

"The skinny one, damnit."

"Oh, her. That's Bertha Darkcloud. Her friends all call her Birdie. But you can forget about her."

"What? What's that supposed to mean?" I was about ready to clobber him.

"She comes from an educated background and wants to go to college. Her father's an archeologist, a doctor or something. Way over your head."

"Yeah, over *yours*, you mean."

I spun on my heels, marched right up to Birdie, and blared out, "Hey, your name Birdie?"

She gave me a who's-this-annoying-cockroach look.

"Yes. So?"

"So this. I'm gonna marry you some day."

Her expression didn't change at all. She just raised her eyebrows, turned her head slightly, and replied, "Over my dead body you will."

Oh, she was always a cool one, Birdie was.

As it happens, my father knew Birdie's mother, Bula, and had got her and Birdie work as extras in a few pictures. Bula was also a drinker, and separated from her husband. Now there's a special alliance among drunks, and I managed to get myself invited along on my father's not infrequent visits to the Darkcloud home. After considerable effort, I started breaking the ice with Birdie. We'd sit and talk for hours about our plans, about me becoming a full-time actor and technical advisor and her telling all about soil and rocks and stuff. A natural match, right? We'd even sleep together while the old man and Bula had passed out in drunken stupors, but all perfectly innocent—with our clothes on. It wasn't long before Bula and my father started insinuating our relationship was something other than spiritual. They were wrong, of course, but we were sensitive, sincere kids and, seeing how we couldn't actually prove our innocence, we decided to get married. Just to spite them.

We jumped into an old Ford I was tooling around in and headed for Tijuana, Mexico. Now this was 1924, and Tijuana didn't look anything like it does today. It first started building up into Raunch Town during Prohibition in the thirties, when thousands of thirsty tourists poured across the border daily, looking for some action. And they got it. Shanty towns sprang up, feeding on tourist sources of revenue. Gambling picked up, whorehouses expanded, and sadistic cops were hired. Venereal disease spread around like flash fires out on the dry prairie. When we arrived, the place was well on its way to becoming the Tijuana we all know and love today. It was just less packed in and more dusty—no paving yet. They had bullfighting, dog racing, cockfights, and other exotic stuff to lure people over the border, even though you could still get a drink in San Diego. They also did a good trade in pornography, particularly the variety dealing with children.

When we pulled into town and I asked around in the streets if anybody knew where we could get married, I met with either laughs or blank faces. I suppose most couldn't speak English. Then we finally found a young boy who said he'd take us to a place where he thought they'd fix us up with a "quick ceremony." For a little fee, of course. He got in and we were directed to this ramshackle joint—looked like a whorehouse on bad times—and I hesitantly gave him a quarter. The boy looked it over for a moment and dashed off down the street. We were greeted effusively by a Mexican with popped eyes, dressed in a sweat-stained suit. Our master of ceremonies. Actually he was a little tall for a Mexican, looking as though he had European blood mixed in. I asked if he knew of a place where we could get married without too much fussing around.

"Yes, yes, of course," he said, grinning. "This is it, follow me, children."

Holding the door open and leaning over far to one side like some broken-down headwaiter, he pointed the way with his open free hand. Birdie was skeptical.

"Iron Eyes, I'm not sure I like this."

"C'mon. What do we know how they do things in Mexico?"

We found ourselves in a room. I don't remember much about it except the gold and red wallpaper was bubbling up in a few places. Our host put his sweaty hands together and looked us over.

"Yes," he said. He had no discernible accent. "Now if you children would please take off your clothes. We have special garments for the ceremony. Don't be frightened, just place your things on the back of that chair and I'll be back in a minute."

I have no way of telling this to make me sound any less imbecilic than I was. I didn't see anything too peculiar about this request and talked Birdie into taking her clothes off with me. What can I say? We were just dumb, trusting kids. I have to add that I found something interesting about this arrangement. It was, after all, the first time I was seeing my fiancée in the buff. She kept her back to me and her arms wrapped tightly around her little chest, but what I could make out was very pleasing. Then our friend poked his head in the door, looked us up and down, and, practically choking in his own drool, asked Birdie to follow him into another room. Alone. "For a fitting." That was it for her. She began throwing her clothes back on and I followed suit. We flew out of that room carrying half our stuff, and as we darted through the front door, I turned and blew a kiss to our disappointed host.

"Sorry. We'll be down for the honeymoon."

People didn't get married separately. That much I could figure out.

We headed back to Los Angeles and hung around at Birdie's mother's house for a few days, trying to think of something to do. Then we stumbled into a possibility. A big rodeo was scheduled for the San Bernardino State Fair and my friend the famous cowboy roper and stunt performer, Monty Montana, was getting married. We stopped by to express our congratulations and told him of our situation.

"Why, hell," he drawled. "Why don't y'all jump on a horse and get married with us, Western style with a cowboy preacher."

"But we're not quite eighteen yet. Will that be a problem?"

"Naw. You let me take care of that—I'll throw in a good word for you."

"How about that, Birdie," I said excitedly. "What could be more perfect for us than a cowboy wedding!"

She looked doubtful, but agreed to it.

Now, all the big Western stars of the time always went to the San Bernardino fair for the rodeo. It was unpatriotic not to be seen there—and showing up didn't hurt the publicity, either. Tim McCoy agreed to be my best man. Tom Mix was there, too, dressed in his usual all-white, spangled outfit, together with Hoot Gibson, Buck Jones, Art Accord, Ken Maynard, and a hundred other lesser names. Some of my Indian friends from the studios made it. They were all drinking, laughing, and whooping it up with the rodeo performers, and I was happy and proud they were all my friends. Birdie and I had on the Indian equivalent of our Sunday best—she a delicate white deer skin dress with beautiful hand bead work, and me the white buckskin worn by Chief Joseph of the Nez Percé. We were all set to mount our horses at the stables near the arena gate, and Hoot Gibson cupped his hands together, offering Birdie a boot up onto her horse. He had been drinking pretty heavy.

"Okay, squaw lady. Up you go."

Now I really don't think he meant anything derisive by calling

Birdie a "squaw." It was just his way, the silly fool. And he had been drinking. But it just wasn't something you said to Indian women anymore, leastwise somebody like Birdie. She glared at him, reared back, and, instead of putting her foot in his hand-stirrup, kicked him flat against the forehead. Women have strong legs, I want to tell you. It made a loud, flat "thwop" sound and sent Hoot sailing. He bounced off a fence five or six feet away and took a few steps forward, but he'd already passed out. His legs buckled, and he crumpled into the dust. Birdie ran off into the stands. I jumped off my horse, and Tim was already leaning over Hoot, gently slapping him on the cheeks. He moaned. Tim looked up and smiled.

"He'll be all right," he said. "He's been kicked in the head by horses. You'd better see after that girl of yours."

I caught up with Birdie somewhere in the grandstand. Without even trying to persuade her to come back, I sat down beside her and listened to her quietly sobbing for a minute.

"He didn't mean anything by it, Birdie," I said after a while. "But that was one beautiful kick. Good thing you had your moccasins on. You might have left the heel of a boot stuck in his forehead."

We giggled and hugged each other, and she calmed down a bit. I made a mental note not to ever get this woman too angry at me, though.

"Look, Iron," she said, matter-of-factly, "why don't we just get married Indian style? We can always get papers from the state later."

Perfect idea. Why hadn't I thought of it? We contacted an Indian chief friend of ours who had been helping Birdie's father gather specimens on his archeological expeditions. His name was Chief Thunderbird, a very tall, distinguished looking tribal leader and medicine man. We arranged for a ceremony at his sweat lodge up in the hills surrounding Pasadena. (Sweat lodges are the ceremonial equivalent to a steam bath, where Indians cure each other of certain ailments.) In a few days, we were standing before the chief, our hands bound together with rope. That's where the expression "tying the knot" came from, I believe. Indians from all tribes were gathered around us. The chief held the peace pipe up to the heavens, pointed it down towards mother earth, then to the four corners of the world. This indicated that all were now to pray for the whole earth and all living things, including our enemies. A blanket was placed over our heads, and as the peace pipe was passed around, each participant blew smoke towards us, blessing our union. Then the blanket was removed, the rope untied, and the chief declared us married. A feast followed. As evening fell we bid everybody good-bye and they watched us go off hand-in-hand, some of the elders shouting out encouraging remarks to me of a sexy nature. In the old days we'd be going off to the tepee of Birdie's mother. As it was, we were settling on her mother's house back in Hollywood. But first, a stop by my father's place.

"All right, we're married," I said, my voice firm with revenge. We had marched into the house together and found him in the kitchen, still sitting at the table in his usual drinking spot with a half-empty whiskey bottle. His head was down on his chest. "What've you got to say now?"

He lifted his head groggily and gazed at us through bloodshot eyes. He laughed harshly. "So?" he said, and laughed again. "Am I supposed to *care?*" Then he laughed till he started coughing. I got so mad, all I could think of doing was knocking his block off, but Birdie grabbed my sleeve.

"Let's go, Iron Eyes," she said, quietly. "Leave him alone."

We left, with him just sitting at the table, alternatively laughing and choking.

We spent our wedding night at Bula's, which you can imagine was just a hair this side of romantic. Fact is, I had the damnedest problems with Birdie. She was not only stubborn and hot-headed, she was also extremely modest and shy. A lot of Indian women are. Never could figure it out. First of all, I wasn't allowed to take off my clothes.

"What's the matter, Birdie? We've seen each other already. Down in Tijuana."

She was lying on the bed, fully dressed, her arms crossed in front of her again. "Don't remind me. And that was different—you didn't want to—lie with me."

"Yeah, well I do now," I said, slipping in beside her. "This is what folks do when they're married."

I kissed her, gently, and that didn't seem to have too great an effect, so I kissed her again a little rougher. Then we started wrestling around a bit, and just as I'd get one arm pried loose, the other would swing up into a defensive posture. She *was* a cool one. Just didn't want anything to do with me of a conjugal nature. I was slowly making progress, though, her resistance gradually breaking down, touching her here and there, and she was responding. Just as it seemed I was well positioned for a final assault—and this is true, I swear it—an earthquake hit! There was a loud, low-pitched rumble as the room shimmied and windows warbled in their panes like jello. We heard a woman screech.

"It's the end of the world! It's the end of the world!"

It was Birdie's mother. We heard some things crash in the kitchen, dishes falling to the floor, but by now we were running out the front door. Good thing we still had our clothes on, for the most part. Bula came stumbling out behind, and ran into Birdie's arms. I put my arms around both of them as we sank to our knees and prepared for the end. But it stopped. It was a good-sized quake, but the buildings around us were still standing.

And that was an interruption Birdie didn't recover from. We spent most of the rest of our wedding night wrestling and flipping about in bed, but no dice. She wasn't about to let herself in for another earth-moving experience. I finally gave up and fell into a fitful sleep. By morning, we felt we'd both had enough of married life. I went straight out and looked up Tim McCoy to explore an offer he'd made earlier for a world tour with the Indians of *The Covered Wagon* prologue. This time he was promoting *The Iron Horse* for Fox. The day after that, Birdie was down at the dock with Bula, both cheerfully seeing me off. I was on my ways to the South Seas. And I wouldn't get to know my wife of two days for four years.

3

THE OCEAN looked to me just like a rolling blue prairie. The wooden deck of the liner *Monterey*, bleached almost white from the salt sea air and sun, was heaving up and down, up and down through the gently rounded hills of the Pacific. A fine mist, feeling a little like Oklahoma dust, washed against my face. Only it wasn't salt water but the wind-blown breakfast remains of one of my fellow Indian travelers.

Six of us were leaning over the rail, violently relieving ourselves of the same meal. Eggs. I paused from my own wretchedness long enough to wipe my face and bawl him out. "Can't you control yourself? Watch it!"

"I can't control myself, brother," apologized my friend, his long black braids fluttering windward after his discards. "That's why I'm here."

Terribly seasick we were there, on our way to the South Pacific Islands with 28 other Plainsmen of the Colonel Tim McCoy and His Indians Road Show. Traveling second class below the water line with our cabin next to the kitchen and its periodic wafts of what smelled like fried dog (which, as we'll see later, I'm well familiar with) didn't help settle our land-loving stomachs any. Nor the cramped quarters. But I was in my late teens, bursting with a lust for adventure and happy in spite of my misery. I was roaming the prairie again, like my forefathers! I would somehow survive this boat ride.

It was the fall of 1924, a year after the tremendous success of *The Covered Wagon*. When the movie made its last showing at Grauman's, Lasky had decided to ship the whole prologue off to London for its premiere at the Pavilion Theater, in Piccadilly Circus. I didn't make it on the first trip but my brother did, and I understand it was quite a bash. Apparently some of the elder

Arapahoes, unhappy with the curt mannerisms of their rooming house landlady and the watered-down, overcooked English food, had themselves a drunken, body-painted war dance and feast. Right in the lobby. They broke up furniture for campfires (after having earlier been refused firewood for their cold, damp rooms) and, downing gin by the bottle, roasted steaks out in the middle of the Persian rugs. Rawther a bloody mess. By the time Tim arrived and got them all settled into a quiet little war dance in one of the upper rooms, considerable damage had been wrought. The landlady, understandably, was hysterical with fear of these men. They were, after all, genuine if somewhat aged warrior veterans of the great Indian Wars, and acted the part.

The show—the prologue, that is—was a smash, too. They stayed on in London for almost a year.

Actually, a number of the old Western stars toured with some kind of Wild West show during off season at the studios—Tom Mix and Buck Jones among them. Tim's Indians became popular, as he put it, with these "plains warriors not having to do anything for a change except be themselves," and he accepted offers to have them promote other Westerns, touring as a complete act with cowboys and villains, too. This tour I was on, for *The Iron Horse*, was Tim's first since *The Covered Wagon*, except we were headed in the opposite direction this time.

We arrived in Tahiti after thirteen days of open sea. I had been sick practically the entire time and was in no condition to fully appreciate the fantastic beauty of this paradise. I do remember feeling something like I'd died and been half-reborn in the grandest Happy Hunting Ground (the other half too sick to make the trip). Tahiti is the biggest and most important of the French Polynesian islands, over 400 square miles. Grass huts built up on wooden poles, white sands surrounding lagoons filled with shimmering, sky-blue water. Fantastic mountain ranges, volcanoes, tropical fruit trees, sugar cane. Huge men and women, the latter all running around in skirts made from tapa cloth, the bark of the paper mulberry tree, pounded to make it soft. The women were stripped to the waist, thinking it is just as silly wearing cloth cups over their breasts as American women might feel about, say, covering their face all day like the Arab women. (But Tahitians have taken to covering their breasts and American women are now letting theirs hang loose.) This was the Tahiti before airports and resort hotels, before the people were made French citizens, in fact.

I still felt terrible, though. In fact, I could barely walk from my prolonged sickness.

"I still don't feel too good, Iron Eyes." My Indian friend Clarence Charey echoed my feeling exactly. He looked a peculiar shade of greenish-red. "I feel like I want to die."

"Yeah, me too. Why not find some local God to sacrifice ourselves to and get some mileage out of it? Maybe bring the islanders good luck for a few years or something."

The native kids, apparently used to dealing with seasick travelers, offered us a drink called *kava* which they pound from the dried root of a plant by the same name. They would bring it to you in a special ceremonial cup and indicate you're supposed to down it all at once while patting your stomach. Then you chant *kava, kava, kava*. What could we lose being near death from nausea anyway? I'll be damned if we didn't drink the stuff and feel a hundred percent better.

Our first night in Tahiti, Clarence and a few other Indians, some of the cowboys, a couple crew members of the *Monterey*, and I slipped ashore at the capital city of Papeete. We found our way into one of the nightclubs which dot the waterfront area. There were girls dancing naked on the bar, which they didn't seem to think anything of. They seemed to be enjoying themselves a lot. We drank beer and the Indians, myself included, danced with the girls for everybody's entertainment. At about four in the morning, we staggered out into the moonlight and, with warm Pacific breezes caressing us, fell asleep in the sand. One or two of the men had girls with them. I was too shy—and drunk—to ask one to join me.

We didn't do any kind of formal act in Tahiti, but as the governor wanted to meet "the American natives," he came aboard the day we were leaving and shook our hands. Of French Polynesian stock, he was a magnificent looking man, at least six feet five inches and wearing a white suit. Then, we shoved off for an island just southwest of Cook, Rorotunga. I was, of course, sick again. Clarence and I wobbled on shaky legs up to the natives and asked for more of that *kava* juice. Fixed us right again. I settled myself down onto the soft sand and lay in the sun, trying to bake the sea out of my system, and Clarence disappeared. Later, he showed up with a girl who he said had been "smiling at him." She couldn't have been more than fourteen or fifteen. And she was beautiful—a great shock of bushy, black hair atop a full-featured face, golden brown skin, perfectly formed breasts, and the biggest damn feet you ever saw. Come to think of it, all the Polynesians had big feet. Never could figure it out. Now Clarence was several years older than me and extremely good looking in the classic Indian fashion with sharp, hawkish features like my father and bright, cheerful eyes that drove the women crazy. Me, I think I had the plainest-looking poker face I'd ever seen on any man. I was shy and self-conscious, needing egging on before even approaching girls. That was certainly the case when I met Birdie. For whatever reason, though, this Rorotungan decided she liked me over Clarence. As I lay in the sun, she stood over me. Smiling. Her name was Terara Tara. She was on her way with a few other natives to any island where they would find temporary work as cooks, waiters, what have you. The officers of the *Monterey* would allow a certain number of nonpaying passengers aboard if they slept on deck or in the empty swimming pool and didn't beg for food from the regular passengers.

That night, the Indians and the rest of the cast went ashore to whoop it up with the barroom girls who would dance naked and drag them upstairs for a while. In fact, most everybody was on shore except a skeleton crew. Terara came on board to meet me.

We didn't speak much at first. Didn't have to. She told me she had been with men before and I believed her. She placed her hands under each breast.

"Touch me."

I obliged, and right there on the deck, in soft tropical moonlight with the gentle sound of waves lapping the sides of the ship, I discovered my manhood. Not a bad introduction, if I do say so. She stayed with me all that night, just talking to me in the most lyrical, sing-song voice you ever heard. She sang beautiful songs, which were stories about how they had journeyed to the islands. I in turn sang some Indian songs for her. It was all very sweet and uncomplicated.

In the morning we set sail and she was with me again the

following night before getting off on another of the dozens of little islands splayed throughout the South Seas, to work, maybe raise a family, and be forgotten. I was certainly sad to see her go. Many years later when I was back in that part of the world on another tour I tried looking her up. No one had ever heard of any Terara Tara.

Next stop for Colonel Tim McCoy and his Indians: Auckland, New Zealand. Now, in those days I used to walk around in beaded moccasins, Levis, and a loud reservation-style shirt. Sometimes I wore a beaded tie that a friend in Los Angeles, White Horse, gave me. I had my hair long and braided in the traditional manner of the Northern Plains Indians. Whenever we landed in some new exotic port we Indians would stir up quite a commotion, as you can imagine. But here in good old Auckland, we felt right at home. Everybody thought we were Maories, the natives of the bush that paint themselves green. Come to think of it, they did look a little like one of my wife's uncles, a medicine man.

Auckland was the first place we performed our act formally in a big public theater. It consisted mostly of telling something of our life story in signs, while Tim interpreted. Then we'd do some dancing and sing Indian songs. On this particular trip the great stuntman and later second-unit director, Yakima Canutt, was with us doing various tricks and playing the lead cowboy. You remember all those B Westerns in the thirties and forties where the hero would jump from his horse to the back of a stagecoach in pursuit of the villain and start fighting, fall between the horses, and have the stage run over him, grab the rear axle, pull himself up, and finish the guy off? That was Yak. Small wonder he went on to put together such memorable action scenes as the chariot race in *Ben Hur*.

For my own part, I would do a little stunt where I'd fake shooting an arrow into a white man by releasing the bow and flipping the shaft behind my back. Had the natives convinced, I'll tell you. They'd all squeal with delight, "Where is it, where is it?" Then I'd slowly pull out another one, carefully take aim on one of the cowboys and—pow!—let him have it right in the gut! Of course he was wearing an arrow-proof vest fashioned from balsa wood and steel. I was the first to develop this particular stunt later for the movies—maybe because they trusted my marksmanship. It was outlawed eventually, though. An actor took an arrow in the leg at the hands of another archer of unsteady aim.

On to Sydney, Australia, for a big rodeo.

We went hunting for wild boar in Australia, and I saw my first kangaroo. These animals move at fantastic speed on those hind legs—the faster they go, in fact, the less energy it takes, as the forward momentum gives them more bounce. I saw some clear a six-foot fence at what must have been thirty miles an hour. I also found an infant kangaroo, maybe abandoned by its mother during a high-speed chase by predators. I named him Joey (all young kangaroos are called a "joey") and took him all the way back to San Francisco, where I donated him to the zoo. I also had a chance to do some big game hunting in South Africa, our next stop. This was long before many of the species were in danger of extinction. I hunted with a bow, and I stuck with animals like pigs and small fowl. It never seemed like sport to me to shoot a magnificent creature like an elephant, which not only presents an easy, slow-moving target but has intelligence to match the average California citizen. Well, with a few exceptions.

We made a few more stops in Africa, and then it was up to Paris. All the Indians climbed the Eiffel Tower as a publicity stunt, and we did a dance around the top. That was a sight these French folks got a kick out of; thousands were out to greet us. I can't say as the Eiffel Tower impressed me much, though. When you think of it, it looks like an overgrown Los Angeles radio station plunked down into an otherwise beautiful city.

Of all the Europeans we encountered, I would have to say the Germans were the most enthusiastic Injun lovers. Just the sight of two dozen painted warriors, singing and dancing and screeching in one of their beer halls, sent them into a kind of wild-eyed frenzy. They started singing and dancing and throwing beer on each other, all arm-in-arm. They're really something, those Germans— especially the Berliners. Germany still has a fascination with Indians; they read about them, their generals (especially in World War Two) studied Indian guerrilla tactics, and they all go to Western movies regularly. In fact, the Germans regularly crank out Westerns, themselves. They have their own Duke Waynes and everything.

[53]

We made a long stop in London, England, where we played the parks and theaters. The English seemed to take a particular liking to watching me skewer a cowboy with my fake arrow-shooting. They all whistled in delight. Then, after almost a year of traveling the globe, it was homeward bound! The first thing I did after landing in New York was call Birdie. I asked her to join me at Tim McCoy's ranch in Wyoming, where I planned to spend the winter (it was now the fall of 1925). She agreed, and trooped all the way up to Thermopolis (close to Lander), but not to get together with me so much as skulk about. Apparently she'd gotten word—how is completely beyond me—that I'd been unfaithful. Women have some kind of radar built in when it comes to sexual matters. It's really amazing. We passed the time in a state of lukewarm friendliness. We dined together at Tim's lodge, went on fishing trips, laughed together socially, but she'd have nothing much more to do with me. Which is to say we hadn't as yet consummated our marriage. And after a few days of this, we'd had enough of each other. She went back to California and continued her studies in archeology with the distinguished Indian historian, Dr. Mark Harrington of the Los Angeles Southwest Museum. I spent the winter freezing my behind, hunting elk with Tim. At night, I curled up next to a woman I met in town and swore off marriage altogether. Being almost twenty, I figured I was already too old for such nonsense.

In the spring, I was happy to get back to warm, sunny Hollywood, thaw out, and start making movies again. My father had, at least for the time being, abandoned the film business and opted for returning to my mother's side in Oklahoma. He also swore off drinking, but unfortunately my mother didn't believe it. When she found out he was on his way home, she grabbed up the kids and took off. He ended up chasing her across half the country and contracting pneumonia before catching up with her in Orange, Texas, where she had an aunt. My mother never could resist caring for somebody ill, so she took him in.

My father had left behind all his props and Indian outfits, telling us we could do what we wanted with them. I added to our collection a trick horse I picked up for a pretty good price from one of the studios, and began doing more stunt riding and falls. Falling off a

horse going full gallop is mighty tricky business. Before they outlawed it, directors would simply tie the animal's forelegs together
to one end of a rope, the other to a peg in the ground. You'd spur the
poor animal to run for a short distance and both come to a bone-
crunching flop in the dust. Another variation was called the "Running W," where ropes were strung across the horses' path for them
to trip on. I think the worst of them was simply running a wire
from a foreleg up to the rider, who would give a yank at the
appropriate instant and send the horse crashing down. The rider
would always know when the fall was coming, of course, and roll
out of it. The horse might break its neck, which wasn't uncom-
mon. In all fairness, the rider might, too. Or get a hoof in the groin.
The fee for taking these falls was seven dollars and fifty cents. (It's
up to about $300 now.) The horse got room and board. In the late
teens, the ASPCA got after the studios and outlawed horse-falls
using contraptions like the "Running W."

The advent of horses trained to fall on cue didn't mean the riders
were any more willing, though—at least not yet. Professional
stuntmen were a rare commodity in the early days and didn't make
a strong appearance till stars were commanding such high salaries
that injury to them would be bad news economically. It was at first
just extras taking the tumbles off horses, or leaping off cliffs. But
there was many a time when the Indians we hired would, understandably, pull their horses up to an abrupt stop before "falling,"
swing a leg over and just sort of half fall, half jump off. Didn't make
for good cinema. Some of the more curious among them even
refused to play dead properly, and would constantly raise their
heads and have a look around to see what was going on. The camera
faithfully recorded everything, and if you look carefully at the
action sequences of some of these old films, you'll see what I'm
talking about.

I got into the act for specialty items, when the camera would
focus on one particular activity. With tomahawk in hand, I jumped
from my horse onto the back of cavalry officers. I shot arrows into
stagecoaches, through an actor's hat or into his gut. I led war
parties on train raids and, after wrecking and pillaging, rode off a
cliff, head first, landing on my shoulders and rolling. All the while,
I did war whoops. After sound came in, practically all the whoops

you've heard when the Indians dance around campfires or charge the wagon are mine, pre-recorded. Never did get any rights to those whoops. Would be a millionaire by now if I had.

When I wasn't worried about how the Indians would perform on camera, I was dressing up white men to play their role. One of them was a young beanpole named Frank Cooper.

We had been on location up in the fake hills of what is now called the Paramount ranch, near Hollywood. I was introduced to Coop—standing there shivering in his loincloth—by Lane Chandler, also among the white "Indian" actors for this particular film, called *The Vanishing American.* It was directed by George E. Sykes and starring Richard Dix. Lane and Coop were both from Helena, Montana. They both appeared in a whole string of little quickies at Paramount. Lane was also a good friend of Tim McCoy, which is how I came to know him, and he went on to a brief stardom which flickered out in the early thirties.

Coop, as his friends called him, lasted a lot longer. We all know he won two best actor Oscars for *Sergeant York* and *High Noon*. We know he became something of a symbol for everything people believed was good and pure in this country. Critics may tell you his acting was stiff and limited, but that didn't matter to us. Coop had something special, an instant likeableness that made men smile and women swoon. But who was he, really? Damned if I know, and I knew him thirty-five years. I can tell you he was the most self-conscious man I ever knew. Despite what appears as his aw-shucks spontaneity on the screen, or his famous understatement, whatever, he always knew what he was up to. He was always *aware* of himself. And I think every Cooper mannerism was connected in some way to his lifelong struggle to overcome his own shyness, anxiety, and sense of awkwardness.

Frank Cooper was raised on a ranch up near Helena, Montana, a place called "Last Chance Gulch" at one time because it had been a gold miner's shanty town sprung up around an actual gulch. Coop recalled that, although the gulch had been thoroughly mined, "the cracks were fished with darning needles," and after each spring flood he and his friends would always find enough gold to keep them stuffed with candy for a week. Frank's father was busy with a law practice, his mother with photography, and they gave the boy a pretty free hand. He had his first riding lesson from a local character named Roy Smith who looked a good deal like Buffalo Bill. "No one knew where he came from," Coop said, "and when he disappeared one day, no one knew where he went and no one ever found out."

One day little Frank walked in the kitchen and shouted an obscenity at his mother. Instead of washing his mouth out with soap, she decided he had to get away from the likes of Roy Smith and obtain some culturing. She packed her bags, took him to England, and enrolled him in a boarding school. There, Frank let the classical disciplines of Latin drift in one ear and out the other while he retained an interest in art. When he returned to Helena three years later, he could draw a pretty mean horse but was behind his fellow classmates in the academic subjects. To add to his problems, he had piled a layer of British accent over his Montana drawl—in addition to growing about a foot—making the gangly, shy boy seem strange indeed. He made up for his oddness by becoming the class clown, and he was soon bounced out of high school for cutting up in class.

Frank finished high school in another town and took a few courses at a local college. He befriended a student crippled with polio since childhood. One day they went for a ride in a Model T especially equipped for hand operation. The brakes failed at the top of a hill, the car slid backwards off the embankment and rolled over, smashing Frank's hip. While recovering, he found it was less painful to ride horses than to walk. Favoring that hip, he developed a kind of silky-smooth riding—and walking—that later became one of his trademarks. He also later discovered that riding was the worst thing he could have done while the bones were trying to knit themselves together. He suffered pain on his one side for the rest of his life.

In 1922, when he was twenty-one, Frank Cooper enrolled in Grinnel College, Iowa, as an art student. He fell in love with the campus queen, who didn't find anything too marriageable in the Montana plainsman who was too shy and nervous to carry on a decent conversation. Rejected, Frank headed west after two years at Grinnel, deciding it was time to find work. He landed his first acting job driving a tourist bus in Yellowstone National Park. To

[57]

scare the passengers into forking over bigger tips, he grimaced and exaggerated the difficulty of negotiating the hair-bend turns, pulling, straining on the wheel, and yelling, "Okay folks, ha-a-a-ang on!" He also tried various kinds of selling: advertising, real estate, family photography. He failed at everything, including painting curtains for vaudeville theaters. Vaudeville was on its way out, being replaced by movies.

One day Frank was strolling along the avenue in Hollywood when he bumped into a couple old cowboy friends he knew in Montana. They were pretty mangy-looking, as though they had spent the day rope-tied by their ankles to the saddle of a horse, dragging through the dirt. They explained they were making ten bucks a day falling off horses for the movies. All Frank had to do was show up at a place called Gower Gulch, although he'd only be making five at first. Gower Gulch was the corner of Sunset and Gower where, on one side of the street, you found a drugstore with benches lined up out front. Perfect for lounging in the sun. The cowboys that hung out were called, not surprisingly, "drugstore cowboys." Across the street was a bar where the action stepped up a bit—poker, fights, women, even gunplay. These cowboys that acted in the movies of the twenties were, for the most part, the real thing. Right off the ranch. And they wore *loaded* guns. Up and down both sides of Sunset were located the studios where all the quickie movies and serials were cranked out on a weekly basis. It's also where the quick-buck producers and hucksters waited in their lairs. The whole setup was called "Poverty Row," with Gower Gulch as the sort of spiritual center. Every day you would see something of a circus parade up and down Poverty Row: cowboys, midgets, beautiful women. It was really something.

The movie Frank Cooper was to try out for was *The Vanishing American*. What the hell, he thought. If I can ride a horse, I can fall off 'em. And five bucks is more than I've got now. He showed up for work and, as the story goes, they didn't need any more extras. Another friend of his named Slim Talbot, also from Montana, had been falling off horses in some senior capacity. He had gotten the other two guys jobs. Slim is supposed to have stepped aside to let Frank Cooper have a day's work, although I was on this picture and never saw anything of the kind. I suspect this was a story churned

out later by one of the Hollywood publicity magazines, as other
"interviews" with Cooper print him saying his first movie was a
Tom Mix vehicle called *Dick Turpin* and, to round it out, as a
South African guerrilla fighter in a film depicting the Boer War. I'll
settle it right here. He told me that chilly morning in 1925 that this
was his first time. He said, with disappointment, that he thought
he was going to be a cowhand as he stood before me in an Indian
G-string, which I'd given him to play an Indian in *The Vanishing
American*. He went ahead and fell off a few cliffs with me and 500
other Indians for this picture. Then he went on to be a cowhand in
several others.

His father thought he'd grow out of it, but instead Frank Cooper
grew into the movie business. While continuing to get himself
banged up from various kinds of falls—mostly off horses—he
scraped together every cent he had and filmed his own screen test.
It featured him galloping up to the camera on a horse, jumping off,
leaping a fence, and taking a deep bow, sweeping the ground with
his ten-gallon hat. You could barely make out his face through a
cloud of dust. He also found himself an agent who, because she was
from Gary, Indiana, suggested he change his first name to Gary. He
didn't argue, even though he didn't like it too much. That was
Cooper, always affable. As a compromise, he encouraged his
friends to call him "Coop."

Coop's first real break came through his father, who had been
doing some legal work for the father of Marilyn Mills. Marilyn was
doing pretty good in the two-reeler Western department, some of
which I had worked on with her. The two men arranged for Coop to
meet her, and Coop played a villain in *Tricks*, complete with
penciled mustache. It wasn't long before he ceased being a "corral
buzzard," as we called the drugstore cowboys. He was in the big
time now, earning fifty dollars a week playing a heavy to Marilyn
on screen, her lover off.

"You ride very well," said John Waters, "and you move well too
. . . you ought to be making a name for yourself one of these days."

Waters was a big producer at Paramount who, with Coop standing next to him sweating, was looking at Coop's little homemade
screen test. He was unimpressed with his other screen credits to

date, but there was something about the way Coop moved, like he was moving without moving anything. Nervous, Coop gulped during the interview. Waters said if he kept the gulp, that would serve him well, too.

In a matter of months, Coop began landing bigger, more important roles. He played opposite his idol, Ronald Colman, in *The Winning of Barbara Worth*, where, after having been out in the desert for weeks, he ran up a flight of stairs, crashed through a door, and fell at Colman's feet. The director was supposed to have thrown dust in Coop's face to make it more realistic. He appeared briefly in *Wings*, the first movie to win the "Best Picture" Academy Award, and that launched him into leading-man roles.

I hadn't as yet appeared before the cameras in anything other than action stunts and bit parts. It was Coop who encouraged me to do more, to start developing character roles for myself.

We were on the set of Victor Flempng's *The Wolf Song*. I think he was playing the friend of a mountain man, portrayed by *All Quiet on the Western Front* star Lewis Waldheim. Coop and I were standing behind the cameras together and he said, "Go on, get in there, get in there," all the while poking and teasing me. "Tell Fleming you want to do some real acting."

"Why don't you tell him, you're so crazy about the idea." I had my own share of shyness in those days.

Coop ambled up to Fleming and mumbled something in his ear. Fleming looked over his shoulder at me, then came over and barked, "All right, Iron Eyes, you play an Indian talking to Cooper here in this next scene."

Before I had time to get nervous and chicken out, we were standing in front of the camera. At the command "Action!" I made some hand gestures and spoke in an Indian dialect. Coop stared at me intently, nodding his head in seeming comprehension. Then he simply babbled, "Ya bla bla bla bla bla, ya bla bla," pointing off in the distance, his long features reflecting the grand sweep of land and adventure before us. I nodded in solemn agreement and said something else. The scene worked perfectly—without sound— and Fleming loved it. My days as a real actor had begun.

Coop's talents weren't limited to acting, though. In fact, making one movie after another bored him to death and he often talked excitedly with me about most anything else—hunting, cars, women—anything to keep his mind off the film business. In addition to being a crack shot with both gun and bow (I taught him to make his own bows Indian style), he was an amateur taxidermist and had his place cluttered with stuffed rabbits, hawks, and other small game. He also rendered some pretty decent charcoal sketches of animals and people around the sets that interested him. I've still got one he drew of me. For some reason, though, he was particularly interested in eagles.

My brother happened to have been raising some eagles we found in Texas while en route home to Oklahoma. In those days, according to the ranchers, the big birds were bounty game because they'd swoop down out of the sky, knock a rancher's lambs or calves on the head, then rip them open and devour them. (I personally have never seen eagles attack such big quarry, but that's what they say.) We found a flock of the fierce "winged wolves," as they were called by the Aztecs, hanging upside down on a farmer's fence, dead. We asked if we could have them for their feathers. The rancher obliged, and also gave us several live ones that had survived his traps—all with broken talons. My brother found himself in 5he eagle-nursing business.

One day Coop dropped by the garage and, his eyes glistening with excitement and admiration for the birds, asked if he could sketch one of them right there on the spot. He usually carried his pad and charcoal with him.

J.W. took one of the biggest out of its cage and, when he held him on his forearm, Coop saw the mangled talons. He was noticeably pained. "Mind if I take this bird home with me?" he asked shyly. "He's a beauty and I bet I could fix his feet up. Whad'ya say?"

Off he went, this carniverous animal with a six-foot wing span and a beak capable of breaking bone perched on his arm. Coop was still living at home with his parents, who had moved to Los Angeles, and there was no room there for any eagles. So he took his prize directly to the living room of the woman he was seeing at the time, one Lupe Velez. Lupe's blood temperature hovered somewhere close to boiling all the time and she never took to delicate language. She came home, saw our national emblem atop her china cabinet, and screamed, "Get that goddamn steenking bird out of here!" Funny part of it is, the fan magazines concocted some story about Coop sending a pair of "love birds," *two* eagles, to his girlfriend Lupe Velez, and that she kept them in a cage in her backyard. I had been over to Lupe's many times and never saw any kind of bird cage in her backyard, but for decades, stories persisted about how the two exchanged exotic animal gifts like that. Amazing how "inventive" them fellers at the fan magazines can be. Love birds or no, Coop came back the very next day looking a little hangdog and gave the eagle back to my brother.

"I'll stop around from time to time to see how he's doing," he said, edging himself out the drive.

That reminds me of the first time Coop met Lupe Velez. We were preparing to shoot on location for, again, *The Wolf Song,* up around June Lake in the mountains. It was the winter of 1928 and there was about two inches of snow on the winding mountain roads. By this time Coop was pulling down a hefty salary with Paramount and had himself a custom Duesenberg sports roadster so long that, as he put it, "I have to start turning corners in the middle of the block." I was struggling along in my little Ford, winding out first and second gear. Coop waited for me around every bend to see that I made it okay. We finally arrived, but still had a little time to kill before filming started, so a bunch of us took off for the lake to do some fishing. Some of the folks were having problems with the tackle, not knowing what they were doing, but Coop and I were landing trout about a foot long, one after the other.

Lupe, who had been flirting and joking with some of the guys until our fishing prowess caught her eye, sashayed up to Coop with her hips swinging about two feet in either direction.

"Hey, handsome," she said, "mind eef I try that?"

"Huh? O-oh, you mean this, this fishing here. Why, sure, sure you can. Just step over here and hold this here rod right there. That's it. Now . . ."

Yeah, he was shy with the women in the early years, but he certainly did manage okay with a little encouragement. Lupe, providing enough encouragement for twenty shy men, proceeded to tuck herself comfortably into his arms and there they were like that, Coop teaching her how to "fish" with himself all wrapped around her.

[62]

"You know," he murmured, "you're one hell of a good-lookin' girl. You gonna be on this here picture long?"

Evidently Coop hadn't as yet read the script. He would have seen she was playing a feature role as an Indian girl.

"Well," she mimicked, "you're one goddamn good-lookin' cowboy. I theenk I'm gonna be around this here peecture as long as you are."

They caught a lot of fish together that day.

We hauled our catch up to the lodge we were staying at to have it cooked for dinner. That evening, when we all gathered in the huge dining hall, Coop and Lupe went into the kitchen to see if the chef was preparing the fish as he liked it. Well done. When the cook left the kitchen to talk with us, as Coop told me later, they started making love. Right there with all the steenking fish. When they emerged, rumpled but still intact, Coop sat down. A combo started playing some kind of rhumba music, and we settled back to enjoy it while we ate. Lupe apparently wasn't hungry—not for the fish we were eating. She grabbed on to one of the support beams with both her hands and, planting her feet on either side, started grinding her pelvis into it in perfect rhythm with the music. I'll tell you, the men at the table looked almost frozen in utter fascination, mouths open slightly, food dangling on forks suspended with shaking hands. Even the women were entranced. Coop just sat there staring at her, mechanically stuffing fish in his mouth and saying periodically, "God*damn*!"

She was one hell of a dancer, that Lupe Velez.

This went on for about a half hour till a big car pulled up to the lodge. Somebody at the table managed to tear his eyes from the spectacle before us—which by now had progressed to Lupe going from pole to pole, varying her routine with much imagination and downing one drink after another—and yelled out, "Hey, there's Tom Mix!"

"What?" cried Lupe, stopping her gyrations and putting her fists on her hips. "That sonavabeech is *here*?" The band had stopped playing.

Now this is the first time I'd heard a woman use language like that, at least in public, and I must say it gave me quite a jolt.

"That's my man," she said, addressing all of us. "I go wid heem.

[63]

But he was not supposed to be here unteel tommorrow, that sonavabeech."

In waltzed Tom Mix, dressed completely in white from his huge Stetson to his white fur coat to his white, hand-tooled boots. He almost glowed, appearing like some kind of snow king or the Good Fairy Godfather. Acknowledging folks he knew with a friendly, easy nod, he clomp-clomped up to Lupe in those boots, spurs clinking rhythmically.

"Well, what's the matter?" he said, "You ready to go down off the mountain or what?"

"No!"

"You've been drinking again, Lupe."

"Yes."

They carried on this little "conversation" for another minute or so when suddenly Lupe grabbed Coop up from his chair, threw her arms around him, and, tossing her head back with a wild laugh, cried, "Play the museek! Play the museek!" The band started up again, and she started substituting a lucky Coop for one of those posts.

Tom Mix just stood there looking foolish for a minute, then said, "Jesus, give *me* a drink."

During the four years that Coop and Lupe were living together he went from about 180 to 140 pounds. You can read where he had been working himself half to death at this time, developed ulcers, and got jaundiced. Well I say it was the result of his steady diet of hot, Mexican food and that red-hot, beautiful Mexican woman. (Although I should mention he ate a big can of sauerkraut each morning. Said it helped keep him regular. . . .)

Dark Spanish women—or women a bit roughhewn—were Coop's chief weakness, in fact. Lupe used an odd name for these girls, calling them "chippies." But with her accent it sounded, appropriately enough, I suppose, like "cheepies." Whenever Coop and I were about to take off she'd huff, "So-o-o! Off cheepy chasing again, heh? You goddamn cheepy chaser you. Get out, get out!" And she'd come after us with a broom or whatever was handy, all the while Coop whimpering, "Yes ma'am, yes ma'am," ducking the broom and laughing as we ran out the door. After Lupe Velez it was Carole Lombard, who could swear on a par with Lupe, and

Coop would croon, "Oh, you're a real woman, I really like you," and so on. That's why it was such a surprise to all who knew him when he married blue-eyed, social registerite Veronica Balfe. He seemed to go through a complete change. They did almost everything together for years, her being an outdoor enthusiast like him, and Coop and I didn't go off on our little trips to Mexico too much. We still hunted together quite a bit, though.

Years later, they separated for a while, and Coop went back to some of his old ways. He also took up drinking tequila, never having been a drinking man before. I was in Mexico City making a movie called *Trailing Canoes* at the Cherabusco Studios, the largest film outfit south of the border. Coop called me one afternoon at my hotel. He was at Cherabusco, too, making *Vera Cruz* with Burt Lancaster.

"Iron Eyes, why don't you come down and have a sandwich with me. I've got to talk with you."

I went over to the studio, and there he was. He looked terrible, chain smoking, one cigarette after another, and downing tequila. His hair was out of place—that was never like Coop—his color was ashen and his nose looked swollen. I'd never noticed it swelled up like that before, either. I don't know if it was from drinking or what.

"What's the matter with you, Coop. You look awful."

"Aw, hell, it's that goddamn Burt. Can you believe he's trying to tell me how to act? *Me?*" He actually choked back tears. "I don't want anybody telling me how to work but they're all giving me the business, I guess."

"Who's giving you the business? Who you mad at?"

"Oh, I don't know. Guess I'm mad at everybody," he said, his voice trailing off.

A little later, my producer, W.R. Frank, joined us. We started in on some small talk—it was obvious to W.R. something was bugging Coop. Out of the blue, W.R. said he'd never been unfaithful to his wife during thirty-some years of marriage. This seemed to perk Coop up a bit.

"What? You mean you've never cheated on your wife? Not even in a foreign country?" he said, feigning astonishment. "Well, let's see what we can do about that."

We started joking about all the fat Mexican girls working in the kitchen—Coop never could stand fat women—when suddenly Frank said, "Hey, look at that doll over there." He was pointing out this vision of Mexican loveliness with a shimmering, milky-white complexion. Coop sprang out of his seat and brought her over for an introduction. Her name was Sarita Montiel.

"Sarita, this is the famous producer W.R. Frank, and he's making a picture called *Trailing Canoes* starring Iron Eyes Cody here."

She said, "Meester Frank, you made the peecture *The Devil and Mr. Webster* with Walter Huston?"

Frank's eyes lit up, acknowledging he did.

"Oh, I liked that peecture very much. So you the producer, eh? Well," she said, pointing a determined thumb at her bosom, "I want to be a star."

We all got a laugh out of that one. But Coop apparently was impressed. He went ahead and *made* her a star. Used her in *Vera Cruz*, in fact. He also went with her a good while before returning to his wife. To my knowledge he didn't wander from her side at all after that.

Three years later we found out he had cancer.

As you can gather, women were high on Coop's list. He wasn't one of the true Hollywood wild men, like Errol Flynn. I would say his character was basically too taciturn and gentlemanly for extremes. Once we overheard the goings-on in his dressing room when a particularly aggressive young lady had barged in on him asking for his favors. She stripped off her clothes and waited impatiently while Coop was just talking to her, prying into her personal life, trying to find out where she was from and what interested her. Finally, she stormed out, announcing to anyone within earshot, "When I want a man to make love, that's it. No wine and dine, no nonsense. Him, all he wants to do is get to *know* you."

Right up close to women on the list was hunting. He went all over the world stalking game with famous people, including his friend, Ernest Hemingway. I mentioned he was equally competent with a bow as a gun, and the great archer Arthur Young gave him one with a ninety-pound pull. The three of us would often go out together and Arthur taught me how to shoot "archery style," drawing the long bow to your chin and aiming down the arrow. (Indians used short bows, which they pulled back to their chest for a quick "snap" shot, easier for use while riding a horse.)

Coop liked hunting small game the best—grouse, pheasant, ducks, partridge—because he thought they stood a better chance against you. And he always ate what he bagged, never killing for the sake of killing. He had the finest collection of guns of anyone I knew, spending a good deal of his time cleaning and oiling them himself. The only other things he lavished the same attention on were his cars. For all I know he may have been one of those nuts to go after the tire treads with a toothbrush, he was that fussy about them. Half the time when you went to his house unannounced, there he'd be in the driveway, dressed in jeans and an old shirt, polishing one of his many exotic breed of automobiles.

But above all else Coop was a laugher. I don't think many people remember him as a practical joker but I say they just didn't know him. He loved to create crazy situations for people, sit back, and laugh his head off. While never getting anybody in serious trouble, a lot of his pranks were nonetheless not exactly innocent. When on the set of a Western, he surrounded himself with three or four stooges—rough, gristle-and-bone cowboy extras he would constantly bounce jokes off or play tricks on.

DeMille and the others who worked closely with Coop liked making him laugh, too. Half the time he was all keyed up and not able to do his dialogue with any conviction and they knew getting him cracking jokes and giggling would help him relax. When he was loose and feeling himself, he was, as we all know, a fine naturalistic actor.

Once, probably to research some joke intended for me, he asked a group of Indian actors what the sign language for "Cherokee" was. Now, contrary to popular misconception, Indians have a pretty lively sense of humor. With poker faces they intoned, "Ah, Cherokee. This is it," giving the universally familiar close-fisted, raising-the-forearm obscene gesture.

The next time Coop saw me he said, "Hey, Cherokee," giving the new sign.

I didn't react, just deadpanned incomprehension.

"C'mon, this means 'Cherokee,' doesn't it?" He was genuinely disappointed.

"Coop," I said with a sigh, "what are you talking about? That means . . . you know, 'screw you.' It doesn't mean 'Cherokee.' "

With that he exploded with laughter and staggered away, repeating to himself what I'd just said and then laughing again. I thought he'd drop dead from the sheer exertion of it. It wasn't long before everybody on the set was giving each other the new sign for "Cherokee." Indians and whites, actors and directors, set designers and hands. I must say it did tend to relieve some of the pressure-cooker atmosphere of making movies. Nobody, including myself, was really offended. Coop just had a way about him and you'd have to try awfully hard to get mad at him.

He did go a little too far with a joke one time, though. At least *I* don't think it was funny, being at the brunt of it.

We were on location. The great stunt man and character actor Frank McGraff (Frank later played "Cookie" on TV's *Wagon Train* all those years) and Coop had found a scorpion, pulled its stinger out, and put it in a match box. I was atop a hill on my horse about to lead some Indians on a charge when Frank came galloping up beside me. The director yelled into his megaphone, "Okay, ready? Action!" Frank slipped the box into my shirt, tapping the top open.

"What the . . . what the hell are you doing?" I was already starting off with 200 warriors down the hill.

"Just give it to Coop when you get to the bottom," he called back, riding off to the side out of camera range.

I ignored it till about half-way down when suddenly I felt something crawling around my stomach. Having no idea what it was but suspecting the worst, I thought the last thing I should do is start swatting; not only would I ruin the scene and give them that satisfaction, but whatever it was would bite me for sure. Riding smoother than I think I ever rode in my life, I gritted my teeth and made it through the take.

At the bottom of the hill I very slowly reached in and, gently, pulled out this scorpion, not knowing that it had been de-stingered. I had been in Mexico and seen kids play with these little monsters, though. When I asked if they were ever bitten they said no, you just let them know you're not afraid. I tried letting my scorpion know I wasn't afraid.

Frank rode up with an expectant look on his face but I had the goddamned thing safely back in the box and tossed it at him.

"Here," I said with as much dignity as I could muster, "I think you lost something."

Then I rode off. Frank told me later that Coop asked him impatiently, "Well, what did he say, what did he say?"

"Nothing much. Just threw it at me and rode off."

Another disappointment, but good for a few laughs, anyway.

The only other guys in Hollywood I knew at this time with a taste for practical jokes like Coop were Yakima Canutt and Roy Rogers. Once, Yak walked up to Roy, stuck a gun in his belly, and said, "Howdy, pardner." Then somebody standing directly behind him blew off a real gun. Poor Roy's eyes almost jumped right out of his head.

But nobody loved to laugh and joke around more than Coop. Maybe nobody else needed to, like him.

VVVVVVVVVVVVVVVVVVVVVVVVVVV

4

Now I'D LIKE to mention something right from the start. It's to do with drunkenness. Booze, as I'm sure you'll soon gather, plays a central tragicomic role in this book. There's no way around it. Hollywood is deeply mired in one kind of mind-bending substance or another. It was and still is primarily alcohol, but lately I'm sure you've read about the avalanche of "snow" that has descended on the city. Actually, I think the reports of cocaine abuse are exaggerated, but it is definitely inching its way into the sinuses and minds of many people out here. Why all this drinking and snorting in Tinsel Land? Why do people who lead supposedly glamorous and exciting lives, who have plenty of money and are adored by millions, find the need to escape so often? I'm sure it has something to do with the tremendous pressure of making movies, the pressure to stay in the public's good graces, the pressure to stay young forever, to always be "on," to always be charming and entertaining. I know actors who, even at the breakfast table, feel they have to be a one-man vaudeville act between sips of coffee. Add that compulsion to the boredom of making movies, all the sitting around waiting for technicians to ready a shot. Top it off with the silliness of the whole thing, the fact that acting is something that children do, really. If you keep it up into adulthood, always acting as somebody other than who you really are, you'll not only have a pretty hazy self-image but an immature one at that. This not knowing who you are can be painful stuff—can even drive you bats—so what better escape than drink?

And who more susceptible than *Indian* actors? The poison of alcohol had already made strong inroads into a dessicated Indian culture long before Cecil B. DeMille ever filmed *The Squaw Man.* This isn't to say, of course, that all Indians are victims of alcoholism (many Indians won't touch the stuff), but the ones that do drink to ease the boredom, to kill off the pain of not knowing who they are, seem to do a pretty good job of it. I've known Indians who'll drink themselves into a stupor, wake up long enough to find another bottle, and start in over again. I'm not about to explain this tragedy to you; for that you might start with *Bury My Heart at Wounded Knee* or when the first white explorers met their first Indians. What's more, my own story isn't really a reflection of Indians per se, any more than the shenanagans of some white actors are a reflection of white America as a whole. Or, I don't know, maybe it is—you'll have to decide that one, depending on your politics or your view of America itself. I guess all I'm saying is that this is the story of *my* life and it's a story about Hollywood. The Indians who participated in acting out their role in the myth of the American West, including myself, *became* part of Hollywood. You might say we were sort of swept up in it, and bought the fantasies the Dream Factory turned out. The Indians we hired as extras were also swept along with the joy of being paid decently at something which was, really, a lot of fun: riding horses, shooting, and yelling.

But what about the way Indians have been depicted on the screen? The excessive violence, the stereotyping? That gets back to the entertainment business versus historical documentation. It isn't that, at least with the aggressive tribes, there wasn't fighting and scalping (although I should point out that the French were the first to introduce scalping to the New World). Where the movies were chiefly inaccurate was in showing Indians seemingly doing nothing but. It's a little like deciding all Americans are blood-thirsty savages on the basis of news clips of the war in Vietnam. There is a side to Indian life rarely shown in the movies, the day-to-day existence of hunting and child rearing, of calm and beauty and oneness with nature. We're seeing more of the Indian as a human being now as a result of struggling with studio bosses and powerful directors. When I first started in the film business, I had no power and was there to do what I was told: to make *exciting* Western entertainment. And in the days of the big studios, you either did what you were told or you didn't work. So we made movies, we "gave them what they wanted," as movies always did and continue to do. The stereotyped movie image of Indians as child warrior didn't begin changing until general awareness set in after World War II.

So, that said, let's get back to our story.

As you can imagine, when there were problems with extras in the early days of moviemaking, both white or red, directors practically tore their hair out in frustration. I think James Cruze actually lost about half of his aleady thinning locks by the time *The Covered Wagon* was finished. (Incidentally, no sooner was *The Covered Wagon* completed than the producers were slapped with a $5 million law suit for defamation of one of the historical characters—the family sued.) Many of the directors dealt with problems on the set in only one way: pure orneriness. John Ford was one, for sure. So was DeMille. But probably the meanest, orneriest of the lot was W.S. "Woody" Van Dyke.

Tim McCoy had just been signed up by MGM and we were off on a remote location in Wyoming doing some action scenes for his first full-length feature, *War Paint*. It was 1926, a year after Coop made his debut in *Wolfsong*. Tim pointed out in his biography that he had a good idea what it would be like working with Van Dyke when he sat in on a story conference with writers and assistant directors. Everybody took turns giving his idea of how the story might be told, and Van Dyke sat there with his chin in hand, a scowl on his face. Finally he interrupted.

"Any of you geeks know what the hell you're talking about?"

There was silence around the table.

"That's what I thought," he said. "McCoy here and I are going to write this goddamned thing ourselves."

They were up all night working on the script for *War Paint*, which isn't that formidable a task when you remember there's no dialogue, just story line. The "shooting script," giving directions about camera angle and so on, was generally improvised as they went along.

One of the scenes called for a band of Indians to charge down upon Tim and I, with me playing his friend and scout. One of the Indians was a full-blooded Apache named Frank Hill. Frank had been drinking a little, which only added enthusiasm to a personality already as wild as any plains warrior of a hundred years ago. He was so enthusiastic, in fact, that when the Indians circled us, whooping and screeching, Frank stuck the barrell of his 45–70 right in Tim's face and pulled the trigger. As was often the case with "blanks" in those days, the powder had dried and caked, causing it to explode with enough force to knock Tim right out of his saddle. At the instant it went off, I knocked Frank's barrel back with my arm, and instead of turning Tim's face into a charred stump, it took off a little piece of his ear and peppered the back of his neck with small powder holes. He lay on the ground, bleeding and unconscious, and the Indians, noticeably pained, quietly gathered their ponies in a ring around him. Frank had turned his gun around and was examining the barrel with a puzzled look on his face.

"More bite than thunder," he said, summing up.

Van Dyke threw his script on the ground with great violence. "No, no, *no!*" he roared. He ran up to Tim and kicked him on the heel of his boot. "You weren't supposed to fall off the horse, you stupid bastard. Now you've ruined a beautiful shot, goddamnit."

I slid off my horse, grabbed Tim under his arms, and pulled him to his feet. He groaned.

"Well, at least you're alive," snorted Van Dyke in disgust. "Thalberg will be pleased to hear that, anyway. Now get ready for another take. Iron Eyes, put him on his horse," he said, and marched back to his director's chair.

"Tim, are you all right? Think you can . . . Tim?" He slumped in my arms. "Mr. Van Dyke, I think we'd better get Tim to a hospital. He's bleeding pretty bad and he passed out."

"*What!* Whaddya mean he passed out? Put him on the goddamn horse anyway and let's get on with it!"

The Indians stared at each other. One of them murmured "*Niatha,*" which means "Smart like spider." Deciding we were in the employ of a madman, I lay Tim out gently in the dust and called for a stretcher.

During one summer when we weren't making films, I hit the road again with another traveling circus. This one was called Buck Jones' Wild West Show, fashioned somewhat after Buffalo Bill and Tim McCoy's Wild West shows, with many movie cowboys and cowgirls. Monty Montana and I were specialty acts. And, like Tim McCoy, they went broke with it. Damn thing never made a dime.

Traveling shows were, first of all, often at the mercy of unscrupulous promoters. Keeping ahead of the performances, these "advance men" were supposed to set up bookings, advertise, and collect the gate, and then rendezvous with us at some point and divvy up. Too often, they would mysteriously disappear. In all honesty, they were both white men *and* Indians, the latter making good salesmen because of the novelty, I suppose. One Indian promoter, a tall guy named Mo Besmart, once left at least fifty Indians, including myself, waiting for our salaries on his wife's front lawn while he skipped off to Las Vegas. The generous woman served every one of us dinner that night, but I can remember many a time having to hock our Indian costumes just to get money to put food in our stomachs.

The Buck Jones Show (as we'll call it for short) was outfitted almost entirely with people and equipment used in Buck Jones' Westerns. With the exception of the Indians and their costumes, which I provided, all the horses, cowboys, cowgirls, and props were movie regulars. Buck had for himself an entire train, with the show's title sweeping majestically across several cars in gold lettering. Pretty impressive, but apparently our would-be audiences didn't agree. The turnout opening night was dismal, about one-third capacity in the huge tent we had pitched outside Los Angeles. Then it was on to Winimucka, Nevada. It's one thing to flop in Hollywood, but Winimucka? Everybody was already so dispirited at this early juncture they almost all took to drink, including the Indians. We were all so drunk by the time we got to Las Vegas we provided the most entertaining show to date, complete with pratfalls, off-cue entrances, forgotten and/or slurred lines. I was to lead an "attack" on a stagecoach, where some of us were to fall on cue at the moment shots were fired. Indians fell off their horses *before* the shots, most of them from laughing so hard they couldn't hang onto the reins. The audience loved it. On top of it all, this was an extremely uncomfortable trip. We slept on lumpy bunks in un-air-conditioned cars, the dusty, furnace-like air blowing in from the desert, and we spent most of the time traveling. Most everybody drank just to take the edge off those awful train rides, to say nothing of our lackluster performance at the box office.

Buck Jones had made some decent little Westerns at Fox, much along the realistic lines of William S. Hart. Or at least he looked the part, being rugged, handsome, and not too flamboyant in his dress. Most of the other "Big Five" followed in the slick tradition of Tom

Mix. Buck had sunk at least $200,000, a fortune in those days, in this traveling circus. He also bought a new Packard which, with his wife, Dell, he followed us in from town to town. As we were pulling out of Las Vegas, some railroad officials pulled up in a black sedan and ordered the train stopped. A little man flanked by two big sheriffs stepped out of another car and demanded of Buck $3,000 payment for renting the train locomotive. This was news to me—I thought he owned the whole damn thing.

"Three thousand dollars?" he roared, "For *what*?"

"You know perfectly well for what," said the little man, somewhat nervously. He glanced on either side at the burly cops for reassurance. "You made three stops and did three shows. Your contract calls for payment of $1,000 each performance. These gentlemen and I are here to see to it you haven't, shall we say, forgotten anything, as I haven't heard from you since you left Los Angeles."

"Well we haven't made a cent yet, barely able to make salary, so I can't pay you nothin'. If you wanna do anything about it, I'll take on the whole lot of you, right here."

That was Buck for you, always ready to fight anybody. It turns out the little man settled for Buck's Packard in lieu of payment instead of a punch in the nose. But now Buck and his wife had to ride on the train with the rest of us.

We headed north from Las Vegas, up across the northwest tip of Arizona and on into Colorado, stopping every few hundred miles for a show. We did one performance a day, and each was as bad as the last. Buck, who had remained optimistic up till Las Vegas, was now beginning to show signs of wear. His wife complained about the train ride constantly, and he was developing a mean streak in the treatment of his horses. That was unusual for him. He was also getting distrustful. When it came time for payday he stationed one of the performing clowns, armed with a shotgun, by the paymaster, who was deaf and dumb. The clown's name was Ike Lowen, who went on to become a big circus clown. In addition to making sure there wasn't a rush on the paymaster, Ike was also given instructions to "fill that little prairie turd full of buckshot" should he come around demanding more payments on the locomotive. When it got down to paying the Indians—low man on the totem pole, as usual—they ran out of funds after only half had received their salaries. I thought for sure that would do it. The Indians were gonna bust some heads and people would get killed. To make matters worse, one of them had deposited $500 with the "bank" when he was drunk, and now of course it was gone. He was threatening to burn the whole train down, and the other Indians were grumbling and cursing to themselves, or trying to find out from the deaf and dumb paymaster when they'd get paid. Buck showed up, but he didn't help matters any by telling everybody to shut up and stop complaining, that they'd get paid after the next show and if they didn't like it they could get the hell out. All was not lost, though. Monty Montana's father was along on this tour. He was a part-time preacher, somewhat along the lines of an Oral Roberts without the mass following. He stood up on the back step of a railroad car and I'll be damned if he didn't commence preaching to all of us.

"My friends, if you will just calm down and listen to me for a moment, that's right, just a moment of your time for Jee-suss. For y'know, Jee-suss under*stands* you're plight, he under*stands* you've been drinkin' and fallin' offa your horses, he under*stands* you ain't been paid. Jee'sus understands you've been *bad!* And it's only Him that can save you!"

Finally Buck came up to me.

"Look, Iron Eyes, this is your department. Why don't you say something to them?"

"I don't see as there's much to say, Buck. They want their money, not religion. Money's *your* department."

But as Father Montana droned on, the crowd, still grumbling, started to disperse. He had worked himself up into quite a passion by now, but his congregation had dwindled to two or three Indians, and they had fallen asleep.

By the time the Buck Jones Wild West Show had made it to Pueblo, Colorado, we'd about had it. Buck gathered us all together and said he was leaving for Los Angeles the next day, and that he was sorry nobody could get paid this time because the show was flat broke. The only thing he could offer was an IOU and a free ride home. For obvious reasons, nobody seemed too broken up. That afternoon, in fact, we gave a pretty spirited little performance to the handful of people who showed up at the gate for the last show.

Then, in the early evening, a car with the back half sawed off and replaced with a kind of huge trailer pulled up. It was a bunch of whores out of Pueblo, what you might call an advance scouting party. They were all dressed in tight, slinky dresses, and heavily made up, but still very comely looking. All blondes. It happens I was standing around talking with a small group of my closer Indian friends, and the driver walked up to me and smiled.

"Hi! You guys are Indians, aren't you?"

"That's right," I said wearily.

"Well, we sure do like Indians," she said heartily, and looked over her shoulder at her colleagues. "Don't we, girls!" A chorus of laughter and general agreement came from her colleagues.

"That's nice, but we're broke, so you're wasting your time. In fact, the whole show is broke. We're gonna pull out tomorrow and head for home."

"Izat so?"

She grew serious for a minute, and looked me up and down knowingly.

"Hell, why don't you come with us, then? We'll see you get home okay. We just *love* Indians."

I guess I should mention here that I went along on these circus tours more for the adventure than anything else. I didn't need the money, or whatever money I thought I might make. I had, in fact, just been talking over with my friends the possibility of doing a mini-prologue to Western movies, telling stories, dancing, traveling from town to town, and working our way back home like that. The only problem was we had twenty-four dollars between us, and this was before the days of easy-access checking accounts. We looked at each other, grinned, and I shook hands with our new benefactor. In an hour we had loaded a few things in the back of their wagon, I had a guarantee from Buck that my costumes and props would be delivered safely to my Paramount warehouse, and we were off.

We were, literally, "on the other side of the tracks" in Pueblo, since the city had an actual red light district in those days. Our hostesses turned out to be ex-Mormons who had "gone bad," as they told us, but they were the sweetest women I've yet to encounter. Real ladies. They had a smartly decorated house and a regular clientele, no bums or heavy drinkers allowed. And they did have this genuine passion for Indians that I won't pretend to understand. It was all we could do to drag ourselves away from their beds.

[77]

After their generosity, including loaning me money for a car, they asked for nothing in return except to be thought of from time to time.

"Just remember us, boys," said the driver who had first approached me, waving us off. "Say something good about us to that Big Spirit of yours."

About ten years ago this same lady was running for some local political office, after having spent the larger part of her life as a successful madam. Evidently she found success in the political arena simply by carrying over the skills acquired in her former profession.

It may surprise you that we were fairly successful with our little prologue. It certainly did surprise us. The theater owners, when they didn't slam the door in our faces, were pleased to do business. We dressed up and paraded through the town, and I'm sure theater attendance picked up considerably. We hardly made any money—enough to get by on—but, what the hell, it was all in fun.

When we got back to Hollywood, I spent another year with the studios and was fast approaching twenty-one. (It was 1928.) I suspected I was about grown up, because now I was getting an urge to settle down. My wanderlust was certainly ebbing. I thought it might not be a bad idea to look up my wife and see if she'd have anything to do with me. I dropped by the Southwest Museum in Los Angeles, where her mother told me she was working as an assistant. Sure enough, there was Birdie, down in the basement, marking specimens.

"Excuse me," I said, "But aren't you Mrs. Cody?"

She paused, lifted her head a moment, and, without looking at me, went back to pasting labels on pieces of rock. "Yes-s-s," she said, stretching the word out to a fine, sarcastic edge. Always a smart aleck, Birdie was. "And I suppose you're Mr. Cody?" Then, spinning around, she glared at me icily. "What do you want?"

"Well, uh, how about going out to dinner tonight?" The direct approach. I could think of nothing else.

"*What?* You disappear for four years, spend your time with all those girls—and don't think I don't know about it, either—then have the nerve to march in here and just ask me out?"

"C'mon, Birdie. How old were we when we got married? I just

[78]

thought you might like to join Chief Thunderbird and a whole group of us for dinner."

You'll recall it was the chief who had married us. He was now a successful lecturer, making about $500 for each speech he gave to various groups—PTAs, historical organizations, colleges, you name it. That was fantastic money in those days, and as business was brisk he now had himself a big brick home up on the hills and was always entertaining people. At the mention of his name Birdie went through the most amazing transformation, she being an admirer of his. She seemed to get angrier and softer, both at the same time. Then she just exploded with an exasperated "Ugh-h-h-h!" and turned back to her work. I knew I had her.

"Well, what do you say? It's just dinner."

"Oh, I don't know. . . . I suppose if you insist. Tell you what, why not come to my grandmother's for dinner?"

"No, no. You know how the chief likes to entertain. Big deal planned. It's all set."

"I think we'll all go to my grandmother's," she said, turning back to her work and humming. At this moment she was indistinguishable from the rock specimens.

"But . . . what's the point in . . . Okay, okay. We'll go and see the chief to get his opinion. Birdie? Birdie, are you listening to me?"

"Oh," she said between her humming, "don't forget to bring something for grandmother. You know how she feels about that sort of thing."

Well, I did manage to eventually drag her over to Chief Thunderbird's. It was on the way. He'd supply much needed reinforcements, I thought.

"Chief Thunderbird, you remember my wife, Birdie?"

"Yeah," snorted the chief, appearing to almost back away. "Yeah, I know her." Birdie had this unique talent for making certain men squirm and clam up by seeing into them. She had worked with the chief since our marriage and apparently left quite an impression.

"You want to go where?" he asked, "Grandma Dark Cloud's house? She don't like me."

"Oh, that's okay," piped Birdie cheerfully. "She doesn't care much for Iron Eyes, either. You'll both feel right at home."

So, off for dinner to grandma's house with the ten Indians. Birdie did the cooking. Everything she served the chief and our friends was delicious—fried bread and plenty of beef. Everything except what was put in front of me, which was burnt to a crisp.

"Birdie," I said, "so this is why you wanted us here. I've tasted your cooking before and know you're good at it. Right now you're cooking like your drunken mother."

With that she stood up and slapped me, crying, "That's my mother you're talking about!"

"Yeah, and if my drunken father was here he'd tell you the same thing!"

She pointed a finger at the charred lumps on my plate. "Eat it then. And *like* it." She stomped away from the table and curled up on one of the cots in another room.

Indian men consider it weak to show outward signs of emotional distress over domestic matters so, although the steam was coming out of my ears, I managed to shrug it off. We all continued our meal as if nothing had happened, chatting with the chief about the finer points of stalking deer. Then we sang songs for a few hours until I started getting sleepy myself. Edging away from the table, I tiptoed into the room Birdie was in and lay beside her. Grandma Dark Cloud's little dog jumped up on our legs, and the three of us slept peacefully. The contingent in the kitchen stayed up all night (perfectly customary for an Indian gathering of this sort), singing songs, laughing their heads off, and enjoying themselves.

We woke early in the morning and Birdie, seeing me beside her, leaned over and gently kissed my cheek. She smiled.

"How are you?"

"Okay, I guess. My stomach feels a bit heavy is all. Must be something I ate."

She giggled. "Let's bury the hatchet, shall we?"

And we did.

Later, I jumped off that cot, my heart bursting with joy, and went in the kitchen to join Thunderbird and our friends. They were still going strong.

"Thunderbird," I said, slapping his back with manly good cheer, almost knocking him over, "let's sing some crazy songs."

He regarded me suspiciously. "What do you mean, 'crazy'?"

"You know, love songs."

"Ah-h-h," he said, nodding his head and grinning. "I know just the thing."

We launched into an old Indian courting song, intended to poke fun at your loved one. It's sung by all tribes, each in its own language. Translated, it goes something like this:

> Oh yes I love you hon-ney, hi-hey-ho
> I don't care if you're mar-ried, hi-hey-yo
> I will come to you to-night, hi-hey-yo.

Okay, so who's claiming we're especially romantic? All I can say is Birdie came out to sing along and cook us up some hot cakes. They came out perfect, not a single one burnt. I figured we had made up.

I was sure I wanted to *stay* with her, though. Then we were on our way up to northern California that very day. She had some research to do on a famous medicine man named John and suggested we drive up together in my car. We made it around nightfall and Birdie mentioned I should buy some groceries for these people, that they were especially poor. Medicine men live like church mice, you see, often from hand to mouth and barely surviving on donations and the charity of others. Then she started singing some weird Indian songs I'd never heard before.

"What's that you're singing, Birdie?" I asked, pulling off the road in front of a tiny house with a tent pitched next to it. She looked at me, her eyes sparkling.

"Oh, I'm singing John's songs, some that you'll hear tonight. He's going to make everyone laugh. He's going to sing songs that will make the spirit flow amongst us. You'll feel all of life under your hair and in your hands."

She took my hands in hers after we came to a stop. I could already hear the chanting and rhythm of drums from inside the tent. I know this sounds corny, but I looked at Birdie and felt she was right inside me somehow. I can't explain it any other way. And that I wasn't alone and that I would never be alone. When we got inside, the feeling increased in intensity. A little like your insides are warm and crawling all around. It's what they mean when they say a medicine ceremony turns you inside out. John then prayed for three straight hours. He didn't say anything was good or bad, and didn't place people above the other living things on the earth. He prayed for our enemies as well as our friends. He prayed for everything—birds, snakes, even bugs that bite you. Then we all joined in. I can't think of anything more humbling than praying for a damn gnat, but I did, and I felt the spirit creeping into my bones. For three hours, we prayed and prayed. Some people started moaning and saying they were healed in some part of their body. Everybody was healed in the soul. I know this kind of thing isn't unique to Indians. The Spirit is there for all people who learn to reach out to each other, Christians, Buddhists, Hindus, whatever. Some call it God, we call it the Great Spirit. Same thing, wherever you go.

When we were hungry—and everybody seemed to get hungry at once—we all moved into the house and sat ourselves down on the living room floor. An old woman stood up and, with appropriate solemnity, announced, "It is now time to eat."

We were served up plenty of fried bread and meat stew. Birdie and I were famished from our long drive and stuffed ourselves, happily exclaiming with full mouths how good everything was.

Birdie's mother, Bula, was there, too, sitting next to us. Looking about to see if anyone was listening, she whispered to Birdie, "I think we've been eating dog meat."

"What?"

"Dog meat. We've been eating dog meat."

Birdie nudged me to indicate her mother may have been drinking and said with a patient sigh that she probably meant cheap hamburger meat like we would buy for the dogs.

"No, no. I mean *dog* meat. Meat from a dog. And I'm not drunk, so don't ignore me."

We looked at each other, then down in our stew bowls.

"Come to think of it," I said weakly, "it is a bit on the sweet side. I thought it was maybe rabbit . . . or squirrel."

We got up, went into the kitchen, and saw a bloodied towel draped over something big on the table. Birdie slowly lifted it and there, attached to nothing but a long rib cage, spinal column, and tail, was the huge shaggy head of a dog. We had been gorging ourselves on German shepherd!

Birdie instantly became violently ill and ran out in the backyard.

I managed to contain myself, barely, and ran out after her. "C'mon now, Birdie, try to control yourself. We can't get sick and insult these people."

"But . . . (gasp) . . . did, did you see it? Horrible. Have *you* ever eaten a dog like that before?"

Well, actually not like that. I had tasted dog meat, but it was at a ceremonial event of the Sioux. They raised special little white dogs in a secret way—nobody can look upon them except the medicine men—and you're given just a little bite. Something along the line of the Christian Communion. Here with these Northern California Indians—who wear their hair short and dress in ordinary white man's apparel—we had been feasting on this animal from who knows where. Or how long dead, for that matter.

After Birdie finished relieving herself we tottered back into the kitchen and John was there to greet us.

"Is something wrong?" he asked, noticing Birdie's sickly pallor.

"Wrong? No, no nothing wrong. Say, John, uh, how did you come about this dog here?"

"Him? Oh, about an hour before you folks arrived a car hit him right out front. The poor dog, we took him into the house and tried to save him with my best medicine, but he died. Then I had a vision. In my dream the Great Spirit told me to take this dog and have a feast on him. So the dog provided food for us. The old woman, she told you, didn't she?"

"No!" gasped Birdie, about to convulse again.

"Hmmm. I told her to tell everybody and that if you did not like dog, not to eat."

"We didn't see you for a long time," I explained. "We heard nothing."

"Yes, I had to go out and pray, of course. I took some of the meat and gave it to the Great Spirit."

Nothing will keep an Indian from his prayers when it comes to offerings like this. Buffalo meat, deer meat, dog meat, whatever, you'll wait fifteen or twenty minutes and let the food get cold before touching it. Doesn't mean a damn thing to an Indian. Also, it's rude to refuse food of any kind from an Indian, and we were out of place. No explanations from John were necessary.

This is the Medicine Way.

VVVVVVVVVVVVVVVVVVVVVVVVVV

5

IT WASN'T LONG after I got back with Birdie and back into the
movie business that my father decided his home wasn't back on
the ranch with my mother. He preferred celluloid to horses and
corn. He was also still hitting the bottle. It wasn't too much of a
drawback, even though he'd already gotten a bad reputation for
drinking on the job. A good many of the upper crust in Hollywood,
the big producers and directors, still liked him and offered him
work. More important, he knew more Indian chiefs than we did at
this time. It was an easy matter for him to round up, say, 500
braves for a major Western, just through his friends.

One day in the early fall of 1929 I was in the wardrobe department at Fox Studio sorting through our costumes in preparation for
a big Western to be shot in Arizona. Beyond that I didn't know too
much about it. In marched Raoul Walsh with a huge, serious-
looking boy of about twenty-one.

"Iron Eyes, say hello to Duke Morrison."

"I think I've seen you around here before," I said, shaking hands.
"Haven't you been propping for Jack Ford?"

"That's right. And I think I've played cards a few times with your
father. Thomas Longbloom, isn't it? Tall, good-looking guy, long
hair like yours?"

"Yeah, that's him all right."

"Not much of a card player. He can hold his liquor, though."

"He's had plenty of practice."

"Look," said Walsh, "Duke here needs a buckskin outfit that
looks like it's been on the trail a few months. I'd like some Indian
beads worked into it. Can you fix him up?"

"Sure thing."

Walsh left us, and this six-foot four-inch ex-football player for
the University of Southern California proceeded to describe in

minute detail exactly how he wanted to look for his premiere role in the movies, including shortening the jacket to make him look even taller. Prop men, those who were responsible for ashtrays in their exact spot for a particular star's whimsical manner of flicking his ash, or seeing to it that the chair collapses at the moment the villain (or good guy) is hit over the head, certainly knew their way around the wardrobe department. I hit it off fine with Marion "Duke" Morrison, later to become John Wayne.

The movie I was preparing him for was one of the biggest gambles ever undertaken in Hollywood, a million-dollar epic Western only two years after the revolution in sound, which most people thought had killed off the genre. Most except William Fox and Raoul Walsh. With the advent of sound, microphones had to be concealed in fixed positions and cameras put in these heavy, soundproof booths so their noise wouldn't be recorded. Since this limited mobility, you had great difficulty capturing the most important ingredient of Westerns—the *action*. But Walsh, using the Fox newsreel sound truck and a lightweight mobile camera, shot the first successful Western talkie for only $100,000. It was called *In Old Arizona*, with Warner Baxter as the Cisco Kid. My father and I did the technical advising, and it was a big hit.

The studio bought a story about the Oregon Trail and contracted Walsh to make "the biggest Western of all time," *The Big Trail*. They didn't use the old silent stars because everybody thought they couldn't talk worth a damn, so they went East and hired Broadway actors such as Tyrone Power, Sr., Ian Keith, Tully Marshal. Taking these New Yorkers out of their habitat, plunking them out in the middle of the desert, and sticking a camera in their faces for the first time was Walsh's first big mistake.

Walsh had hoped to cast Coop for the part of the frontier scout, but Sam Goldwyn, who had promised him, changed his mind at the last minute and put Coop in *The Winning of Barbara Worth*. Who would be right for the rugged part of the scout besides the usual cowboys, who could ride and shoot okay but were drunken sods who couldn't count past three?

Now I've heard the story of Duke's landing the part for *The Big Trail* about a dozen times from as many sources, including Duke himself, but I still don't know for sure if it was John Ford who made the initial recommendation, or if Walsh discovered Duke on his own. Anyway, Walsh screened Marion Morrison by putting him next to two stars of the film and rolling the camera, to see how he'd react. The scene was taken from the script, of which the two stars had a copy but not Duke. They were to ask him various questions about the long road West. Did he know the way? What kind of Indians would they encounter? How many miles between this particular watering hole and another? And so on. Scared and sweating, Duke at first gave hesitant, mumbled answers until he got mad and started making up his own questions, yelling, "Can *you* handle a gun? Can *you* ride a horse? Could you *kill* a man?"

The producers liked the screen test, but didn't know what to do about his name.

"Marion Morrison? What's he, a fairy or something? That's no name for a leading man," grumbled Winfield Sheehan, the new head of production at Fox.

"We've got to have a good American name," said Sol Wurtzel, another big producer.

Walsh was an American Revolution buff and knew his generals, including "Mad Anthony Wayne."

"How about Anthony Wayne?"

"Nah, too Italian."

"Okay, we'll Americanize it. Tony Wayne."

"Now he sounds like a fairy again."

"Well, what's the matter with just plain John? John Wayne."

And there you have it.

In a few weeks I was on a train with the entire company for *The Big Trail* bound for Yuma, Arizona. Some of *The Big Trail* was shot there, the rest up in Yellowstone National Park, the Grand Tetons, Sequoia National Park, Jackson Hole, and even the Grand Canyon. Walsh had erected a replica of a frontier settlement on the Apache reservation out there, intending to use some of the indigents for extras. Big mistake number two.

The first thing everybody did when they got settled into the routine of rising before dawn, makeup at seven, and being on the set at eight was to get stoned drunk. The New York actors, used to dropping into bed around dawn after an evening on the boards and long hours of nightclubbing, were miserable on location in the desert. This was their first exposure to moviemaking; they didn't like the idea of breaking up the continuity and couldn't understand why scenes were shot out of sequence. Their timing was all off. They hated everything about movies—including Walsh—and drowned themselves in whiskey the whole time they were there. Cheerfully joining—and supplying—them was my father, who kept a bootleg runner going back and forth from the location to Yuma. It's incredible that anything was accomplished at all.

Walsh himself had a little surprise pulled on him. When we got to location Sheehan and Wurtzel were there to greet him with this gigantic camera. *The Big Trail* was to be shot in 70mm "Grandeur Screen," the first departure ever from 35mm. William Fox, a genius, gambler, and crazy man, had decided that audiences were ready for the big screen, and what better movie to debut his grand vision than *The Big Trail*? The only problem was that there wasn't a single theater in the country equipped to handle 70mm film except Grauman's Chinese, where the picture eventually opened. But, hey, minor details, right?

Anyway, this just added to Walsh's woes. "Goddamnit," he would say, stomping around the set looking frayed and about to explode, "I'm up to my ass in drunks! This is no way to make a picture!"

My father and I were charged with hiring Apaches, dressing them up, and getting them to perform as extras for these strange white men with their nonsense machines. No problem. It wasn't long, though, before they took my father's and everyone else's lead, and started off the day's shooting with a shot of booze. Then another one. We all settled into a routine of sloshing in whiskey from one take to another, day after day.

One afternoon Duke came into my tent (we all had tents on location in those days) and told me he had a really bad case of the runs. He looked about ten pounds lighter and his complexion blended nicely into the off-white dust all around us, I thought. Except for those haunting, pain-ridden eyes of his.

"I've been puking and crapping blood for a week now. You Indians got anything I can take for this shit?"

Now at this time John Wayne wasn't anything like the character he managed to turn himself into over the years. None of that swagger, rolling hips, and dropping his g's. Standing before me was a very sick, confused kid with decent manners. I say "kid," but actually he was six years older than me.

"Jesus, did you tell Mr. Walsh? I don't really have anything for something as serious as that. We do have this remedy where we take the rattler from a snake and—"

"Huh? No thanks. I'll manage."

And that's just what he did. He always drove himself to his limit, whether it was creating a role or destroying himself.

On the last night of our work in Yuma I hit the sack early, exhausted after a day of trying to direct drunken Apaches reeling crazily in their saddles and chasing runaway horses. My father spent most of the time sleeping off the night's drunk in Yuma with the rest of the crew (there was a whorehouse in town which kept him and everyone else pretty busy). I was awakened by a rough jab in my shoulder.

"Hey, Indian, geddup. We're being attacked by Indians."

"Hmmmmmm." I opened one eye and peered at two glowing, mean little slits carved out of a red jack 'o' lantern face. It was Duke, delicately holding a bottle of hootch in the crook of his index finger and obviously feeling very good.

"Right . . . Indians attacking . . . "

"I'm serious, damnit. C'mon, geddup. You godda help chase 'em away. Nobody knows 'em like you," he managed, staggering slightly as he flicked the jug to his lips. With me staring in amazement, even in my half-asleep stupor, he chugged down a good pint of that rotgut booze.

"Jesus, Duke, take it easy," I said, shaking off sleep. "I thought you were supposed to be sick. Keep that up you'll crap your stomach out."

It occurred to me that it *did* sound like a war going on somewhere in the vicinity of the set—a lot of war whoops, screeching, and yelling amid the thunder of horses' hooves. There was occasional gunfire, and everything sounded like it was getting closer by the minute. Duke gave me an I-told-you-so nod. I jumped up and ran to the flap of my tent. At least fifty Apaches were on horseback, riding round and round the set shooting real flaming arrows into the fake scenery! Half were carrying jugs of whiskey, waving them

in the air. The air was filled with dust and smoke, the set already
lighting up the desert sky with ten-foot flames. The Indians looked
magnificent, their morning's war paint still intact and war bonnets
trailing behind them like banners. A few members of the company
were out, running around yelling, "Injuns, Injuns!," an occasional
rubber arrow bouncing comically off a head (we used rubber arrows
for shooting at people, real ones for inanimate objects). The other
folks were mostly cowboys falling all over each other, as drunk as
the Indians and laughing till they'd choke on the dust, ashes, and
smoke whirling about in the blood-red light from the fire. Then
they'd take a shot or two at the "attackers" with a blank-loaded
gun.

"Ya-a-a-a-hooo!" they'd yell, draw a bead, and shoot.

Well, let me tell you, it was the most fantastic thing I had ever
seen. Something just snapped in me, maybe from all the pressure
and drudgery of the filming. Maybe I just needed to join the fun.
Whatever, I let out my very best whoop, turned to Duke leaning on
the tent pole, and let out another.

"Yip-yeeeeeeeeeeeaaaaaaaa!"

Duke was a little too gone to appreciate my enthusiasm as he
just looked at me with a blank expression, shrugged, and quietly
went back to his drinking. I pushed by him, grabbed a dozen rubber
arrows and my bow, and, still in my underpants, ran out, jumped
on my Appaloosa horse, and, bareback, rode off to war. It was the
wildest fun I think I've ever had in my life.

After we'd pretty much demolishd the set we charged over to the
supply train and rode round and round, round and round, laughing
and screaming our lungs out. A few of the more spirited of us
savages started shooting burning arrows in the baggage cars and in
a few minutes they, too, leaped into flames. Burned 'em right down
to the axles.

I was so swept up in all this I can barely remember what happened the rest of the night. Some of the Apaches would eventually
fall off their horses, stagger off, and drop in the dust, passed out
from the hooch. The cowboys had yelled and laughed and drank
themselves to sleep, and the rest of the company was hiding in the
tents. I must have eventually run out of steam and, in a dream-like
state, let my horse take me back to my tent. I pulled back the flap

and there was Duke, spread-eagled across my cot and snoring like a bear. I didn't bother with the hopeless task of removing his bulk, so I curled up in a blanket on the earthen floor. I fell asleep instantly and dreamed of my forefathers racing across the plains after buffalo.

That was the most memorable event while filming *The Big Trail*. Apparently figuring the Indian attack was just one in a series of disasters that had befallen him since taking on the project, Walsh let bygones be bygones and didn't fire my father or me. We managed to drag ourselves through the rest of location shooting and completed the interiors back in Hollywood in time for the film's grand opening at Grauman's Chinese Theater in October 1930. And it really *was* grand! Can you imagine a movie opening today with searchlights sweeping the evening sky, famous stars arriving in Hispano-Suizas and Duesenbergs, throngs of hysterical spectators cheering and groping to touch one of their gods?

The governor's slip should have served as an omen to John Wayne. The publicity people at Fox got hold of him, had him grow his hair down to his shoulders (that's right, John Wayne!), dress up in a ridiculous cowboy outfit, and parade around telling lies about his past. I was there at Fox to help him climb into his yellow, elaborately tooled boots, a green plaid shirt and beaded jacket (my beads again), leather chaps, and a huge white ten-gallon hat. He had two guns in a belt holster and a Bowie knife in a sheath.

I thought he was the most pathetic man I'd ever seen. "Don't make me do this," he protested, "I feel like an elephant in a red dress." He looked on the verge of tears.

They sent him on a tour all over the country and I understand when he got to New York the more sophisticated newspeople there tore him to shreds. They printed mocking photos of him with arrows pointing to his wristwatch, saying, "Apparently this frontiersman never has to worry about the right time." Fox staged a kind of bizarre press conference for him in Central Park, where he would demonstrate some of his frontiersman skill. He actually was a good knife thrower, because a Fox stuntman had given him lessons before they started filming *The Big Trail*, including teaching him to throw a lariat and handle a gun. They put him on a spirited horse that shot across Central Park West (then with about half the tall apartment buildings it now has facing it), got loose from him when he dismounted, and galloped off! The press had to be satisfied with his knife throwing.

When he couldn't stand it any more, he cut his hair, quit the tour, and came back to Los Angeles. The movie was doing miserably at the box office, and Fox dropped his option. And that's when he really started drinking. Of course, I had already seen him display his talent for imbibing on location, and it certainly rivaled the level of poison my father could pour into himself. In fact, John Wayne could take booze of just about any variety—beer, whiskey, wine, everything all at once—better than any man I've ever known. For the next forty years of his life, not including the softer stuff, he drank at least a quart of whiskey every day.

For the nine-year period between *The Big Trail* and when John Ford picked him up for *Stagecoach* and made him a real star, John Wayne grubbed around Gower Gulch in Poverty Row. After *The Big Trail* flopped, the studio moguls buried the "A" Western for what they thought was for good. Poverty Row picked up where they left off. We cranked out movie after movie, serial after serial, working sunup to sunset, six days a week, except during the seven-day week "emergencies." We did a twelve-episode serial, five hours of viewing time, in three weeks. We did a feature-length film in six days. Location shooting was so rough we considered it lucky to get tents to sleep in. In fact, it was during a "no-tent" night, sleeping out in the open under an ice-cold desert sky, that Duke met the man largely responsible for teaching him the familiar characterizations we associate with him today. The drawling, hesitant speech and that famous hip-rolling walk of his were all pure Yakima Canutt. On this particular occasion we had worked well into the night, and were scheduled to get up again at the crack of dawn.

"Y'know somethin'," said Yak to Duke, after sitting down next to him at the campfire and handing him a pink bottle he'd been sipping from, "it sure don't . . . (nod of the head) . . . take long ta pass the night out here, does it, kee-yid."

Duke took a long pull on the bottle, handed it back, and said, "Sure . . . don't."

That was it. They were friends for life, and Duke Wayne had himself a role model.

After Republic pictures was formed from a hodgepodge of independent Poverty Row companies in 1933 and started turning out Bs with at least some semblance of character and plot, Duke began getting a name for himself among the working people in the South and Southwest who couldn't afford any other type of entertainment. He was the Burt Reynolds of his time. They called him the "Hero of the Five-Reelers." He was making $1,500 a picture, and finally married the Mexican woman he'd been pining away over ever since his college days, Josephine Saenz. But instead of settling down, he just took to drinking more. He sometimes showed up on the set so drunk I would have to wire his legs to the horse so he wouldn't fall off the saddle! He gathered around himself a tight group of cronies, Victor McLaughlin, Ward Bond—who went to USC with him and got his first part in *The Big Trail*—an odd assortment of drunks, often for card games, my father, and John Ford.

Even though John Ford stopped drinking and took up religion in his later days, he was never exactly what you'd call a nice guy. In fact, he could be downright sadistic at times, especially with regard to his sense of humor. Like Coop, he was a practical joker. And for some reason, he seemed to take special delight in tormenting poor Ward Bond. Maybe it's because Ward always considered himself star material and resented playing character roles opposite Duke in Ford pictures. Or maybe it was because, in Ford's eyes, he was just so big and ugly.

We were on the set of MGM's *They Were Expendable,* and Ford hired a beautiful, aspiring actress to play "star struck" with Ward. Her role was as a waitress at our table, always seeing to it Ward got served first, keeping the rest of us waiting. She'd compliment him, coddle him, ask for an autograph every time she saw him, and swoon if he touched her hand giving the pen back. All this, of course, had something of a head-swelling effect on Ward. He glowed and puffed himself up, and spoke about some big offers that were coming his way from "directors who know talent when they see it."

The act was carried on for a couple days. Then our "waitress" told Ward that her husband, who worked for the railroad, would be coming home tomorrow. Tears welled in her eyes as she said this was their last chance to see each other. She offered to have him come around her place that night. He was to bring a watermelon and a six-pack of beer. Ward accepted, though he couldn't understand the need for a watermelon. That night, he trudged up the path leading to this lady's house, a big watermelon under one arm, a six-pack under the other. Clumsily, he knocked on the door, and she called sweetly, "Come in. It's unlocked." He juggled his load and, probably delighted she had left all the lights off, opened the door and walked in. He was met with a barrage of gunfire—from blanks. Ford and company had been waiting for him. Poor Ward let out a yelp, threw the melon and beer into the air, and ran down the walk. I still don't know if he ever learned the truth. He looked so glum and mean the next morning that I was afraid to ask.

These kinds of pranks were going on all the time with characters like Duke, Ford, and Ward Bond. When pressed, they would speak highly of each other, especially Ford, who always said he "loved that wonderful guy," Ward Bond. And Bond was always there to help when Duke or Ford were in trouble of any kind. Or so drunk they couldn't move.

"Now remember, five's the limit, driving or no driving. I've seen how you get when you're around that Duke Wayne, and I don't want to have to carry *you* home."

"Sure, sure. You know you can depend on me, Birdie."

She thought about that for what I felt was a few seconds too long. She reached a conclusion with a firm nod of her head.

"Yes, I suppose you can be trusted," she said, giving my hand a little pat.

We were on our way to a typically extravagant Hollywood party, this one honoring Judy Canova's first Republic picture directed by my friend Frank McDonald. She was to be the guest of honor and John Wayne was to officially greet her. Dressed in black tie with my still-long hair, I thought I cut a pretty dashing figure, but Birdie, she was perfectly beautiful in her dark green, sequin gown and her hair piled on top of her head. Birdie and I agreed that as long as she would drive, I could do some drinking with "the boys." But five was the limit, or else she'd grab me up by twisting my arm around my back and drag me home (or so she said).

This thing was being held in a huge barn that had been converted into a ballroom, or maybe I should say it was a fancy ballroom with glass chandeliers and a thirty-foot bar made up to look like it was once a barn. We were met when we pulled up with the usual throng of Hollywood gawkers. Of course, I don't flatter myself into thinking they were there to gasp and weep over Birdie and me, but I was starting to get some recognition even then. It usually went something like, "Hey, there's the Indian I saw in . . . Gee, but he looks familiar." I managed to get myself photographed a lot, and with those big, old-fashioned light bulbs flashing and popping, and all the people around cheering (sometimes they even set up bleachers!) it certainly was exciting for us.

We made our way through the police line and there at the bar to greet us was Duke, looking well on his way to a big binge.

"Iron Eyes, Birdie—hey, my Indian pals. C'mon over. Wanna introduce ya to a friend of mine." He waved us over with that funny, stiff-waisted movement of his. He was with Ward Bond and someone, or something, that looked about seven feet tall.

"Meet the heavyweight boxing champion of South America, Arturo Godoy."

This is the same Arturo Godoy that Jack Dempsey had just finished pummeling, although he looked none the worse for it. His tiny eyes were set deep into mounds of flesh that seemed to have no distinctive features whatever, except to give the impression of indestructibility.

"Hello," he boomed in a voice like playing a record on a much slower speed.

We sipped drinks, chatted politely, and waited and waited for Judy Canova to show up. Duke was getting restless.

"Where th' hell is she," he said, throwing back a martini with one gulp. "Whadda we gettin' stood up or something? Hey, Arturo, betcha I can drink more of these things than you can."

"Ah, a contest, a contest," chimed in Ward. "Bartender, mix up a couple pitchers of martinis for my friends here!"

Well, let me tell you, they layed into those martinis like I've never seen anyone drink before. I think I must have counted thirteen or fourteen apiece, polished off in one or two gulps one right after the other, before they even started staggering. Finally Duke said, "Jesus, ain't anything gonna slow you down?" Then he spun that big guy around by the shoulders, got him in a bear hug, and lifted him right off the floor. He squeezed till I thought something would pop in his head—Duke's, that is, because it didn't seem to be bothering Arturo a bit. Just before Duke let go he let out a blood-curdling howl, like a wounded animal.

"Haw haw," said Arturo with a stupid grin. "Didn't hurt at all." Then he grabbed the pitcher of martinis, chugged three or four good gulps and, with that same ridiculous grin but his eyes suddenly glassed over, started listing to the left.

"Tim-ber-r-r-r-!" yelled Ward, cupping his hands to his mouth.

Arturo plowed through about two tables and six chairs before crashing to the floor in a seven-foot heap. A hush came over everybody at the bar as we all just stared, wondering if he was dead.

"Ah, he'll be all right," snorted Duke, waving him off, "but I ain't beat 'im yet. Gimme that pitcher."

He gulped almost half the damn thing. Even Ward Bond, who could drink almost as much as Duke, was amazed, whistling in appreciation.

Duke slammed the pitcher down, staring into the mirror over the bar with those pained, narrowed eyes, the upper half of his body swaying in tight little figure eights. Then one of the managers came over. He was sweating nervously.

"Mr. Wayne? Mr. Wayne, sir?"

Duke just continued swaying and looking into the mirror.

"Mr. Wayne, Miss Canova's car just pulled up. Are you . . . can you greet her now? Mr. Wayne?"

"Huh? Who're you?" he mumbled, looking about with a confused, childlike expression. "What's goin' on here. Where am I?" He took two steps away from the bar, staggered, his arms groping for imaginary holds of air, and fell sideways on one of the tables. There he lay, his feet still touching the floor, moaning and just staring off into space.

Ward gave me a poke. "Iron Eyes, we gotta get him out of here before the press sees him like this. Gimme a hand, will you?"

The manager looked hysterical. "But who's gonna greet Miss Canova?"

"You greet her. C'mon, Iron Eyes."

"Birdie," I said, "go in and find Mr. Yates. Tell him Duke had an accident at the bar—slipped and fell or something—and that we're taking him home. He'll officiate over the ceremony himself, probably."

We tiptoed around Arturo, who was snoring peacefully on the floor, each took an arm over our shoulders and half carried a semi-conscious John Wayne out the back door to Ward's car.

"You can go on back in," he said after we had Duke settled into the front seat. "I can manage him. I've done this plenty of times before."

I used to go hunting on occasion with Duke and Ward, but I wasn't too crazy about it. They would bring along their bottles, merrily drink away, and, without knowing it, become dangerous. Once, when Ward went over a ridge to flush out some game, Duke stumbled into the same vicinity. Thinking the disturbance in the bushes was a bear or something, he let him have it with his shotgun. Ward spent the next few days in the hospital having pellets taken out of his neck and back.

Duke was also a practical joker, and if his pranks ranged a little on the mean side there was a side to him which usually made up for it. I remember once we were on the set at Republic and this Mexican guy who chauffered everybody around announced he was getting married on location in Durango, Mexico. This was a town that Duke had bought up practically lock, stock, and barrel, all for producing his films. The chauffeur introduced his pretty, young bride, who flashed a knowing, come-on eye at big, handsome Duke Wayne and his buddies. What they did was get this guy—I think his name was Carlos—drunk and hide his wife right after the wedding ceremony. These cowboys Duke hung around with in those days were wild as hell. Most of them actually were just removed from actually being cowboys and just a tad on the callous side. They'd do anything for a laugh. Later, when Duke became a real star, he displayed another side of his personality: his boundless generosity. As a kind of reparation, Duke set poor Carlos up in his own business down in Mexico and supported him for life. He did that virtually with dozens of people, spending untold millions. Everybody said of him that he was the easiest touch in Hollywood if you needed cash. If you were broke, hit up Duke Wayne for a few thousand. If you needed a down payment for a new car, he'd give it to you, no strings attached. He was without a doubt the most generous man I ever knew.

But getting back to the thirties and the struggling years, Duke also tried co-producing some of his own films. But half the time his crew were too drunk to finish the thing, which ordinarily took about five or six days. Real cheapies. They cost maybe a whopping $1,000–$2,000 a day. He had opened up his own little studio in Gower Gulch, and they'd rent equipment from the bigger outfits, mostly Disney. This must have lasted only a year or two, and then Republic was keeping him fairly busy up until John Ford began taking serious notice of him.

Duke also made his stage debut in a play called *Red Sky at Evening*. At the dress rehearsal he polished off a bottle of Scotch to steady his nerves a mite. Then he made his entrance and, in accordance with the story, the leading lady screamed and smashed a breakaway vase over his head. Well, Duke reeled about, looking pained and confused and impressing everyone with his "natural" acting ability. Then he blurted, "Where am I? Where the hell *am* I?"

Those lines weren't called for anywhere in the script. And that single performance ended his stage career.

During the mid-thirties, since Duke's income from acting was at best unsteady, he tried his hand at a number of sidelines. Not too many people know it, but in addition to selling real estate, which he was miserable at, he even tried prizefighting. But after getting himself bounced around the ring he gave that up quick enough. Aside from not really getting anywhere in films, he was also having problems with his new wife. When he was working he'd come home too exhausted to even speak with her, and I don't think they ever had anything in common, anyway, except a physical attraction. Duke Wayne was wild about Mexican women, physically. But Josephine was a pious Catholic, and her idea of a good time was inviting the parish priest over for tea. To add to their troubles, they had a child in 1934, and by 1939 three more had come along.

In the later thirties, though, his career started taking an upswing. Republic signed him to bigger contracts, recognizing, if not his acting ability, his uncanny drive, sheer determination, and his developing discipline. It seemed like the man could never run out of energy and believed in doing everything in the extreme, whether it was drinking, acting, or just being a man. He was playing cards once with my father and his usual cronies when he started rambling on about his philosophy.

"I'm gonna play a real man to the best of my ability. Too goddamned many early Western stars were sissies—and that includes your Tim McCoy, Iron Eyes. Too goddamn perfect. Never drinkin' or smokin'. Never screwin' beautiful women. Never havin' a fight. Some goddamned heavy might smash him over the head with a chair and he'd just stand there lookin' surprised, never fightin' back in the same spirit. Too goddamned sweet and pure to be dirty fighters. Well, I'm *gonna* be a dirty fighter in my pictures if that's the only way to fight back . . . "

And on and on. You can think what you will about this brand of super-macho, but I'll tell you, he *was* ready to back it up. He did gain respect of a kind, slowly and painfully. While other actors constantly took abuse from strong directors, never did anyone say anything to Duke Wayne's face, with the exception of John Ford.

"Jack" Ford and John Wayne had been friends all during Duke's Poverty Row years, in fact. We used to all go off for fishing expeditions on Ford's hundred-foot ketch, which he called the *Araner.* Duke was invited on these expeditions more than anyone.

"When you learn to act someday, I'll put you in a good picture," he would tease. Ford was the only one who could get away with remarks like that to Duke.

Ford was responsible for helping turn Duke's life around, not only as an actor but as a man. For one thing he allowed no drinking on the set, and no women (except, of course, actresses). When we started shooting *Stagecoach* in Monument Valley, in October of 1938, he immediately started ridiculing and bullying Duke in front of the whole company. And these were real film stars, the first Duke had ever worked with: Thomas Mitchell, Claire Trevor, George Bancroft, John Carradine. He'd call him a dumb bastard, a big oaf, and say things like, "Can't you walk *normal* instead of skipping around like a goddamned fairy?" It's true that working with Jack Ford could be pure hell, and he was a sadistic man if there ever was one, but there was also a reason behind most everything he seemingly did for the sheer hell of it—at least while working.

a photo album
from the private collection
of
IRON EYES CODY

This is me at fifteen,
already a "veteran" of
three years in Hollywood.

And this is my future wife
Birdie, age eleven, having a
lesson with her grandfather.
The picture was taken in 1917.

I used to hunt rabbit right outside my home in the Hollywood Hills.

Tim McCoy on an indoor set at MGM in the mid-twenties. I think this shot is a perfect evocation of the era: stagy, melodramatic, and maybe a little silly, but always noble.

To
Iron Eyes
with my best regards

Tim McCoy
1930

Tim McCoy
1977

Here's my favorite picture of Tim, signed in 1930 and again in 1977.

ela Lugosi, sometime after donning
ne old cape and pointed teeth,
a movie called CHANDU.
otice the staging of the shot:
rms, legs, clubs, everything in harmony.

I played Bela's "native" friend
in CHANDU, and saved his life.

*Birdie proudly showing off one of her archeological finds,
in this case two ancient arrows. She's also a few months gone
in her first pregnancy here.*

Newspaper clippings from Birdie's "giant sloth" discovery in 1930.

Along with Gary Cooper, Jimmy Cagney also got his start playing Indians.
And he was just as unlikely. Here he is being sprayed with bole armenia,
with me the next victim. (Being nondiscriminating,
the studios sometimes sprayed Indians along with the whites.)

The finishing touches.

ABOVE: *At the Ringling Brothers, Barnum & Bailey Circus,
with some of my clown friends. That's Lou Jacobs on the right.*
BELOW: *Here I am in full Hopi snake dancer regalia,
along with my favorite pet rattler.*

All the snake dancers. That's Sean Bradley on the far right, rear.

Coop in a scene from DeMille's NORTHWEST MOUNTED POLICE.
Relieving him of his pistols is Mala, my Eskimo/Jewish friend.

*Coop with one of his Indian girl
friends while filming* UNCONQUERED.

Demonstrating the new sign for "Cherokee"
near Coop's ranch in Helena, Montana.

Taking a break during filming of THE SEA WOLF,
with Edward G. Robinson and John Garfield.

This was taken during the war years,
and I think I aged about ten years during this period.
Could be just because I never did like wearing a suit, though.

Roy Rogers and I giving the Indian sign for "two people who grew up together".

Birdie in white buckskin.

We got started on a new family. This is three-month-old Robert.

Our growing clan by the family car.
Arthur is the smaller of the two boys.

My friend, beautiful Paulette Goddard.

"Get in there and burn
[h]ell out of her," says
[C]ecil B. DeMille to me. . . .

. . . And that's what
I attempted, till
Paulette landed a kick
between my legs.
She was criticized for
"overacting" in this film.

ABOVE: *Can you tell them apart? The masks, that is. They are Indian death masks—
the one I'm holding is an original, C.B.'s a reproduction.*
BELOW: *Indians engage the cavalry once again, this time on
the football field. The quarterback about to receive
the ball from me (playing center) is the great Jim Thorpe.*

At a jamboree of 50,000 Boy Scouts.

ABOVE: *Bob Hope and Jane Russell in trouble in* THE PALEFACE.
BELOW: *Playing Crazy Horse, the great Sioux chief,*
about to lead an attack. The movie is SITTING BULL.

On location with the late Steve McQueen for NEVADA SMITH.

With Lee Van Cleef filming EL CONDOR *in Spain.*

"Go ahead, cut me with the damn thing," he said under his breath. He's a gutsy guy, that Richard Harris. Sparing no pains for effect, he helped make A MAN CALLED HORSE *wonderfully authentic.*

ABOVE: *J. Haikey, Ellen Corby, and Will Geer of "The Waltons".*
BELOW: *"The Fonz" (Henry Winkler) and I signing autographs for children at the Rancho Los Amigos Hospital."*

With Frank Sinatra and John Ferrer,
president of the Los Angeles City Council,
during the presentation of the
Humanitarian Achievement Awards.

*The Duke, just months
before he passed on.*

ABOVE: *I renamed President Carter "Wambler Ska" ("White Eagle" in Sioux),*
and placed a handmade eagle feather headdress on his head.
The press thought that this was pretty amusing
and the photo was flashed worldwide.
BELOW: *A couple of old actors reunited.*

A contingent of Indians and I went to Rome to meet the Pope.
Of all the world leaders I've met, he was
the warmest, the most human.

Sandy.

He would, simply, do *anything* to bring out the best performance an actor had to deliver. He was ruthless in the pursuit of excellence. In Duke's case, Ford knew perfectly well that behind all that swagger was an insecure man, completely ill-at-ease amid these stars. By constantly riding him, he knew that he'd either get him broiling mad, which was what he was after, or break him completely. Also, the rest of the cast started feeling sorry for Duke and rallied around him, inadvertently building his confidence.

Next to my role as Crazy Horse in *Sitting Bull* and the medicine man in *Man Called Horse*, the work I did in *Stagecoach* was a high point for me too. Monument Valley is located in the huge Navaho reservation in southern Utah, which has some of the most spectacular scenery in the world with those huge, colorful rock formations and vast desert plateaus. Nobody had ever shot a film there before, since it was one of the most inaccessible spots in the country: no telephones, roads, bridges, and a hundred miles from Flagstaff, Arizona. We had to lay plankboards over the dirt paths and sand, which the trucks had to follow carefully or sink. The Indians in the valley weren't doing too well as sheepherders and farmers, having been hit the last few years by particularly bad winters. It was my happy duty to hire hundreds of them as the Indian extras for *Stagecoach*. Most people say the beautifully drawn out, hair-raising chase scene in this picture is the most exciting one ever filmed, Indian or otherwise. Typical of Jack, these Indians probably would have worked for a day's food, but he saw to it they were payed at full Hollywood wages.

Under Jack's direction, Yak worked out all the action scenes. Because I was the expert archer on the set, I rode alongside the coach when it made its dash across the dry lake, shooting arrows into it and through the windows. We used real arrows for that scene, substituting quick-reflexed stuntmen in the coach for the stars.

Stagecoach not only launched John Wayne as a leading man in "A" pictures, it brought back the "A" Western in full glory. I worked with Jack in all his Westerns starring John Wayne, including *The Searchers*, *She Wore a Yellow Ribbon*, *Fort Apache*, and *Wagonmaster*, and I'll tell you more about him later on.

While Duke continued to work for Republic Pictures many years after *Stagecoach*, the quality of his pictures improved greatly. He even tried to stop drinking for a while, but picked it up with a vengeance after his second marriage—again to a Mexican—started going sour. Duke was in and out of marriages and affairs with many women, but he stayed pretty much wed to the bottle all his life.

Now I could go on and on with drinking, brawling, and womanizing stories about Duke during the next thirty years. But as you can imagine they get kind of repetitious, tending to cloud over his better qualities. He was a devoted father to his children: somewhat old-fashioned, in fact. He was the hardest-working man I ever met in this or any other business. He was a loyal friend—for life, if you got on the good side of him. Like he once said to me, "Iron Eyes, I never forgive an injury and always remember a kindness." The least said about his jingoist politics the better, except that it was, again, a reflection of his doing everything in the extreme whether it's love of country, fighting your enemies, whatever. He was one of those people who lacked the ability to see anything in other than clear-cut terms, terms leading to action. He embraced life completely on his own terms, and he often loved it to death.

His acting ability? I know there's a lot of very intelligent people out there, critics and such, who say John Wayne had no acting talent at all, that he just moved and rode horses damn good and grimaced for the camera on cue. They often quote Duke himself, who said, "I don't act, I *react*," and also that he just "played himself." Well, I don't pretend to be a judge of real talent, but I never met an actor who *ever* plays himself, mainly because I never met one who had any damn idea who he was in the first place. So the ability to act with perfect ease like Duke did so well must have something to do with talent. When John Ford was asked once why he thought John Wayne was so successful, the director of *The Grapes of Wrath, How Green is My Valley,* and *Mister Roberts*, the director who never said anything nice about anyone if he could avoid it, replied, "Duke is the best actor in Hollywood, that's all."

6

"Birdie?"

"Hmmm."

"Birdie?"

"What."

"Are you listening?"

"Iron Eyes, I'm right here listening as always. Whenever you open your mouth, I'm listening. The chief speaks, I hear."

Birdie put her sponge down next to the sink (she spent at least half her life, it seems, with a sponge in her hand) and turned to me with elbows akimbo, a teasing half-smile on her face.

"Ah, you hear the voice of authority. That's good."

I leaned back from my Indian stew, mostly beef and corn, and puffed philosophically on my pipe.

"Birdie, let's have us a child."

"What?"

"See, you're not listening. A child. A kid. Let's have one of 'em."

"You must be crazy."

She turned back to the sink, grabbed up her sponge and attacked the countertop with much violence.

"Birdie, I think you did that already."

"Did what already?"

"The countertop. You already wiped it. Keep that up and it'll disappear."

She threw down the sponge. "All right, why?"

"Wh—how do I know? When you rub something like that it'll just fade into nothing. The only thing around here fading from *not* getting that kind of attention is my—"

"Ha ha. Very funny. Why do you want a child, Iron Eyes?"

"Why not? You like kids. I like kids. What the hell are we married for?"

[101]

"Good question. Look, Iron Eyes, we've been over this before. I have my career. You have your Hollywood girlfriends—and your career. Where would we find time to raise a child? You're too much like a child yourself. I should think you'd be satisfied with your own company."

"Now, c'mon, Birdie." I eased out of my chair and, standing behind her at the sink, gave her behind a little pat and touched her shoulders. She had the shoulders of a fullback, that woman. "I don't want you working. I have plenty of money for the both of us."

"That's not the point."

"What's the point? Say, how about a little glass of wine. You know how you like wine. Just a sip or two and then we'll—"

"Iron Eyes," she said, stepping away from me. "The point, the one we're discussing, is that I like my work. Like you. I want my career to grow. I didn't go to college and work in that museum basement so I can minister to a bunch of screaming, ungrateful little brats. Besides, I don't understand why you should want a child with me. The way you get around, you must have at least four or five planted out there somewhere already."

"Birdie, that's not true and you know it."

"Know it? I know nothing of the kind. Who was that slinky blond I saw you talking with at that last Republic party?" She pointed the sponge at me in what I thought was a fairly threatening manner. I reasoned I'd better watch my step.

"What, her? You can't be serious. She's just another serial actress. We were discussing business."

"While whispering in her ear?"

Well, our little talk continued along these lines for some time. Actually, I knew she didn't mean what she said about "screaming brats." There's nobody who loved children more than Birdie. And it's the women who hesitate out of caution that make the best mothers. She was rightly concerned lest I continue running around with other women, that neither of us would have the time to devote to proper child care. And while money was no problem for the time being, she had no faith in the movie business or my ability to keep up a steady pace. All this together with the natural reluctance of Indian women in general to venture into sexual territories, no matter how hospitable and safe the terrain. I respected her for it, really. She showed a lot of sense for her age, which was twenty-three. When you think of it, it's these women who are all gung ho about children, proceed to disgorge five or six of them before they're twenty-five (and unfortunately often before they're married) who spend half their time screaming at the "little brats." They make the worst mothers. So, the upshot was Birdie agreed to "think on it." Beginning that night, after a valiant resistance, she surrendered to our thinking on the matter in great earnest.

This was 1930 now, some months since Duke made his debut in the Wild West big time with *The Big Trail*, Coop had snarled, "Smile when you say that" to Trampas in *The Virginian*, and a gap-toothed, big-eared twenty-nine-year-old named Billy Gable—soon to be known as Clark Gable—did his first screen test in a G-string, a flower behind his ear and painted with bole armenia for a MGM movie called *Never the Twain Shall Meet*. Gable was rejected for the part. By 1930, the cycle of "epic" Westerns started with *The Big Trail* had run its mini-course with one more large-scale sagebrusher, *Cimarron*, before flopping in the dust from overweight, making room for the trimmer "Bs." It was the B Western, in fact, that reigned throughout the thirties. They were the vehicles that served as springboards for many Hollywood careers, including Gable, Cooper, and Duke Wayne, and it was this steady need for anything to do with Indians that gave me a kind of monopoly business. I have 50,000 feet of stock footage which I loaned to the studios, hundreds of costumes to rent, I acted and directed action sequences and did pretty good for myself. Which is why I could think about having a kid.

About a month after we talked about it, Birdie took off on what was expected to be another routine anthropological dig. This time it was in the Gypsum Cave area of Nevada, about twenty miles from Las Vegas, which at this time was just a little ranching and mining town. These expeditions served a dual purpose. Funded by the Southwest Museum, California Institute of Technology, and the City of Los Angeles, they provided valuable clues as to the first human inhabitants of this continent, as well as turning up priceless Indian artifacts. Birdie was appointed field secretary to the Southwest Museum, which meant that out on a dig she had considerable authority. One day in June on the Gypsum Cave dig, she found a stone spearhead which proved to be over 20,000 years old. But more important to the larger paleontology community was

what it was lying next to: a perfect skull of a giant ground sloth—
the first ever discovered and the first to demonstrate that humans
at one time actually hunted the twelve-foot, bear-like monsters.

Of course, the last one to hear about any of this was yours truly. I
opened the *Los Angeles Times* on the morning of June 7, 1930, and
there was a big Associated Press article and pictures of Birdie.
Really knocked me out, I must say. I was so proud of her. Then, no
more than a day or two later, I got a long distance call from Birdie's
anthropologist uncle (her father, Arthur C. Parker, and uncle were
both Ph.D.'s in the field). He was calling from Las Vegas.

"Iron Eyes," he shouted after exchanging a few amenities. Some
people always feel they have to shout when calling long distance.
"Why did you do it?"

"Do what? And you don't have to shout, I can hear you fine."

"Knock her up," he said, still shouting. Uncle Ray was never one
to look for delicate ways to get something said. "You shouldn't
have knocked that girl up."

"I don't know what the hell you're talking about. Knocked who
up?" I frantically searched my memory for any possibilities outside
Birdie. Oh no, could it be the seventeen-year-old movie extra?

"Why, Birdie, of course. You shouldn't have gotten her pregnant.
What's she gonna do now, out here in the middle of nowhere in the
middle of the biggest find in decades, and she's sick."

"Are you telling me Birdie's pregnant? *My* Birdie?"

"You didn't know?"

"Of course I didn't know. I'm the last one to know anything
around here. And what's this about a giant sloth? Is that a big deal
or something?"

"Come to think of it," he said, lowering his voice, "she is acting a
little strange. Like she doesn't believe it."

"What? Speak up, I can barely hear you now."

"I said she acts like she's not pregnant. My wife Edna's looking
after her okay, though. She says she's definitely knocked up."

"That's wonderful! Just what we've been hoping for!"

"*You've* been hoping for, you mean. She's got a brilliant career
ahead of her. You've got a brilliant career. What did you want to go
and screw it up by having children for?"

"Wait a minute, Uncle Ray. Since when have you taken such a
keen interest in our careers? Are you sure it isn't anything to do

with all the reporters hanging around, just fascinated with your damn bones and pickaxes, giving you all that publicity? What is it, grant-writing time, Uncle Ray?"

"Never mind that. I'm concerned for your wife's health. You better get yourself out here."

He didn't have to ask me twice. I threw some things into the Ford, roared off into the mountains, and immediately got lost. Had the damndest time of it winding around on those old mountain roads.

When Birdie saw me walk into her tent, her eyes danced with happiness for an instant, then switched gears into the old suspicious glint. She was dressed in some kind of long-sleeved undershirt that looked like English riding pants, an Indian belt with a knife and scabbard, and knee-length moccasins. My desert Lady Hiawatha.

"Iron Eyes, what are you doing here?"

"I came to take you back."

"Look, if that's all you came out here for, you've wasted your time. I've got months of work to do here. Maybe a year."

"Oh, I see. You plan on having the kid out here in the bush, Indian style. Well, that's admirable. Just set the old shovel down one afternoon, squat behind a handy cactus, and—"

"What kid? I don't know what you're talking about," she said, looking down and fidgeting with her balloon-thighed pants. Just then I was overwhelmed with a feeling of affection for my brave, beautiful young wife. My *crazy*, beautiful wife. It's amazing how many thoughts can zoom into your head all at once, you know? In this case, it was: I'll never be unfaithful again, we'll get out of this place and drive off into the sunset, set up a big, happy household in Hollywood, start a collection of noisy, bouncy little kids, and live happily ever after. All in the space of half a second. I stepped forward to hug her, feeling sure she was thinking the same thing, and she stepped back.

"I'm not having any child," she said flatly. "It was a false alarm. Nothing to concern yourself about."

"False nothing. Uncle Ray told me—"

"Uncle Ray's wrong. I should know, shouldn't I? I'm not pregnant, Iron Eyes."

She looked at me fleetingly. I couldn't tell whether I saw pain or humiliation, or whether she was just lying or what. That woman was more complex than an ant colony. Later, I spoke with her uncle, and he said he thought she was lying, but that she wasn't as sick as she was and was continuing with her work as usual. I hung around for a day or two, Birdie ignored me as much as possible, and then I headed back to California. I was disgusted with the whole thing and cursed myself for bothering.

Four months passed. The usual letters arrived from Birdie, the occasional phone call. Meanwhile, the giant sloth find had received worldwide publicity and Birdie was granted a permanent position with the Southwest Museum as an Assistant in Archaeology. She had launched a career for herself, all right. She subsequently wrote dozens of articles on ethnology and paleontology in national scientific journals, a book on ancient Indians of Ecuador, got listed in *Who's Who* and enrolled in the National Roster of Scientific and Specialized Personnel as an ethnological researcher and writer.

But for the moment, not a clue as to whether or not she was pregnant.

Then one day she showed up at the front door. Just like that, not a word's notice.

"Guess what," she said, standing in the doorway and choking back the tears. "I'm pregnant."

She was at that. Her belly was already so swollen that those English pants could barely contain her. She looked so innocent and confused—and vulnerable. All that hard nose, tough-girl swagger had disappeared. Or so I thought. I held my arms open and walked toward her.

"Don't touch me!"

"Wha—Birdie, *now* what's the matter?"

"Just don't touch me." She burst into tears, ran past me to our bedroom, and slammed the door. Click, went the lock.

Well, I didn't know what to do. I pounded on the door, pleading with her to open it so we could just talk. No dice. I called doctors, doctors, doctors. They all said it was just something she'd go through, that she'd "come around eventually." Of course, she did finally come out, but just to either leave for the museum or to go about cooking and cleaning. I told her we could get someone to help with the housework, but she gave me such a if-you-bring-another-woman-in-here-I'll-kill-you look that I thought it wise not to mention it again. She dutifully went with me to her periodic checkups. Everything was fine, fine, fine, but where was Birdie? I was getting scared she was losing her head, I'll tell you. Either that or I was. I almost stooped low enough to see a psychiatrist, and that's something no self-respecting Indian would ever do in those days. The idea of an Indian talking to a perfect stranger about personal matters like sex and marriage would be tantamount to a white man standing up in the middle of a church sermon, dropping his pants, and relieving himself on the old lady sitting in front of him. Indians are stubborn as hell about this sort of thing, and that, I think, is one of the main reasons we have had to a large extent such difficulties assimilating. But more on that later.

Birdie spent her entire pregnancy not talking to me. We would have guests over and she would be her usual animated self, with her women friends in particular, with everybody but me. They'd even laugh and giggle about her pregnancy the way Indian women do, as though everything were perfectly normal. Gary Cooper dropped by one afternoon, and he noticed something wasn't quite right immediately. He took me aside, planted a reassuring hand on my shoulder, and, talking softly out of the side of his mouth, warmly confided his opinion of the situation.

"Looks to me as though she hates your guts."

"Oh, is that all? And I thought it was something serious."

"But what it is actually," he said, narrowing his eyes and his voice growing conspiratorial, "is she loves you, but in protection of the upcoming kid she doesn't want to let on. She's afraid you're gonna fly the coop again, and she's preparing herself for it."

"But she's the one that takes off. Most of the time she's not even around. She doesn't want to be the mother of our child, she's more interested in fossils of sloths."

"Nope, just the opposite. Take my word for it, kid." He shaped his finger into a gun, stuck it into my shoulder, and made a clicking sound with his lips. "It's pure mothering instinct at work here."

What the hell does he know about it, I thought. Spends all his

time chasing after women. I felt the major obstacle to our con-
nubial bliss was Birdie's work at the museum. In fact, I began
to be obsessive about it. I'll get her to quit that job if it takes summoning the Great Spirit to do it, I muttered to myself. Looking
up at the heavens, I shook my fist. And where the hell are you
in emergencies like this? You're never around when you're
needed!

Birdie gave birth quickly, easily, without any fuss. But not
without a little last-minute drama. She had been sitting in the
living room, knitting, her forearms comfortably resting on the
mound of life within her, when she gave a start and dropped her
needles. I had been particularly edgy these last few weeks, as I
suppose all first-time expectant fathers are, and when she gave out
a little "oh" it was as though someone had pulled the old gun-in-
the-gut, bang-behind-your-back routine. The newspaper I was
reading flew from my hands like some huge, flimsy bat.

"What? What is it? Is it time? *Now?*"

She bit her lower lip and nodded her head. "You expected a
calling card?" she managed, grasping the arms of her chair. "Damn,
I dropped a stitch."

"Never mind about *that*. What should I do, what should I do," I
stammered, pacing the room. I snapped my fingers and pointed at
her. "I'll get the car, drive it up the front lawn to the front door. You
stay here, don't move a muscle."

"Actually I thought I'd take a little run around the block."

That was the first pleasant wisecrack I'd heard in months. God,
it sounded great. I leaped in the car and roared up to the front door,
forgetting this was January, the rainy season out here. I helped her
in the front seat, jumped in, and threw it in gear. The wheels just
spun in place, stuck in the damn mud! By now Birdie was too far
gone even for wisecracks, just sat there quietly toughing it out.
That's when I knew it was serious. Cursing, I jumped out and
grabbed up anything not resembling mud I could find—sticks,
stones, leaves. With my hands covered with muck after stuffing
this junk under the wheel, I hopped in and tried it again, this time
rocking back and forth. It held, more or less. I spun onto the drive,
sending a shower of mud all over the front of our house, and raced
off.

Two hours later, I was gazing down into two gleaming little black beads, set in a perfect, tiny face. A beautiful baby girl! Birdie looked as though she'd just had a mild workout in the gym, flushed with color, only a trace of perspiration. It was all they could do to keep her in bed for the usual amount of time; she was ready to gather up her child, pay the man, and vamoose. She showed the tenderest affection for that kid when we got home. Wouldn't let her out of her sight. But can you believe it? She still wasn't talking to me! That was it, I'd soon put a stop to this nonsense. A week later I put a call to the museum director, Dr. Frederic Hodge.

"Iron Eyes, hello, dear friend. What can I do for you?"

"Dr. Hodge, you and I are good friends, we've known each other for years, right?"

"Of course."

"And I don't have to remind you of the time I've put in on your committee, all the fund-raising activities I've helped you with?"

"Well . . . no." He smelled a big favor coming up, rightly enough.

"Doctor Hodge, I'd like you to fire Birdie."

"*What?*"

"Fire Birdie. Her work at the museum is eating away at our marriage. Pretty soon there's not going to be anything left to even feed to the hogs."

"Iron Eyes, I wish you hadn't asked me that. What seems to be the problem between you two? You can tell me."

"You want to know the problem? The problem is she's never around. She thinks of nothing but her damn specimens. And I wish she'd never found that damn sloth head bone. It's gone to *her* head. You know she hasn't spoken a word to me in over six months?"

"Well, I'm sorry, I'm afraid firing her is out of the question, Iron Eyes. Frankly, I don't think it would solve anything between you, either. Tell you what I will do, however. I'll see to it she spends some time at the museum and not out in the field, although that's where her true strength lies. Best field scientist I've ever worked with. But I'm sure we can find something for her to do here at home, at least for the time being. Give you both time to dig around and find out what's really the matter."

"And you won't tell her—or Dr. Harrington—it was my idea?"

"Of course not. Couldn't."

"Thanks, Doc. When's the next committee meeting?"

A few days later I came home from the studio and found Birdie in the kitchen pounding steak with the back of a meat cleaver. She gave it one last shot, which shook the countertop, and fixed me with a look that might have frozen the balls of an angry bull.

"I'm down in the basement of the museum again, as if you didn't know."

"Down in the basement?" I said, innocently, carefully. "No, I didn't know. But that's not so bad, Birdie. Now maybe we'll have a little time to get to know each other. See, here we are talking, just like normal people."

"Normal nothing." She pointed that meat cleaver at me. It was inevitable. I put my hands up, ever so slightly, and stepped back a pace or two, with her advancing steadily.

"You got me down there, didn't you. Who did you talk to, Uncle Ray?"

"Now, just a minute, Birdie. Slow down a minute here. What are you talking about, 'sent you down there'? Nobody sent you anywhere to my knowledge. And take it easy with that thing, will you?"

"Or maybe Dr. Hodge?" she snarled, still advancing. "That's it! You told Dr. Hodge to transfer me, didn't you?"

"No, Birdie, honest. It was his idea."

"Ah *ha*! So you did talk to him."

"Damn," I said, snapping my fingers. "All right, all right. So I talked to him. It's only because I see us drifting further and further apart, Birdie. And now we've got a child to think of. Say, what are we naming her anyway," I asked, trying desperately to change the subject. It's Indian custom to wait for naming the child until aspects of character reveal themselves. For instance, Birdie's Indian name is Gy Yea Was. Means elusive, hard to find. I seemed to have distracted her for a moment.

"I was thinking of Wilma. But don't try to change the subject."

"Oh, Wilma, that's a nice name. Wilma. Very brave, fertile-sounding. Yes, I like it. She'll probably like having a father around, too. Don't you think so, Birdie?"

"You know I've a mind to kill you with this thing, so don't try and worm out of it," she said, brandishing the cleaver before my face. But the light of humor had begun to return to her face. Was it possible she was becoming her old self?

"Listen, Iron Eyes," she said, lowering the cleaver. There was a peacemaking tone to her voice, a little weary and resigned, too. "You can't help being who you are anymore than I can help being me. What do you say to going fifty-fifty on this thing? The child needs caring for, I'm aware of that. I could have just as easily managed out in the field with her, and you know it. As for us, well, we get along okay in some departments, not so good in others. It's the 'others' that concern me, Iron Eyes, so if you want to run around with other women, fine. I'll run around with other men. Fifty-fifty."

That wasn't exactly what I had in mind, and I told her so. At least she put down that damn meat cleaver, however.

"What's the matter? You got what you want, didn't you? I'll stay home and take care of little Wilma and you're free to do what you want."

"And what about us? What, are we just pals now or something?"

"If you mean are we going to be sleeping together, we'll just have to wait and see."

"Oh, wait and see now, is it? Well, you're probably right. After all, it's only been six months. Not too much time for separation at all. We don't want to overdo it in the bedroom, do we? Might be too much of a strain."

And that was the end of that discussion. What happened was she kept her end of the bargain, stayed home and took care of Wilma, let me come and go without question, went out occasionally—but I know without men as she's not the type—was a perfect hostess to guests, even spoke to me occasionally. In short, started driving me nuts. After about six months of our "fifty-fifty" bargain, I lit out on another tour with Tim McCoy.

We steamed out of port in Long Beach and, this time, I wasn't to return for a year and a half. This was 1931, you'll remember. You didn't just whiz about in jets in those days.

Birdie and I exchanged letters which, by fractions of degrees, got warmer and warmer. At least she was communicating and occa-

sionally asking my help in certain situations. One day she wrote
and said her uncle, John Big Tree, had moved in with her. "I don't
know what to do with him," she said. "He just sits out on the porch
and drinks all day, making all kinds of noise and disturbing
Wilma." I wrote back and told her to send him to the Tonawanda
Indian reservation in New York, that I would pay for everything.
Indian reservations. The Red Man's nursing home. Big Tree isn't to
be pitied, though. He dried out on that reservation and it wasn't
long before he was back out here in Hollywood, doing bit parts we
could get for him in the movies. And, unfortunately, back on the
hooch. He eventually was selected as one of the Indians to pose for
the Indian head on the buffalo nickel. Became quite a celebrity. I
think it was in the late sixties that he finally made it to the big
time, "The Johnny Carson Show." He lived to be 104.

When we were in Canada, we ran into some kind of tax problems
with the authorities which I won't pretend to understand, except
to the extent that we almost went broke letting everybody see the
show free. Not long after that little display of charity, we were
home in California, which was fine with me. I was dying to see my
daughter. When I pulled up in the drive, there to greet me was the
cutest little two-year-old Indian doll I'd ever seen. She opened the
door and, with a mischievous grin, said, "Hello Chief Big Nose."

"Heh, heh, nice little girl."

"Big Nose," she screeched again, then put her hand to her mouth
to hide the giggling and ran to her mother.

"Well, look who stopped by for dinner," Birdie said, smiling
widely.

"Birdie, you've been poisoning that girl towards me. What's this
'Big Nose' thing?"

"Why, you've been off with Tim McCoy so long, she doesn't
know who you are, I suppose."

"The way you treat me, who the hell wouldn't be off. You got me
goin', kid." I squatted down, opened my arms, and said, "Wilma,
this is your daddy. Come here and give us a kiss, darling." She
looked at me, winced, and ducked behind her mother's skirt.

"Try calling her 'Tomato Soup'," said Birdie, grinning at me.

"Tomato Soup? Big Nose? Sounds like a cartoon casting party
around here," I mumbled.

"Uncle Big Tree started calling her Tomato Soup because she loves tomato soup."

"Oh, well that makes sense. That explains everything."

"Guess it stuck with her. Go ahead, try it."

Well, she did cautiously waddle over and give me a kiss when I called her Tomato Soup. We got along fine after that, in fact. And Birdie? She had her humor back in full force, I'll say that much.

"So, how was it? How many girls did you have? Who were they—anyone I know? I hope they don't call me some day and tell me about another addition to the family."

That kind of thing. The woman was hard on me, I'll tell you. Not that she didn't have cause, but I felt I had cause, too. I guess that's what's the matter with half the relationships nowadays. Each thinks the other is screwing him or her. It's that simple. And this went on with us for years. We got along okay on the surface but more or less went our separate ways—she to the Southwest Museum, me to the movie studios. This was a time when the sirens of Hollywood were the most alluring to me. In fact, I was there eagerly listening to every shrill note.

7

PROBABLY SOME of the shrillest, most alluring notes to be struck in Tinsel Land didn't come out of Hollywood at all, but from a place on top of a hill about 200 miles north. No book having anything to do with old movies is complete without mentioning the Enchanted Hill of William Randolph Hearst, and his estate on top of it called San Simeon.

During the Depression years of the thirties, it's often assumed that the movie moguls were raking it in faster than the theater owners could pop popcorn. Entertainment does good when times are bad. The truth is that the Great Depression was *so* bad it even cut into Hollywood profits, and some producers feared bankruptcy. A lot of the smaller companies came and went during this time. Poverty Row certainly experienced the pinch.

But most people did manage to scrape together the dime needed for a few hours of escape. And while most were dipping into the cookie jar or chopping firewood on weekends to come up with ten or fifteen cents worth of dream money, one man was busying himself contemplating how to spend *hundreds* of millions accomplishing much the same thing. Hearst, to me, is synonymous with the side of Tinsel Land directly across the tracks from Gower Gulch and yet very much part of the same territory. In his castle, Hearst stayed aloof from the troubles of the world yet seemed to love contact with all varieties of people. With his newspaper empire he influenced and sometimes controlled world events. Yet he never even met half his editors during the time when I knew him. He lived in fantasy, like most of us, but in his case he never had to cough up the price of admission because he owned the movie. And the theater.

So much has been written about Hearst—I count six biographies, an autobiography, and countless mentions of him in the deluge of Hollywood memoirs of late. No one agrees on exactly who this kindly, generous, aloof, vicious, rapacious, possessive, fatherly, loving, shy, boisterous, sentimental megalomaniac was. Can't figure out why, myself. He was just a simple, average guy with a perfectly normal dream, except he actually began carrying it out in earnest. He wanted to own the world, is all.

You may think it presumptuous of me to speak so casually of a man who, while not great, was certainly big enough to crush me like some bothersome little spider crawling across his fifty-four-foot dining table. Well, the fact is, I never asked to be invited to his castle in San Simeon, he asked me to come—on several occasions. I don't fool myself into thinking it was because we were good pals, or that his altruistic penchant for helping underprivileged Americans was a'hankering for expression. What I think he did have in mind was a fondness for Indians in the *abstract*. I'd also push that a step further and guess that this detached appreciation was typical of his feeling for all humanity—"nice critters, but for Lord's sake, keep 'em at a distance." We all know he collected things as a way of life. I wasn't a person to him, certainly not a friend, but rather an exotic ornament, another little something to hang up on and decorate the limitless wall space of his massive ego. I speak of Hearst as I do because, while he inspired awe, I had difficulty respecting him all that much.

Besides, the man who bought up half of Hollywood just to create a film career for his girlfriend was too sentimental to squash a spider.

Or a zebra. Hearst's well-known fondness for animals revealed itself most emphatically as you wound up the six-mile driveway to his palace atop La Cuesta Encantada—the Enchanted Hill. Along the way a dozen or so reminders that ANIMALS HAVE THE RIGHT OF WAY were painted on conspicuous signs. A section of his 250,000 acre estate, an expanse of territory half the size of Rhode Island, was fenced off to contain the world's largest private zoo. It was complete with thirty varieties of flesh eaters and seventy grazing species, everything from elephants and tigers to monkeys and yaks. All for the private enjoyment of this one man. On this first trip I was sitting next to Ronald Colman in a Rolls Royce, while Tim McCoy commandeered us.

"Ron," I said, nudging him in the ribs, "is that buffalo I see grazing over there or am I dead and this the Happy Hunting Ground?"

"Hmmm?" he replied, vaguely. I don't think old Ron would have distinguished a buffalo from a gazelle. "Why, yes, I do believe it is. Fascinating. You don't suppose they're dangerous?"

"Hell, they just look tasty to me," I said. "Sure wish I had my bow along."

Tim took his eyes off the winding road and fixed me with his famous glare, but kiddingly. "Yeah. You feed on one of his buffalo and the old man himself will feed you to the lions. I understand they need plenty of red meat."

"Ha ha. You're funny, Tim. You should go into the pictures."

"There's really . . . lions about?" asked Ron, scanning the horizon warily.

"Don't worry," said Tim. "All the meat eaters except Iron Eyes here are in cages. Hearst only lets the grazing animals roam about and—"

"Tim, look out!"

At the moment Tim was addressing us on the various beasts roaming the Hearst ranch, I saw an ostrich step in front of the car. Tim braked and swerved to avoid it, the big Rolls tearing off about 10,000 miles worth of rubber from the tires. We barely missed the opportunity to show up at Hearst's castle with a two-legged, feathered basketball stuck to the fender. Funny, I always imagined ostriches to be one of nature's shyer creatures. But this ostrich on the Hearst ranch was bold, barely bothering to step out of the way. I could have sworn it gave us a look of disdain as we continued our ride, a bit more cautious.

Now, for those of you not acquainted with some of the fantastic statistics associated with the Hearst castle, it's worthwhile I think to tick off a few here. Hearst began building his dream home in 1919, and for the next fifteen years or so kept from twenty-five to 150 construction workers busy on it every day. He started with three guest houses, each a palace in its own right and containing dozens of baths and bedroom suites filled with priceless art and antiques. The almost barren Camp Hill was slowly transformed into The Enchanted Hill after years of blasting away at solid rock and shipping in hundreds of tons of topsoil over miles of mountain roads, together with whole forests of fulldsize pine trees, cypress, and a dozen other varieties. Thirty gardeners, under the supervision of an expert English horticulturist, turned the grounds surrounding the castle into a paradise of flowers, shrubbery, and exotic plants.

Meanwhile, in a five-story warehouse in Bronx, New York, Hearst had accumulated over the years a colossal treasure of art, antiques, and sections of whole buildings. He was the largest private collector of art in the world, some say singularly responsible for inflating prices throughout the market due to his almost lunatic buy-at-any-cost bidding practices. Half his possessions he never in his life even set eyes on, but rather kept an elaborate filing system with photographs and descriptions (although the real filing system was in his computer-like mind, and he could recall at any moment some piece purchased ten years ago to fill a particular need—as part of a set in one of his movies, say, or to fill a space at San Simeon). He kept professional art and antique dealers jumping to their feet at auctions all over the world. He bought up entire rooms which he ripped out of crumbling European Gothic castles, had each piece numbered, crated, and shipped over the oceans in chartered vessels. It's joked that, during the Depression, Hearst kept the entire shipping industry healthy with his constant trans-oceanic shuttles. He accumulated thousands of square feet of antique paneling, whole hand-carved ceilings taken from 500-year-old monasteries, staircases, stained glass, Greek and Roman tiles, columns and statues, corbels, choir stalls, mantels, tapestries, cophagi—he filled the warehouse literally to overflowing.

La Casa Grande, the main castle begun in 1930, is almost the size of a Gothic cathedral. It was to contain all the exotic bric-a-brac Hearst had accumulated over the years as a personal monument, from himself to himself. The first edifice you encounter as you drive up the hill are twin towers, but they aren't the original ones. The towers he first approved of, and proceeded to erect at enormous expense, he later decided weren't to his liking as you approached the castle. "Too stark." Had 'em torn down and made fancier. A dozen full-time wood and stone carvers spent years chiseling elaborately ornate balconies and a portico atop a door big enough to let a small ship through. Each tower contains a set of church bells, on top of which rests a dome and crucifix. He was continuously making additions, adding wings—only one of which contains forty bedroom suites, each filled with art and treasure. Deep below La Casa Grande, the art and antique overflow from the Bronx began filling up five sealed vaults, plus another vast warehouse in the nearby village. When these were filled up, his collection just started piling up around the grounds, crated and covered with tarp. Three full-time operators kept Hearst and his guests plugged into each other's rooms and throughout the estate. There were phones hidden under rocks, behind statues, in bushes and trees. Ranging over this vast estate outside the zoo area were over 10,000 head of cattle, some of the top breeds of horses in the country, including appaloosas (my favorite), Arabians, palominos, and Morgans. Thirty-five cars were on hand at any moment to whisk guests to and from the estate. A complete, privately owned train transported people coast-to-coast to attend his parties. A full-time radio operator signaled Hearst-owned planes safely in and out of his private airfield.

The price tag? I don't know as anyone has seriously estimated what the place cost *in toto*. Just to maintain it, including salaries for his legions of servants, ran over $6,000 per day. The cost of his constant construction, which was to continue till the day Hearst left The Enchanted Hill for the last time, was averaged at $50,000 per day. In 1930 dollars. You figure it out.

While you're at it, try and imagine the effect this fairytale-come-true had on a roughhewn character like me. I just couldn't believe what I was looking at. How could one man own so much! On repeated visits, the effect is the same, a sense of unreality, or disproportionate magnificence. I'm told that some of the richest men in the world, pals of W.R. no doubt, were as blown away as I when gazing upon all this baroque splendor. If you're able to put yourself in my shoes, I'm sure you can't imagine the effect it had on the bus load of ancient Little Big Horn Indian veterans and younger braves directly off the reservation! Yep, Tim McCoy had brought along his touring Indians, who had followed us up from Hollywood in a bus. Keep in mind these are the same Indians that tore up the English boarding house some years ago to make campfires, got roaring drunk, and had themselves a war dance on antique oriental rugs. Hearst was a teetotaler. This would prove an interesting weekend, indeed.

Among the first to greet us was Marion Davies, Hearst's mistress and still girlish in what must have been her early forties. She was one of the most charming, full-of-bubbly-fun people I've ever met. I had a crush on her the moment I laid eyes on her. Taking one look at this twenty-odd assemblage of Arapahoes, decked out in their finest native attire, she threw her arms out in an all-embracing gesture, bent her knees, spread her legs slightly, and piped, "Ooooooh! R-r-real Indians. Hiya, guys!" She also had a perfectly charming stutter. Bustling up to Goes In Lodge, the six-foot, four-inch Arapahoe chief you met earlier, she gave him a friendly punch in the arm and said, "Hi, Chief! Welcome!"

"Humph."

Goes in Lodge wasn't being impolite. He was just so stupified by the wondrous castle, and so taken aback by this aggressively chummy woman—something he wasn't used to—that all he could do was snort out his lack of comprehension.

"Say, w-w-what's the matter, Chief? You look as though you could use a drink." She turned to me and smiled, all bright eyes and teeth beaming a thousand watts. "And aren't you Iron Eyes C-C-Cody?"

I acknowledged, flattered she knew me. Then Tim stepped forward and they peck-kissed and exchanged lovey-dovey greetings, old friends who had worked in several movies together.

"Pops is f-f-fascinated with Indians and all those battles and everything," she continued. "He and Tim here have s-s-spoken of you often. I'm sure he'll be happy to meet you."

By "Pops" she, of course, was referring to Big Daddy Hearst.

We all spent some time jabbering out there on the top-tier "veranda," which is all marble and encircled by a hand-carved bannister with little statues and figures spaced along the railing. The view was breathtaking: forty miles in either direction, up and down the Pacific. All of it Hearst's domain, as far as the eye could see.

We shuffled our way through the enormous entrance into a reception hallway with whole trees roaring in what must have been the biggest fireplace in the world. In fact, I remember someone telling me it was over twenty feet high. W.R. was taking one of his late afternoon siestas, so we began an informal tour of the palace, with Marion pointing out little oddities, like what medieval prince owned this vase, where this particular tapestry came from, and so on. For somebody who seemed to regard the whole thing as some kind of elaborate joke she was fairly well informed about the castle. Or so it appeared, but I wasn't paying too much attention. Every room we wandered into would just floor me, the richness of it all was so overwhelming. It must have been an hour, although I honestly can't recall. It actually takes days to see the whole place—we were only shown a fraction of the rooms. We eventually made it to the indoor swimming pool, assembled by hand from genuine ancient Roman tiles into a beautiful mosaic, almost Olympic in size. The outdoor pool is marble, of Greek motif, with classic statues carved by Hearst's own artisans. Some guests were already lounging around the pool. Robert Taylor and Joan Crawford padded over to greet us, smiling widely. Some of the other guests included Lionel Barrymore, John Gilbert, Louella Parsons, Samuel Goldwyn, W.S. Van Dyke, and Dick Powell. In addition to Hollywood types, Hearst generally preferred the company of explorers and adventurers, writers, a few politicians, and the top executives of his business empire. He disliked the company of stuffy people, although some say that was due to Marion's influence. At least, most of the younger folks surrounding him at San Simeon were her friends, including Tim McCoy.

At dusk, we gathered in the dining room for the evening's meal. It's actually a giant monastery refectory, of Renaissance vintage, complete with hand-carved ceiling, giant chandeliers, Sienese banners arched over more priceless tapestries on the walls, and monk's prayer booths extending its entire length on both sides. Another gargantuan fireplace roared at one end, sending eerie, thirty-foot shadows dancing among the ancient relics. A nice, homey touch. Along the fifty-four-foot table were the famous ketchup and mustard bottles and paper napkins. Some Hearstorians speculate it wasn't so much to "keep things simple" that he laid out these basic condiments for his guests, but rather that it reminded him of his youth. Hearst, they say, was so afraid of dying he needed constant reassurance his past wasn't slipping through his aging fingers. He was, at this time, in his seventies. Huddled with a few business types over a long Teletype printout, he looked up and cast his imperious gaze over us Indians as we entered, shyly gaping at everything. I understood at that moment how he could command so much power in the world, as his eyes met mine and the chill made my heart drop to my ankles. But having a decent stare myself (they didn't name me "Iron Eyes" for nothing), I mustered up the courage and gave it back to him. Abruptly he broke into a Cheshire grin, left his colleagues, and lumbered over to greet us. He stood about six foot six, was pear-shaped, and, on top of his deeply lined but still handsome, noble face, was a full shock of gun-metal hair. Like the color of his castle's stone walls. Dark circles under the eyes, which were icy blue, gave him a kind of haunted, sinister appearance, one that maybe he was aware of and tried offsetting with his loud sports jacket and two-toned shoes. Together, he gave an impression of charm, aloofness, and something hard to define, something kind of scary.

"Tim, Tim McCoy! How are you, sir? So glad you made it. And your friends, ladies and gentlemen, welcome all. Now you must introduce me, I've been anxious to meet these native Americans for some time."

We filed by as if meeting a head of state, Tim making the introductions and providing a brief historical anecdote or two. Hearst's reception was enthusiastic and jubilant. He seemed particularly fascinated with the older Indians involved in the Little Big Horn battle, snapping off battle dates and locations as if recalling last week's picnic outing. A lover of history myself, I was impressed. We had a couple of women in our ranks, including a stepsister of mine, beautiful White Bird. She was fresh from having just won some kind of beauty contest in Los Angeles, though I don't recall what it was. Hearst lingered with her a particularly long time, holding her hand and caressing the back of it with his thumbs, speaking softly to her. Then, letting her loose, he spoke with me briefly, saying he'd followed my career for some time and heard so much about me from Tim, and so on. Curiously, he then nudged me with his elbow and said, "We'll have to talk more later, okay?"

"Sure," I replied.

We seated ourselves, the master sitting square in the middle of the long table with Marion opposite. The Indians, including myself, were surprisingly placed midway between Hearst and some of his more dignified, but apparently boring guests. Somehow I expected to be plunked out near the dim, further extremes of the table where the less important people roosted, but importance in the Hearst castle I suppose was determined by how entertaining you might prove to be. While dress was casual, imagine if you can the sight of Indian warriors, not sixty years from bloody battles of the Old West, being seated at a table of priceless china and silver, attended by servants in white tie. A few of the Indians lowered themselves gingerly in the high-backed, somewhat threatening chairs, as if expecting them to bite their behinds. One or two, not believing how uncomfortable they were (originally designed, I understand, to support a knight's armor) stood up, turned, and appraised the damn things with deep frowns, shaking their heads as if saying, "Won't these white men *ever* learn?" We were presented menus, with a fare comparable to any high-class restaurant, and which included a notation of the movie to be shown after dinner. A waiter was always at your shoulder, tending to you like royalty. We started off with modest glasses of California champagne, and very little wine was served through the meal. Hearst kept the booze to an absolute minimum due to Marion's drinking problem, but she had ways of keeping a steady flow. The now-familiar "drink waiting for her in the ladies room," placed there by a trusted servant, is one. She also had bottles stashed all over the palace grounds. As for the Indians, drink isn't necessary to make them feel at home. Just put some red meat in front of them, and they'll dive in. Goes In Lodge, his knife clasped like a weapon in one hand, his fork the other, ripped through two or three steaks almost as thick as telephone books, all the while grunting his approval.

After dinner we all filed into Hearst's private movie theater for a yet-to-be-released film. I might as well confess here I've never been able to stay awake through any movie, or TV program for that matter. A good book will keep me occupied and alert for hours—in fact, I often can't fall asleep after reading. But the flicks? Strictly snoozeville. Especially if it's seeing myself, which I can't bear. You can imagine that, being in this business for so long and having to attend countless premieres, it's placed me in some pretty com-promising positions. Maybe that's why I don't get invited to too many openings anymore. Now I'm not saying this sleeping busi-ness is common to all Indians placed in front of a moving picture. No sir. In this instance, all of us were ushered ceremoniously to the front of the theater. Most of the men by this time had pretty women on either side of them, cooing and touching and giggling. Goes In Lodge must have now realized this was no dream or, if so, he was very much part of it. Never seen him grin so much. But, sure enough, when the movie started, pop went the lights in our re-spective noggins and in minutes every damn one of us was out like drunks after a two-week binge. One particularly dignified chief had his mouth agape, his head resting way back on the back of his seat, and was snoring like a water buffalo. The cacophany of snorts, wheezes, sighs, grunts, whistles, and other ordinary nocturnal musings coming from our quarters must have sounded pretty un-settling to the rest of the guests trying to concentrate on what I vaguely recall was a sloppy romance. Especially if the movie hap-pened to have been one of theirs.

As was their custom, after the film W.R. and Marion climbed into a small elevator and disappeared into the lofty reaches of the second- and third-floor apartments of La Casa Grande. I've never seen it, but I understand that Hearst's study, where he would spend the next four or five hours, is as impressive as the rest of the place. Over the years Marion had familiarized herself with many aspects of Hearst's business, and she spent a good deal of time at his side in business conferences, her opinions always listened to by the fa-therly Hearst. From the study they would retire to the Celestial Suite, the apartments in the base of the towers commanding a 360-degree view of the Pacific and the Santa Lucias Mountains. They had adjoining rooms, and Hearst slept on a huge bed carved from black wood once owned by Cardinal Richelieu.

We guests now felt like we were at a pajama party in an antique fairyland, Mom and Dad having just gone to bed, saying, "Now children, go to sleep and don't make too much noise." There was something about the almighty Hearst that, while compelling you to eagerly toe the line in his presence, made you feel in his absence childish and mischievous. The chatter became racier, the jokes raunchier, the flirting more obvious. Bottles were produced as if by magic, but never openly passed around. And here we were in this giant castle, almost alone! What better place, with our cast of characters, to play Cowboys and Indians! With the older men sitting this one out, we chased each other from room to room, making silly war-dance sounds. There was some flirting and kissing, pinching and shrieks, but not, to my knowledge, anything beyond that. Sex was a no-no at the ranch, unless you were married. Odd, of course, with Hearst living openly "in sin" with a woman half his age.

We progressed to hide-and-seek after a while, and at one point I wandered off into a dimly lit room, bumped into some kind of stand, and sent a huge vase crashing to the floor. Oh no! I thought, breaking into a clammy sweat. The thing is probably worth thousands! Hearst will serve me up for lion meat for sure now. In an unthinking panic, I started gathering up the pieces, actually trying to fit them together. Then, shaking sense in my head and dropping the pieces, I crept out and peeked up and down the corridor to see if the coast was clear. I saw nothing, but heard a "whoo-whoo-whoo" and a woman's high-pitched shriek in some distant chamber. All safe. If the damn thing was discovered, I reasoned with childish guilt, I wasn't about to be blamed for it, or caught "red-handed," so to speak. I found the rest of my playmates, who at this point had thinned out, with some opting for a night dip in the outdoor pool. Goes In Lodge was sitting on the ground cross-legged, a small group gathered around, showing them how to smoke a peace pipe. The "tobacco" used, called *kini-kinich*, is made from seven kinds of herbs, including ingredients from roots, berries, leaves, bark. It has a nice smell to it and bites your tongue like an angry lover, but once you're used to it provides a kind of soothing effect. Indians still smoke it today for that reason. One of the Indians, probably drunk, was swimming in the pool with his costume still on, laughing and splashing water all over a squealing, appreciative audience of women. Another Indian, Chief Yolachi, was telling stories to another group. Still thinking about that vase, I couldn't join in and asked a servant to escort me to my bedroom in one of the guest palaces. I spent my first night at the Hearst ranch in a fourposter bed big enough for three, sleeping fitfully.

While you were free to do pretty much as you pleased at San

Simeon, W.R. and Marion set the pace. Saturday morning we were up fairly early for a horseback ride to some point in the ranch, whereupon we'd rendezvous with a small mule train packed with provisions for a picnic. After breakfast, which was served in bed with another menu, I decided to wander over to La Casa Grande before starting out with the group. I wanted to see what had become of my shattered vase. The criminal returning to the scene of the crime. After about fifteen minutes wandering from room to room, trying to figure out where I was, I finally came upon the familiar hallway and crept into the still darkened chamber. There was the stand and the vase—or *a* vase. No sign of a struggle, no fragments, no fingerprints.

It had been replaced in the middle of the night.

The ride through what must have been a very small portion of the ranch was wonderful. Hearst, a good horseman, led the pack over land that offered the best of California geography: rolling hills covered with shaggy golden grass, multicolored rocks, fissures and canyons carved from the earth by streams during the rainy season, cool ocean breezes and bright sunshine. Usually these outings were overnight affairs, but in this instance we were to make an afternoon of it. The picnic spread included Russian caviar and fine California champagne, plus jumbo shrimp flown in from New Orleans the night before and packed in ice for the mule trip. Wonderful stuff.

Late in the afternoon we returned, most everyone exhausted except W.R. Of course, I'm used to this kind of riding and wasn't fazed a bit by it, but W.R. was in his seventies! Some of us, including Hearst, an enthusiastic swimmer, took a dip in the pool and soon we were all playing water volleyball. Even Goes In Lodge joined in on this one, Indians being keen on all manner of ball games. In fact, he made a damn good defensive guard with his height, but unfortunately almost drowned a few times during the rushes for the ball. I'm not crazy about water myself—in fact, I think I mentioned I can't swim. Staying away from the game, I contented myself paddling around in the shallow end. Suddenly W.R. emerged out of nowhere like some huge, surfacing walrus.

"Say, Iron Eyes, I was noticing you out on the trail today. That was some fine riding on your part."

"Well, thank you, Mr. Hearst."

"Ever ride bareback?"

"Sure do. Many times for the movies. I occasionally like to bareback it for fun, too. Got a couple Appaloosas corraled back in Griffith Park, near where I live."

"Ha ha. Fine, fine." His voice grew softer, almost to the point of inaudibility. Actually, it was pretty high for a man of his size, and scratchy, like a worn phonograph record. I found myself leaning in to hear what he was saying over the din of volleyball players.

"Listen, my boy. About that sister of yours, or stepsister is it?"

"Stepsister. White Bird."

"Yes, yes. White Bird. Now there's a fine-looking woman, damn it. Truly fine. You know something? I could really go for a woman like that?"

Okay, now I know all about the famous Hearst/Davies Love Affair, how they were supposed to be so devoted to each other, with she being the only stable thing in his life. I know how he worshipped her, gave her everything to his liking—including her career—and worried endlessly about her straying from his side. And how he couldn't marry her because of his wife. Also, this was a perfectly normal conversation between two worldly men— although worlds apart—and I don't want you to think I felt otherwise at the time. In fact, I remember feeling flattered and thought White Bird would be flattered, too, when she hears about it. But looking back, it all seems just a touch on the crummy side. At least when you consider the hypocrisy.

"Is that right? I somehow didn't peg her for your type, but I'll mention you've taken an interest in her. You have to understand, though, I don't actually know her all that well and—"

"Oh, I understand perfectly, my boy. And I wouldn't dream of placing you in a difficult position. It is with the utmost respect for your stepsister that I make this, well, proposal. I assure you I have in mind only doing something nice for her . . . or perhaps for your people?"

"Of course."

"In fact, you must know an Indian cause or two that could use a timely infusion of cash. Perhaps a library built, or a school?"

It just happened that a friend of Birdie's, a Kickapoo Indian girl named Myra Bartlet, was opening up the country's first Indian center here in Los Angeles. Birdie and I were donating whatever time we could to this effort.

"That would certainly be wonderful, Mr. Hearst. Myra Bartlet's in the middle of starting up the country's first Indian center with some dedicated friends. We could use anything, land, lumber, stationery, you name it."

Hearst let out a why-this-is-a-mere-trifle laugh, slapped me gently on the shoulder, and, smiling, whispered, "Done!"

I don't know why the most powerful man in America couldn't just go after what he wanted in a more direct fashion. I suppose it was his shyness, another "legendary" aspect of his character. Or maybe it was his being used to having everything "arranged" for him, following an order. In any event, I never got to find out. I'm not sure what was going on in my head at the time; such was the mesmerizing effect the man had on me. I simply forgot to say anything to White Bird. She never knew William Randolph Hearst, owner of empires, self-proclaimed protector of the free world, was sweet on her. And I never got to see any offices built compliments of the Baron of San Simeon.

After our swim, Hearst disappeared with some business executives and the rest of us gathered around the pool after changing for a cocktail. It looked as though Marion had already been drinking. There was a kind of sloshy edge to her still charming, delightful self. She had really taken to our group of Indians, and was jabbering away with them about horses, Indian cooking, pottery, art. There were a few Indians among us who had distinguished themselves in the white world. Chief Yolachi, the story-teller of the previous night, was also a singer with the Metropolitan Opera in New York. In the midst of general conversation you would occasionally hear him pipe up and down the scales. Earlier, he had spent quite a bit of time huddled with Hearst, talking about things I'll never know about, maybe a new wing for the Met in exchange for an eagle feather headdress. (It's against the law for whites to own one now, but not at that time.) Another aspect of Marion's drinking, one a bit more obvious, was making itself apparent. She had loosened up considerably in the swearing department. She was also chatting for some time with my Indian friend, Ira Walker, who is known to imbibe a few himself. I happened to be watching them out of the side of my eye while talking with Louella Parsons—she was planning a piece on Hollywood Indians—when the two of them stepped back a few paces and vanished behind a statue. I guess you know by now that I'm not really one to mind my own business and, well Marion and *Ira*? Impossible. I excused myself from Louella and strolled over to a better vantage point. There was Marion, reaching behind that statue and opening what appeared to be some kind of little trap door built right in the base of the damn thing. She produced a full quart bottle of cognac and, putting it directly to her beautiful lips, took a slug that would have knocked any layman drinker to the floor. She passed it to Ira, who did the same. They looked at each other, giggled, and then Ira placed his hand behind her neck under that golden hair and rather roughly yanked her to him. Laughing gutturally, she didn't exactly resist when he kissed her. I wandered back to the clusters of people about the pool in a sort of daze of jealousy, titilation, and I don't know what.

"What's the matter, Iron Eyes," said Louella. "You look like you've seen a ghost."

"Huh? Oh, nothing. Just flesh-and-blood people, that's all."

On Sunday morning, as we were preparing to depart from The Enchanted Hill and the Indians were climbing into their cars, Goes In Lodge took me aside and said how much he enjoyed himself. Incidentally, he spoke no English and we communicated in signs. Here it is roughly translated:

"I'm glad for you. Did you tell The Man?"

"Yes, with Running Wolf speaking the white tongue for me. The Man said to come back whenever I wished. I gave him my belt in gratitude."

"I'll bet he appreciated that."

"I do not think I will return to this strange place, however."

"Why? Did you not say you enjoyed yourself?"

"Yes. And the young white women who we see in the giant talking pictures, I would like to take a couple back with me for wives. One said she would, but has to ask her husband first. But this place, it doesn't fill you up like lying with our own women or chasing after the buffalo as in the old days. I think if I came back here I might be tempted to stay too long, and this might anger The

Man, who frightened me. He has chased away the spirit in the land and replaced it with himself. That will always make a man feel too big for the world, so he isn't filled up, either."

"Yes, I see what you are saying."

"This Man, very powerful. How can he make water flow up the mountain unless he is now the spirit?"

Goes In Lodge was referring to the big water main that contained water pumped uphill from the reservoir. I saw no need to explain how the water flowed uphill. He knew already.

8

THE THIRTIES are often described by Western film historians as
the "Golden Age of the B." Production costs were kept at a minimum, often using stock footage for action scenes (which, as I
mentioned, I might supply), by carefully dressing up the actors in
studio shots to match frames almost perfectly. There's an art to
deception. Plots were kept simple and formula, with little attempt
at character depth or psychological drama. Simple-minded. I guess
that's what their appeal was, and also why the front-row kids
composed such a large share of the market. In fact, the three
principles making up the Western—Good Guys, Bad Guys, and
Injuns falling vaguely somewhere in between—were so cliché-
ridden, so "they went that-a-way" and "head 'em off at the pass"
corny, that they were really funny. Recently here in Los Angeles
they showed on TV a "Worst of John Wayne" film series. Hilarious.
And I must have appeared in at least half of them. Oh, well.

Making these little sagebrush operas was a pretty rough business. Most were cranked out on Poverty Row, the major studios
confining their activities to what I like to think of as the "B+s"—
really maintaining the quality of the epics, just lacking the extravagance. Poverty Row was where the bread and butter Bs were
made, where the "quickie" got its start. The "spiritual center" of
Poverty Row was Gower Gulch.

I mentioned this little corner of real estate at Gower and Sunset
several times, and it deserves more attention. You could, in fact, do
a whole book on the place, or a movie. When the writers for *Hearts
of the West* were researching their subject, we spent hours together
talking about some of the goings-on at Gower Gulch in the old
days.

I guess the best word you could use to describe the atmosphere at
the Gulch—and all along Poverty Row, for that matter—was

confusion. There were more so-called producers out to make a fast buck, more actors and bit players clamoring for attention and the few roles available, more arguments over who hired who, and more fights per square inch than anywhere this side of a boxing ring. Complete mayhem. The whole place assumed the atmosphere of a twenty-four-hour-a-day Wild West show. Cowboys in cheap, loud Western shirts, jeans, and cowboy boots would sit around in front of the drugstore with their feet propped up on the back of some-body's chair, complaining about everything imaginable. They wore their guns—loaded—slung low at the hips in fancy leather holsters. (Actually, cowboys at work on the range, if they wore guns at all, more often than not shoved the pieces in their pants belts.) When you entered the saloon across Sunset Boulevard, you checked your guns at the door, just like in the movies. Standing two or three deep at the bar was a fantastic array of characters, giving it a kind of carnival atmosphere. It was sure a long ways down the hill from the Hearst castle. There were always the "visit-ing" bit players of just about any caste, including some Shake-spearean types, freaks, weightlifters, winos, salesmen, loud-mouths, and quiet, dangerous looking sulkers. There were women, not whores (well, maybe one or two) or actresses in the usual sense, but honest-to-goodness cowgirls just as tough as the men. They'd drink, swear, fight, and gamble along with the guys, too. The bulk of the clientele were the cowboys described above and Indians, of course. And then there was the occasional celebrity.

By "celebrity" I don't mean a Hollywood star. While Gower Gulch was a hangout mostly for all that supported Western film making—character actors, stuntmen, producers, directors, cameramen, etc.—the stars themselves often did stop around for a drink or two. Rarely a day went by when you didn't see a Tom Mix, Gary Cooper, Errol Flynn, or Duke Wayne, especially Duke after about '33. But they didn't impress anybody at the Gulch. Just more working stiffs, like themselves. By "celebrity," I mean true-blue outlaws and other notables of the *real* Old West, men who, for their own reasons, made the Gulch a kind of second home.

One was Emmett Dalton of the famous train/bank-robbing Dal-ton Brothers. Having survived a spectacular 1892 shootout in his home town of Coffeyville, Kansas, where he and his two brothers tried holding up two banks simultaneously (leaving brothers Bob and Gratton shot dead by the townspeople), he spent fifteen years in prison. Emmett now was in town doing bit parts in the movies. A producer would, of course, play up the fact that one of the famous Dalton brothers was actually appearing in his movie, hoping to parlay some of that notoriety into box office receipts. When you asked Emmett, at this time in his seventies, why he had tried to take two banks at once, and in his hometown where he was sure to be recognized, he shrugged his shoulders.

"Hail," he drawled quietly, "We jus' wanted to git our names in the headlines. Like them James brothers."

Another Gower Gulch frequenter was the great Black heavyweight boxing champion, Jack Johnson. You might know that this is the same man the play and subsequent film, *The Great White Hope*, was based on. Being an avid jogger, he used to run up in the hills around my place with my father. I think he hung around the Gulch as much as he did because it was one place he could come with his pretty, white wife and not be gawked at. But he was gawked at anyway, now that I think of it. Always dressed to the teeth, he would sit at a table with his equally well-dressed wife, who would often be seen gently stroking the champ's genitals.

Probably the most notorious of the characters that hung out at Gower Gulch in the early thirties was Wyatt Earp. That's right, *the* Wyatt Earp. Like Emmett Dalton, Earp was being used in the movies for his name. By this time he was a reedy old man with a huge, drooping mustache who would sit in his rocking chair at his ranch in Riverside when he wasn't at the Gulch. I spent many an afternoon up there trying to get him to talk straight about the old days, but mostly he wanted to just make small talk, or cackle to himself about the folly of human nature. You might ask him a direct question about, say, the shootout at the O. K. Corral and what his real intentions were (there's speculation that, instead of shooting a bunch of outlaws, his brothers, Doc Holliday, and he were clearing the way for a robbery they were planning). He would take a long pull on the corner of his mustache, roll some spittle on his tongue, and with a decisive "thwop!" send it hurdling fifteen feet.

"Can't *re*call."

That would be the end of it. A friend of mine at the Historical Society here in Los Angeles, of which I'm a member, once spent weeks interviewing Wyatt Earp, with the idea of selling the stories to a movie company. Well, Earp allowed for some interviewing, all right. Told a pack of lies on his heroic exploits while a police officer at Wichita and Dodge and, later, a guard for Wells, Fargo and Co. in Tombstone. What he couldn't recall, apparently, was his being on the take with the gambling houses and seeing to it that unhappy losers made a fast exit out of town. This also left Earp free to run a faro game or two on the side at night. Nice, tidy arrangement. Anyway, his life story was sold to Columbia. When the producers came around to Gower Gulch to verify, Earp denied everything.

"Hell, I never said anything like that. Who is this fella said he interviewed me?"

Columbia did manage to unload the story much later, though, but to TV. That's what they based the Hugh O'Brian "Wyatt Earp" series on. Too bad the old fart couldn't have lived to see his myth become truth through the magic of the boob tube. Bet he'd have gotten a good cackle out of that.

I spent a lot of time at Gower Gulch with my brother because we were always looking to hire Indians among the many that hung out. Most were from the East and had never seen a horse in their life, leastwise ride one bareback for the movies. I had to teach them a few basics about horses, in addition to how to "act" like an Indian. I took advantage of the three-dollar meal tickets the studios dispensed for a week's worth of eating. Can you imagine? Three dollars! I hung around with all the extras and hopefuls, sat across from the quick-buck producers in poker games, and negotiated deals. And, of course, argued, argued, argued. Mostly about who got paid how much for doing what. "C'mon bud, I didn't see you on the set that day. Go pick your ten bucks up at the race track." Or, "Was it you who took that fall off the bank roof? No kiddin'. You better see Slope MacIntire. He says he took it and I paid *him*."} I got cheated out of a few bucks myself. I had taken a check to the drugstore to cash against my account. It was cashed, all right, and I got nothing back. My account had been doctored. When I confronted the owner, he said he knew nothing about it. I was about to pounce on the bastard, but he had a couple of gun-toting morons flanking him who looked like they'd fill their own mothers with bullet holes for a shoeshine. I took him to small-claims court, but couldn't prove anything.

When people at Gower Gulch weren't fighting over money it was over who gets hired. It could easily touch off a barroom brawl scene like something out of a John Ford Western.

"Don't hire that goddamn drunk for this role. Take me, I never touch the stuff."

"Hey, who are you callin' a drunk?"

And they'd start slamming away at each other, and it would spread throughout the place maybe because somebody would accidentally poke somebody else's elbow, causing him to slobber his beer. The offended party would turn and, in a half-blind, drunken stupor, slug it out with whoever stood next to him. Before you know it, chairs are crashing over heads, tables are flipping over, and drinks and chips are raining through the air like confetti.

No wonder, then, that there were plenty of shootings at Gower Gulch. In fact, the last two were the biggest, and it wasn't too long after that the Gulch just kind of fizzled out. I think I'm one of the few still around who was there when, in a classic draw, one man was killed, another injured. It went like this.

There was a bit player and stunt man named Black Jack Ward. Everybody called him "Blackie." Although not too big—I'd say about five feet nine—he was surely one of the meanest, toughest dudes ever to fall on his butt for the cameras. There was no stunt too dangerous for him, no role too villainous with his black beard and cold, gleaming little eyes. He also insisted on wearing two guns at all times, and this caused no end of problems when playing opposite the stars. Especially Tim McCoy.

"Goddamnit, Blackie, when you're in my movies you're gonna wear one gun like the rest of the bad guys. I'm the only one that gets to wear two guns."

"Oh yeah? Why's that?"

"Well . . . damnit," Tim would sputter in rage, " 'Cause I'm the good guy. More important, I'm the *star*."

"Shee-it, you know what you can do with your star. As for these guns," he said, backing away from Tim with his hands poised over the revolvers, "I figure if any man wants even one of 'em he has to take it off me."

Now, keep in mind here that these guns were *loaded* and that this character Blackie had a reputation for shooting down men for lesser disagreements.

"For Chrissake," said Tim, waving him off. "What is this, the O. K. Corral? Keep your goddamn guns. See if anyone notices you in the movie."

Crazy nut, that Blackie. The surprising thing is that he was not only repeatedly hired by these stars and producers he always bad-mouthed, but he was one of the most popular extras around. Always under contract. I guess it was because stars like Tim McCoy admired courage so much. Whether or not he had all his marbles, Blackie Ward sure had a full set of brass balls.

One day I was standing at the bar haggling as usual with some producers over what to pay some extras. Blackie was standing straight as a corn stalk at the end of the bar, downing his mescal (a heavyweight booze squeezed from the *agave* fruit) with a single jerk of the elbow. His movements had a kind of military flair to them, an official crispness. He was dressed completely in black, as usual, topped off with a huge sombrero. Bad-guy attire. Suddenly a man I only know as a Mr. Teague barged into the place through the swinging doors, looked about till he spotted Blackie, and marched up to him.

"Ward, you're a no-good, stinking bastard."

Now Teague must have towered nearly a foot over Blackie, who merely paused with his drink for a second, then gulped it down. Then he slowly put the glass down and lay each hand flat on the bar, like two ready weapons.

"You hear me?" shouted Teague. The whole place turned as quiet as night, its attention focused on these two.

"Son," growled Blackie in a hoarse whisper, "you got just two seconds to explain what the hell you're doin' here actin' up like this. And it better be good."

"You been messing with my wife, that's what I'm doing here."

Blackie relaxed a little, but kept his hands free. "Is that all? Hell, I thought it was something important. Tell you what, son, I'm willin' to let bygones be bygones. You just turn around and take yourself outta here the way you came in. Don't want to see you get hurt none."

Some scattered sniggering came from the audience, and that must have tipped the scales for Teague. He let out a kind of strangled yelp and grabbed Blackie around the throat, but Blackie's hands were ready with an open-palmed slice to Teague's groin. Groaning, he let loose of Blackie's throat. Blackie then started methodically working him over with his fists. A couple shots to the stomach. Ducking Teague's roundhouse, an uppercut to the jaw. Blackie was all over the poor man, who was reduced to barely defending himself and stumbling backwards. Finally he fell down and scrambled towards the door, but didn't quite make it before Blackie drew one of his big revolvers.

"Take another step," he snarled, "and I'll blow your head off. You started this, and you're gonna finish it. Get back here!"

Teague froze a few steps from the door. He turned around slowly in an almost resigned manner, like a shoplifting kid just caught with the goods. Of course, by this time the entire place had formed a circle around them and, when Blackie made this last pronouncement, the jeers, cheers, and general clamor of the fight instantly stopped. Teague, his shoulders drooped, walked back. I'll be damned if they didn't start flailing away at each other again. This time, at least for a while, it appeared as though Teague was holding his own. They were both bleeding about the mouth and, if I can remember, one of Blackie's eyes started to puff up a bit as they tumbled about the place, all arms and legs kicking and punching. After about five minutes, Blackie had Teague cornered against the wall and was dealing out some pretty fierce punches to the gut, but Teague managed to slip a punch and, again, run for the door.

"All right," Blackie yelled, "draw!"

Teague turned, drew his gun at what appeared the same time Blackie did, and they fired simultaneously.

Teague winged Blackie's shoulder, sending him spinning half around before falling to the floor on one knee. Unfortunately, Blackie's bullet entered Teague right above the left eye, where a neat, half-inch hole appeared. It exited out the back of his head and blew out his brains, actually splattering the door.

You can read various newspaper accounts of this grim little

chapter in the history of Gower Gulch. To this day I don't suppose they've resolved to anybody's satisfaction exactly what happened. The next few minutes were complete pandemonium. Women screamed. About half the people in the place pushed towards Blackie. Another group stampeded for the door. I was pressed into the mob that ringed Blackie, almost unable to move. There he was, still on one knee and glowering at the spot in the floorboards, saying over and over, "Shit . . . shit . . . shit." As for Teague, another group had formed around his spread-eagled self, admiring the gore and deadly accuracy of Blackie's shooting. A few women were sobbing quietly.

The police arrived, pushed their way in, and started asking questions, but everybody would talk at once, each spewing out something different from the next guy. A couple of small scuffles erupted just over the disagreements. That was Gower Gulch for you. An ambulance roared up. The police took a few names (probably all false) and clapped the irons on Blackie. Then, still growling "Shit!" every two seconds, he was lifted onto a stretcher and carted out. The crowd provided a rousing cheer.

Blackie stood trial and it was a sensation. Not a day went by without the newspapers carrying something on it. Because of the contradictory and, in the view of the defending attorneys, "unreliable" nature of the witnesses, and because no real evidence could be turned up by the district attorney whether or not Blackie actually had been fooling around with Teague's wife, he got off pretty easy. Three years. He served about a year and half before being paroled.

But something happened to Blackie's mind in jail which I guess from the start was wound up a bit too tight. Broke a main spring or something. When he got out he would still come around to the Gulch and drink his mescal with the same jerky style, but his eyes were vacant. Still cold and deadly, but kind of fish-like and flat, and so glassy you could almost see your reflection. He never talked, and he didn't do any more movies. Finally, he just drank himself to death. The last time I saw him was about two years after he was let out of prison. He was sitting on the ground in some back lot alley, propped up against a corrugated tin shed. Flies lazily circled his now shaggy head like tiny vultures. His once immaculate attire was tattered and greasy. His face was grayish-black from soot and it looked as though he was near death. I don't think I'd have recognized him had he not tipped a bottle of rotgut to his blistered lips with the same mechanical jerk of the elbow. The only thing left of tough guy Black Jack Ward.

About two or three weeks after the Blackie/Teague incident, while the newspapers were still cranking out one crazy story after another (one claimed that Black Jack Ward was the devil), a new character showed up at Gower Gulch. His name was Tom Bay.

During the late twenties, Tom was one of the best cowboys in Montana. He was hard-working, spending from sunup to sundown chasing after strays, branding, and doing what cowboys spend most of the winter months doing, mending fences. He caught the eye of a prominent Californian in the business of rounding up wild horses for shipment to overseas markets. Taking a liking to Tom, he put him in charge of the entire operation and introduced him to a few directors, getting him bit parts in a number of low-budget Westerns. Then Tom started hanging around Gower Gulch.

Now it happens, that, in addition to being rugged, fearless, friendly, and well liked, Tom was also good looking. Put it together with this boyish charm that the women went nuts over, and it wasn't long before he was sleeping with everybody's wife in Hollywood. He came to be known among jealous husbands as "The Menace." But his ways were so winning, his smile so "gee whiz, guys, it's all in fun" beguiling that it seemed even they would look the other way. As long as their wives were happy. Then Tom went too far. He started sleeping with the beautiful young wife of an oil-rich Osage Indian. She was a tempestuous, possessive woman who wasn't about to share her lover with any of the other Hollywood wives. As it came out in the trial later, Tom would sneak around to ranch up near "Mixville," Tom Mix's estate, when he was out of town, which was quite often. Of course, even Tom was a little jumpy sneaking around and plugging a man's wife like that. Once he almost shot Ken Maynard, who had come around for a little "visit" himself. Maybe that wife was a little busier than anybody would ever come to know for sure. Finally, he'd had enough.

"Screw this," he told her. "I'm not risking my neck for you anymore. One of these days he'll be standing right there in the doorway watching us, and one of us will have to die. It ain't gonna be me."

So he took up with some other wife. She found out about it, somehow got herself into the house of this woman, and, when Tom entered, shot him three times. One bullet went right through the heart. Then she just calmly sat down in the living room, the other wife screaming at the top of her lungs, and waited for the police to arrive. I've read how after a crime of passion people are often relaxed and seemingly at peace with themselves, as though having just gone for a little stroll in the woods.

Another scandal for the newspapers. This one reached national proportions, with public outcry about the immorality of Hollywood and the need for more censorship, and so on. *Time* magazine got into the act with a big story. She stood trial for about two years, and then finally went off to prison for another six. That was the last I heard of her. Her husband returned to his home town in Oklahoma, never to set foot in Hollywood again.

As for Tom Bay, one newspaper summed it up: "Gower Gulch got rid of The Menace."

Long about 1933, Gower Gulch began cooling off and more police patrolled the area, in effect taming it. Plenty of action still persisted along Poverty Row, but somehow the Gulch was never the same. It had seen its glory days.

Birdie and I were getting along okay as "friends" and decided it was high time we did some kind of double-billing together. We couldn't let rising stars like Clark Gable, Duke Wayne, and the others get a jump on us, could we? We settled on a radio station here in Los Angeles, Warner Brothers' KFWB. This was the biggest station in town, and still is. Our show was called "The Lone Indian," commanding a whopping salary of five dollars for each weekly, hour-long segment. Not bad for them days.

Of course, we were donating our time to this thing, a brainchild of my movie producer friend, Robert E. Calahan, who co-wrote and produced it. If you go back this far, you'll remember these were the golden years of radio. Many of the stars routinely made appearances on the wireless beginning in 1926 when the National Broadcasting Company aired its first show. Been down the tube ever since.

It's interesting to keep in mind that radio was the first *live* mass entertainment. While the pros were performing in them, many showed up drunk. Ordinarily saved from a forgotten line, a drunken slur of words, or temper tantrums by that merciful word "Cut," these folks found themselves in some pretty sticky situations on live radio. No reason for our little "Lone Indian" to be any exception. A typical session at the studio might go something like this:

IRON EYES: Hello, hello! I am the Lone Indian, and we're sure happy to have you with us this afternoon. You all know my wife Birdie—Say hello to the folks, Birdie.

BIRDIE: Hello.

IRON EYES: We've got a really fine show lined up for you today, starting off with our "Story of the Day," An old Creek Indian legend about how the nightflying bat came to be accepted by his fellow animals. Then we'll sing you some authentic Sun Dance songs with my Arapahoe friends, and—(shuffling sound of people entering studio)—In fact, here they are now to . . . say hello . . . (more noises, people talking off mike) . . . Uh, say hello, boys.

ARAPAHOES (in unison):   Hello.

IRON EYES: Good to see you here, boys. Hey wait! Who's this coming, Birdie? (clop-clop, clop-clop of coconut halves, simulating horses)

BIRDIE: Why, it sounds like Uncle Big Tree heading up the Prairie Bob wagon.

UNCLE BIG TREE (somewhat drunkenly):   C'mon, get your goddamn asses moving, you goddamn mules, you. *Ha! Ha!* C'mon, let's go!

IRON EYES (off mike):   "Birdie, get him to cut it out—he's been drinking again." (on mike) Well, hi there, Uncle Big Tree. Looks like you brought a wagon load of singing cowboys with you there.

UNCLE BIG TREE: Sonavabitchin' mules.

[140]

IRON EYES: Er . . . yeah, heh heh. I think Uncle Big Tree here just fell off the wagon, folks. (off mike, hissing to Birdie) "Get him outta here!"

You get the idea. It wasn't all silliness, though, and what I did like about the show was the opportunity to tell genuine legends.

One day, just before Christmas of 1933, we were in the KFWB studio rehearsing our routines just before air time when Mr. Calahan strode in. He took me aside and asked if I wouldn't mind giving a few minutes of the show to a new group just in from Ohio. Four guys were standing at the sound room door, shyly studying the linoleum and stealing glances at us. They weren't in any kind of costume and their instrument cases looked like tattered brown mummies. Decent looking, in a just-off-the-farm way, but not exactly prosperous.

"Well, uh, I don't know. Who are they?"

"Call themselves 'the Sons of the Mountaineers.' The good looking one's the leader. Name's Dick Weston."

"Ever heard them sing?"

"Nope. But a friend of mine has. Says they're really great."

"Have they ever been on air before?"

"Nope. But they've been around for a while. What say we give 'em a chance?"

I shrugged my shoulders. "It's your show."

So these guys tuned their instruments—Dick Weston played the violin—and, when we went on, waited around for their cue. Saving them for the last few minutes of the show, I introduced the "Sons of the Mountaineers, who came all the way from Ohio just to be with us tonight." They opened up with country-Western, which I'm not all that crazy about, but to hear these guys play it turned me into an instant fan. And this Weston dude? Why, his voice made you think you was lyin' out under the stars somewhere with, well shucks, with Sweet Sue.

The station's phones immediately started ringing off the hook. People were asking who these guys were and where could they get their records. It wasn't long before they signed a contract, cut a few disks, and became almost overnight stars. They made a movie debut in a Liberty vehicle, *The Old Homestead*, and Republic then signed Weston at a hefty seventy-five dollars per week. No salary was too high for star material, they figured. It was at the usual publicity luncheon for this contract-signing event that Louella Parsons met Weston, and that afternoon wrote in her column he was the new singing cowboy Western star to rival Gene Autry. For reasons known only to herself, she named him Roy Rogers. The name seems to have stuck.

Actually, Roy's *real* name is Leonard Slye. He changed it to Dick Weston when he formed the Sons of the Mountaineers with Bob Noland, Tim Spencer, and Hugh Farr, the guys "fresh off the farm" who showed up in our studio that day. Roy and I got acquainted. With his income in those early years, he wasn't exactly a wild man about town, confining his socializing and fun to things like inviting his pals over to help him dig a pool in the backyard. By hand. If you've ever had the misfortune to dig ditches in ninety-degree heat, you have a fairly good idea how much fun we had at Roy's place. Mr. Excitement, we called him. I'll tell you this much, it's a credit to Roy's personality that he got a lazy bunch like the rest of the Mountaineers and myself sweating enough to fill that damn pool.

A couple of years before Roy made his movie debut with Republic, a very strange movie was set loose on the American public. It was the first science fiction, musical, Western serial, starring Gene Autry and Smiley Burnette. *The Phantom Empire* came complete with an underground kingdom, robots performing all physical labor, and a society so advanced they could, among other wonders, communicate through "television" and resuscitate the dead. The inhabitants, the "Muranians," were unable to breath air on the surface. So, to see what a real lung looks like, they performed an operation on Autry and took out one of his. I suspect their real motive was trying to get Autry to cut down on his singing.

It was the first time, to my knowledge, that anybody was permitted to play himself on the screen—Gene Autry playing Gene Autry. I think this helps explain some of the Autry mystique, and why my friend Roy Rogers, try as he would, was never able to touch Autry's earning power. In fact, it's a little sad to think that Roy actually played in a few Autry films, one time being forced to sing at gunpoint. Autry made millions and is now a prominent businessman here in Los Angeles. When Roy completed his last picture for Republic in 1951, his salary was an incredible $400 per week.

For several years prior to the war Roy did make good money at Republic. He started dressing fancier and fancier till he became the best-dressed dude this side of Hollywood Boulevard. One outfit might cost thousands, and this was back when you would buy a house around here for that kind of dough. Then, during the war years, Autry began feuding with Herbert Yates, Republic's boss, and refused to do any more pictures while Roy was getting a bigger and bigger buildup. With Autry out of the way, Roy actually became their top-billed star, voted number one among Western moneymakers (moneymaking for the studios, that is) by the Motion Picture Herald. He took on a sort of subtitle, "The King of the Cowboys." His leading lady was Peggy Stewart, his sidekick Gabby Hayes.

"Gabby is a funny guy," Roy told me recently while talking about the old days. "Once he decided to shave off that grisly beard of his, just to see what was underneath. It shocked him so much he went out and hid in the desert till it grew back."

Then, during the 1944–45 season, he teamed up with Frances Smith for his principal leading lady. She called herself Dale Evans. It wasn't long before they were married. Now I don't know if this is known outside of dedicated film buffs, but Dale's first roles with Roy were as loose dance hall girls, trollops, and tough, ranch woman types. Actually, Dale is deeply religious and family oriented. I'm sure she'd had a profound effect on Roy through the years, but not until the gratuitous bloodletting in his films came to an end. When the novelty of musical Westerns began wearing off, and Roy's gentle approach to the cowboy hero became passé, he almost went overboard with fistfights and shootouts—all of a particularly brutal nature. The new "Truecolor," taking advantage of his colorful outfits, also displayed lots of banged-up faces and pools of deep red blood.

All of which leads to a question asked of me a lot these days, now that Roy is back in the limelight: Who the hell is he?

Unlike most of the characters out here—complex, a little crazy—Roy's easy to figure out. We can chalk up to showmanship the unnecessary bloodletting in his later movies and point to other clues. When you meet Roy at home lounging around in jeans and a cowboy shirt, he looks like Mr. Ordinary, so much so he kind of blends into the woodwork, especially when he opens his mouth. I love Roy, but it's the truth and he knows it—he's a plain man with simple tastes. That accounts for the fancy outfits. Roy always needed something extra to make him sparkle, to make him stand out in a crowd. To get to the heart of the man, though, is simpler still. He's exactly what he appears to be. Gentle, kind, Mr. Nice Guy. Just listen to Dale and him sing "Happy Trails." That's Roy for you. There really is something sweet and innocent about the two of them. For all the years I've known him, he never fooled around with the ladies like the rest of us, never took even one drink. Roy and Dale are the essence of clean living, home and hearth, mom and apple-pie America. Who is Roy Rogers? Go and visit the Roy Rogers Museum. Aside from 168 Indian artifacts that I gave him, there you'll find every kind of personal memento from baby shoes to pictures of Dale and him growing up to Roy Rogers comic books. He's a man who loves his home life more than anything. And Trigger and Bullet are still there to remind you all about his glory days.

9

As GOWER GULCH became less important as the production center for making sagebrush operas, fewer people looking for work hung out there, including Indians. We were used to having whites play the part of Indian extras; in fact, this was usually the case in the early days with the low-budget films. So we began surveying other dark corners of Lotus Land. We followed breadlines and picked out among the sad, grey faces those lucky enough—strong and young enough, that is—to qualify. The WPA had just been started up by Roosevelt, and since the work was usually temporary we recruited people employed in those ranks, too. We were paying about three times what these men could expect to earn as laborers, so you can imagine they didn't take long to think about it.

One day, we were scouting out a WPA work party digging ditches for a hospital foundation. It was 1931, I believe. My brother spotted a squat, big-stomached man, who looked to be in his mid-forties, slamming a pickax into the hard, dry dirt. He had short, thick hair, a big, square jaw, and a walnut-brown complexion. There were deep seams in his leathery face, showing he'd been through a good deal. Two men with shovels followed after him scooping up the loosened soil. They had difficulty keeping up. The man with the ax worked like a steam shovel, the breath exhausting from his nostrils in loud snorts with each swing. Silvermoon pointed out the man to me with his chin.

"I think I know that big guy from somewhere," he said. We approached the ditch and Silvermoon leaned over.

"You look familiar. Where have I seen you?"

The man paused in mid-swing and squinted up at Silvermoon through the bright sun.

"Nowhere," he said, and drove the pickax into the ground with a grunt.

Silvermoon snapped his fingers and pointed. "You're Jim Thorpe, aren't you!"

"So?"

"*So?*" Silvermoon slapped my stomach with the back of his hand, not taking his eyes off the man. "Iron Eyes, this is Jim Thorpe! *The* Jim Thorpe!" I was about to reply yes, of course I know who Jim Thorpe is, and Silvermoon blurted, "Jim, what the hell are you doing here?" Silvermoon never was one for being delicate.

Jim Thorpe looked a little irritated. "Something wrong with a man working with his hands?"

"Well, no, but —"

"So unless you got something better, I'm here earning an honest buck." He went back to pulverizing the dirt at his feet even faster than before.

My brother and I looked at each other.

"Excuse me, Jim." I said. "We're sorry to bother you like this. My name's Iron Eyes Cody. This here's my brother, Silvermoon. We're in the movie business and would like to discuss business with you."

Jim Thorpe didn't pause with his work, as though I had been talking to the air.

"That is , if you can ride horses. Otherwise . . ."

" 'Course I can ride," he snapped, taking up the challenge, "Chrissake, I used to break horses."

"Would you consider doing it in front of a camera then? The pay is good, Jim."

The once-great athlete put down the pickax, wiped the sweat off his forehead with the inside of his wrist, and climbed up out of the ditch. I was amazed to see how tall he actually was. Six feet one, to be exact. He only looked squat because he was so solidly packed, the kind of heavy man with muscles hidden behind a layer of fat behind more muscles, all compressed together. He looked both of us square in the eye.

"I have four kids to feed," he said simply. With that, we shook hands. Jim Thorpe was in the movie business. It had been a long slide down since the glory days of the 1912 Olympics in Stockholm, Sweden, when at the awards ceremony, Sweden's King Gustav draped a laurel wreath over him and said, "Sir, you are the most wonderful athlete in the world." James E. Sullivan, U.S. Commissioner to the Olympics, carried the adulation a step further, saying, "He is unquestionably the greatest athlete who ever lived."

Then, dark clouds gathered over Bright Path, which was Thorpe's Indian name. Some say his troubles began with a rookie sports reporter, working for the *New York Evening Mail* who was thumbing through some old clippings from out-of-town papers and trade magazines when he came across one that read: "Jim Thorpe played professional baseball in 1909–10 for Rocky Mount and Fayetteville in the Eastern Carolina League," and put the news on the wire. Jim told me it was actually a guy who he'd once played with in Fayetteville, a pitcher who, after the Olympics had made Jim Thorpe a household word, went to the Amateur Athletic Union with an old snapshot. It was of the Fayetteville team, showing Jim in uniform, riding a mule and grinning for the camera.

There's nothing officials hate more than a man whom they have entrusted with their love being dragged through the dirt. It's like they've been dragged along with him. The people were never against Jim Thorpe after the scandal. They were outraged, in fact, and couldn't understand why he had to give back his medals, his trophies, and have all his accomplishments permanently stricken from the records. And everybody who ever played with him knew he only played for fun, an amateur in the purest sense of the word. It was the officialdom of sports that came down hard because he broke their rules. There would be no light reprimand with the likes of Jim Thorpe, which everyone would promptly forget about. They would have to either break him completely, or back off from the issue altogether. They decided on the former.

Jim Thorpe, the greatest athlete America has ever produced, was, at least in the official sense, turned into a bum overnight.

No one had payed much attention to Jim Thorpe for the two years before we found him digging ditches to support his second wife and their four boys. His first wife, incidentally, wasn't half-Indian like the movie said: she was full-blooded. When the world crashed in around Jim, he left her. He also never had a weakling son that died. Just Hollywood sentimentalizing. In 1926 he married a Scotch-Irish girl with whom he had his four sons, and for whom he was trying desperately to provide. Hollywood has a big mouth. It was only a day or two after we hired him that the newspapers ran a piece on how the great Jim Thorpe was found doing manual labor for four dollars a day, and that he was now embarked on a "film career." As it happens, the Olympics were being held in Los Angeles in 1932. Jim Thorpe wasn't going because nobody thought to invite him. He didn't have a ticket. I'm happy to say that, because of the publicity we inadvertently got for him, protests poured in from around the nation about the champ being excluded from the games. He ended up sitting next to Vice President Charles Curtis, in the presidential box. 100,000 people rose with a thunderous ovation.

One of the first things that became apparent to me when "breaking in" Jim Thorpe to the movie business was his stubbornness. He was truly happy with the idea of playing Injuns in movies, and he had a decent part as Chief Black Crow in a typical B picture.

"You're sure you can ride bareback, Jim?" I said after making him up and introducing him to his horse, sans saddle. He glared at me and, grabbing the horse's mane, threw his bulk up onto its back.

"You just watch old Jim," he said, and galloped off, bouncing a good six inches off the animal's back.

He wasn't a good rider at all. He may have helped break horses thirty years ago on his father's ranch, but I suspect that had mostly to do with running after them, not sitting atop them. But Jim refused to get off that damn horse. He rode till blisters on the insides of his legs got so bad the blood would stream into his moccasins. Duke Wayne admired him immensely—in fact, he seemed on the verge of tears when he saw Jim squeezing that horse's back with his vise-like legs, trying for all his life to stay on. The horse wasn't any too pleased with the way Jim cursed and kicked and fought him. It finally sent the athlete sailing off his back into a bush. Again, he made the papers: JIM THORPE GETS THROWN BY HOLLYWOOD HORSE.

Jim would drink alongside any man he liked, and spent a good deal of time at Gower Gulch with the rest of the boys. Once he got loosened up a bit, he'd start talking about his life, and we all got to know him pretty well. His drinking never appeared to become a problem, though. He would have a few, tell some jokes, and treat us to his stories, usually making light of his achievements. Then one day a man came in who would change all that. Errol Flynn's barroom brawling is probably legendary, being the type of guy who just couldn't resist seeing how tough you were. If you had a reputation, that is. Flynn was a friend of mine and I managed to avoid duking it out with him on account of he always felt sorry for me. Thought I was basically a softie. Flynn knew Jim Thorpe was no softie, though. As he pushed his way into the saloon at Gower Gulch, he faced Jim's massive back leaning against the bar. Flynn had obviously been drinking, but he never staggered about drunk. Rather, you could tell he'd just polished off about a quart of gin from the dancing, madman look in his eyes, that swashbuckling, sabre-wielding, crazy-bent-on-destruction-for-the-fun-of-it look. He gave Jim a little poke from behind, which caused him to dribble his beer.

"Okay, you big sonavabitch. Show me how tough *you* are." Flynn did his famous stance—defiant, screw-the-world, ramrod straight, feet spread, elbows akimbo, and fists jammed into his slim hips.

Jim slowly wiped the beer from his chin, set the glass on the bar, and shook his head. "Dammit!" he said, grinning, "this is just like the Old West around here, ain't it?"

He turned to face Flynn, still grinning, but his eyes smouldered. Now I've never seen Flynn scared of anything, leastwise when his blood was heated up with booze. But I wonder if even he felt a twinge of doubt as he looked into the grinning face of Jim Thorpe and saw something dangerous. Maybe he didn't have time, it all happened so fast. Jim got into a crouch and pretended to throw a left, but held back. Flynn's response was immediate, reflexive, his right flashing out where Jim's smile was supposed to be. But there was only air. Jim had anticipated and ducked, and now had Flynn in perfect position for one punch, one angled roundhouse square on the chin of the handsomest face in Hollywood. I've never seen anybody hit with such force in my life. I think if Flynn hadn't been drinking, he'd have taken it too stiff and his head might have flown off. He was actually lifted off the floor a good foot and sent sprawling on his back. And there he lay, his arms spread out like he'd been crucified. Jim remained in a crouch, the grin gone from his face, his huge shoulders wrapped protectively around his seamed face. This was the old gridiron Thorpe, snorting like a bull. He was watching Flynn now like some animal patiently waiting for a wounded prey to expire. Flynn moaned and started coming around. He propped himself up on his elbows, shook his head, and saw what stood there, ready to go right through him.

"Enough?" said Jim.

Flynn gingerly felt his jaw, and for a few seconds the two of them were locked in a stare war. "Are you kidding?" he said, a smile spreading over his face. For a minute I thought he was going to be crazy enough to continue. "Too bloody much!" He dragged himself to his feet, staggered a little, and shook his head again. "What a punch! Bartender, set 'em up for Jim Thorpe, a *real* man!"

That was Flynn for you. His ways were so winning. He just waltzed up to Jim, put his arm around his shoulder, and acted like they had been buddies for life. The old smoothie could be brawling with you one minute and charming you the next. The grin returned to Jim's face and his eyes softened—after all, this Errol Flynn *was* his kind of dude.

"Jim Thorpe, Christ!" said Flynn, as though only now it had sunk in who he had tangled with. "What are you doing with yourself these days?"

"I'm working with Iron Eyes in the movies. I get to do a lot of riding," he said, laughing.

"Yeah? Well, look here, you can work for me, too. That okay with you, Iron Eyes?"

I shrugged my shoulders. "He's under no contract. He can do what he likes."

It turned out that Errol Flynn used Jim Thorpe in almost every movie he made for years after that day at Gower Gulch. Unfortunately, it also turns out that Jim picked up a lot of Flynn's bad habits. Flynn had an assortment of permanently out-of-work actors, stand-ins, and hangers-on that followed him around raising hell in the bars and busting up parties. Jim became one of them, drinking like a lush, fighting, and screwing girls. With the latter, he had his pick from the bevy which was always trailing Flynn, most of them secretaries and waitresses hoping to either make it in Hollywood or get made. Often, the action commenced at my brother Silvermoon's house. Flynn also had a liking for Silvermoon. I only saw Jim on occasion for these years he was hanging out with Flynn. He'd stop by my house on occasion and have a decent meal cooked by Birdie, and he seemed to look worse every time.

Once, I made the mistake of inviting him and five or six of "the boys" to play cards. We were having a good time for the first few hours, and, as the bottles were passed around, Jim got more and more animated. He was actually quite funny, and had a decent wit about him when he was high. I guess that's the way it is with a lot of people who drink. The guys kidded him about his exploits with women, and how they were afraid with his bulk he'd crush one of them, and we'd all laugh. In disgust, Birdie stayed in one of the other rooms. Then Jim would start getting dour and withdrawn, the alcohol which helped him forget a moment ago now turning on him, as it always does. The lines in his face grew deeper, his eyes went red, and his complexion turned grey.

"Sonabitchin' medals," he'd mumble, "who needs 'em, anyway. I'm still the best! They can't take that away from me. The best, *the best!*"

We were all getting kind of quiet, studying our cards and not paying him too much mind. Then this character who used to be Flynn's main stand-in—I think they called him "Red"—said, "Hey, bud, I'm sick a hearin' your shit about them games. Why don't ya shut up about it and play cards? You ain't the best no more. Damn Injun thinks he can—"

That was all he got out. Jim reached across the table, grabbed him by the shirt, and blasted him. Again, just once. But unlike with Errol (who he said he just "touched" because he didn't want to bang up that pretty face) he held nothing back. I'll tell you, the entire wall next to poor Red was showered with blood and teeth, him having had his mouth practically turned inside out. He also had a broken jaw. Four of us tried to pull Jim Thorpe down and keep him from murdering Red, who lay on the floor in his own gore like a dead man. Jim just threw us off like rag dolls. I still have a big dent in the plaster next to my easy chair where my back slammed into it. The whole place probably would've been wrecked and Red would never have played Errol Flynn again had not Birdie stepped into the fray. Nobody, not even big Jim Thorpe, messes up *her* house.

"*Out!*" she screamed. "All of you, get *out!*"

She started punching and kicking Jim, who just looked at her like some insect. For one horrified moment, I saw that same blank, alcohol-soaked lizard killer look that I'd seen many times on my father years ago. He raised his arm to strike her. I leaped for a tomahawk peace pipe I had hanging on the wall, and, shaking in terror, was just about ready to plant it in his forehead. But that horrible look clicked off in his eyes just at that instant, replaced by something more human. He lowered his arm and stood there blinking.

The other three guys still standing, more or less, gathered up their money and cards, and one of them said, "Yeah, well we was just leavin'. Good game, Iron. Thanks for the whiskey. See you around, Jim." And they scurried out.

Our attention turned to Red.

"Oh, my God," said Jim, sounding like a boy guilty of some prank, "I'm sorry this had to happen at your place, Birdie. Maybe we'd better see about getting old Red here to a hospital."

"Yeah, I think that's a good idea," I said, tossing the tomahawk to the side. "Birdie, would you call an ambulance?"

It wasn't too long after this incident that Jim quit the movie business altogether. He had made quite a bit of money and for once had managed to tuck some away. One day he called on me and said he was going into business.

"Got my eye on a bar up in Burbank," he said. "I always wanted to run my own place. Might be fun."

So he and his wife, Frieda, opened a place in Burbank, which really wasn't half bad. He had it swanked up with fancy tables covered with nice linen, his athletic trophies on the walls (and they covered the walls), and a long, gleaming bar behind which he stood smiling and pouring drinks. For a while it seemed he was going to be okay. Birdie and I stopped in frequently, and we had really nice times. But trouble always seemed to follow Jim Thorpe around in one form or another. He never seemed to be able to get the better side of his nature working for him. He poured drinks, and poured them, and had some himself, laughing and entertaining his friends. But he never bothered collecting money from anybody.

Jim and Frieda held on to that bar together for a few years, not making any money. Finally, she left him, and the bar took a turn for the worse. In addition to the usual freeloaders, a rougher element started coming around. There were occasional fights. The fine linen disappeared from the tables, and Jim still offered everybody credit. He could never just say no to anybody—especially if they took an interest in his sports background. It wasn't long before he was bankrupt, and lost the place.

When the war started, Jim was fifty-three. He tried to enlist but was refused on account of his age. Again there was a long period I didn't see him, being busy in the service myself. I understand he joined the Merchant Marines and helped haul live ammunition to the Far East. Then, just as the war was drawing to a close, he appeared on my doorstep one day with a new woman on his arm.

"Hi, Iron," he said, grinning broadly. He looked terrific, still a little overweight but about ten years younger than when I saw him last. "I want you to meet an old friend of mine, Patricia Askew. We go way back together. Patty, say hello to Iron Eyes Cody."

Patty, in fact, had been an admirer of Jim Thorpe way back in the days when he was smashing his way through lines of 250-pound tackles. She wasn't much to look at, a little on the heavy side with mousy, flat hair, but what the hell. Nothing like a homely girl to put a man at his ease, I always say.

But it wasn't to work out that way. Jim Thorpe's childhood sweetheart hated Indians. I felt a cold contempt on the other side of her smile when we were introduced. She was a fighter, however, and started a whole campaign to get his Olympic records reinstated and his trophies back home. That certainly is to her credit. But she also battled Jim on the company he kept. As most of Jim's friends were Indians, this caused no end of problems and I have no doubt it contributed to his drinking again. For the next five years he continued doing odd coaching jobs. He wanted with all his heart to go back to Carlisle and be head coach there, but the word was out. Jim Thorpe was still hitting the bottle. We went coon hunting together, and he looked worse each time I saw him, very gaunt and pale. If you asked him what the matter was, he just grinned.

"What could be the matter? I feel better than ever."

Then his luck turned again. At the halfway mark in the twentieth century, 1950, America took a look over its shoulder. What about this Jim Thorpe fella? Think maybe he got a bad shake somewhere back there? Hundreds of sports writers were polled nationwide, and the man voted to be the greatest athlete of the twentieth century was Jim Thorpe. One-third of the votes went to Jim, Babe Ruth came next, with Ty Cobb and Jack Dempsey following. Instead of his falling off horses in Western serials, the headlines now read: THORPE NAMED GREATEST IN SPORT. His face was plastered on the cover of every magazine in print and more awards and trophies were heaped on him. He was invited to swank gatherings to make speeches. And, of course, Hollywood was hot on his trail again. Warner Brothers gave the okay for a million-dollar production based on his life because, as Jack Warner said, "Jim Thorpe's story could only have happened in America." He probably was right at that. Jim was given $25,000 for the rights to do his life story. Burt Lancaster and Charles Bickford were signed for the title roles, Phyllis Thaxter was to play Mrs. Thorpe. Then they had to come up with somebody to play Jim's father.

"Why the hell don't you let Jim play it himself," I said to director Michael Curtiz. "He'd be great!"

Curtiz frowned and looked down. "Well, actually, Iron Eyes, we were thinking of casting you. What do you say?"

"Nah, you got the wrong man. Give it to Jim. It would mean a lot to him—and think of the draw he'd be. Besides I'm going over to Paramount to do a big picture with C.B. DeMille." (It was to be called *The Great Sundance*, but it never came off. C.B. got interested in the Bible again and did a remake of *The Ten Commandments* instead.)

Curtiz balked, telling me something about Jim being too overweight and "not right." When the film crew departed for Oklahoma to shoot the opening scenes of Jim Thorpe's boyhood, they left without Jim Thorpe. Wouldn't even use him as a sports technical advisor. And I can tell you it broke his heart, visibly. The big man actually wept. I had to think of something, and fast.

"C'mon, Jim, cheer up. It'll probably stink anyway. What do they know about making movies? Hell, without you in it, it'll bomb for sure."

This seemed to brighten him a little.

"I've got an idea."

"If it means riding horses, forget it."

My idea was this: I couldn't think of anything Jim Thorpe liked more than playing football. So why not form our own football team? Jim was a big man once again, a national hero. Who needs Hollywood? We could tour the country in a bus, play exhibition games, and make a bundle. And that's what we did. We called ourselves "The Jim Thorpe Indians." We recruited a bunch of our Indian friends from the movies and decked ourselves out in costumes taken from my collection. Some of the rest of the old gang, including a denture-wearing Red, dressed in cavalry uniforms. We bought a bus and painted it red, white, and blue, got ourselves bookings through my publicity agent, and off we went to play ball.

I don't think I'd ever seen Jim happier. He really took the whole thing seriously—got into training, lost a lot of weight (his stomach was hard and flat as a piece of slate), and coached us into a fairly decent bunch of football players. I played center, snapping the ball to him while he faded back and fired perfect passes at us, which we didn't always catch. When he ran with the ball, it still took ten men to drag him down. He could kick a fantastic distance, and booted field goals easily from thirty, even forty yards. And this man was sixty-three years old! Our only problem seemed to be balancing the teams—whoever had Jim on their side would trounce the other. We finally teamed Jim up with the worst players (including me) and that almost made things even.

In the meantime, *The Jim Thorpe Story* flopped miserably at the box office. Didn't make a dime for Jack Warner. Burt was terrible (c'mon, Burt, admit it). It was sentimental and false from beginning to end. Jim hated every minute of it and couldn't have been happier to learn it was failing to draw an audience.

"See," he said, winking, "they needed me after all."

But something was happening to Jim. It was almost imperceptible at first, mainly because up to the very end he never let up on his spirited playing. And he certainly never let on that he was in pain. But soon it became apparent to everybody that he was sick. His once walnut complexion turned a chalky, almost ghostly, white. His lips cracked and bled frequently, and he broke out in huge sores around his mouth. Even when it was obvious he was in pain, he refused to stop playing. But one day he was hit with average force on the field, and he just didn't get up. He was bleeding from somewhere inside, and the blood was trickling from his mouth down the side of his face. Somebody called an ambulance. Kneeling beside him, I put my hand on Bright Path's shoulder.

"Think we might knock off for an hour or two, Jim? You've been a little rough on the guys today. They could stand a break."

I thought I saw a glint of fear in the great warrior's eyes, but he pushed through a small smile anyway.

"Sure, why not," he said quietly. "It's all for fun, right?"

The cancer had been eating away at Jim Thorpe's insides for more than six years, they told us at the hospital. He knew it, but never told anybody. It was incredible he'd lasted as long as he did. What, did you say he was playing football up till now? Incredible, they said, shaking their heads. The man must have been made of iron.

VVVVVVV VVVVVVVVVVVVVVVV

10

O NE BRIGHT, SUNNY Hollywood afternoon I was driving to my brother's home on McCadden Place. I had a deer strapped to the right front fender of my car, one that he had shot when we'd hunted together in the hills south of Griffith Park where I live (these same once grassy, wild hills have long since erupted forth with a severe case of pimply condominiums and "luxury" homes). Pulling up in the drive, I notice the front door open and thought him at home. I untied the carcass, flung it over my shoulder, and walked in.

"Silvermoon," I called. "Hello, anybody home?"

No answer. But I did hear some kind of muffled groan coming from one of the back rooms. Meanwhile, the deer had started trickling blood from its arrow wound down the right side of my neck, although I didn't know it. I had hiked it up once or twice, and must have rubbed a little on my cheek. Heading for the sounds in the back, I pushed a partially opened door with my foot. There, reflected in a huge mirror on the ceiling, were two quite familiar rear-end cheeks earnestly pumping away between a couple of shapely legs. The legs, arched up around their host like two giant pink calipers, I didn't recognize. The rear end I knew because it was almost non-existent.

"Flynn?" I roared, trying to scare him. "Flat-assed Flynn, is that you?"

A face emerged from the tangle, unmistakably that of Errol Flynn. Still attached to his bed partner, he raised his eyebrows and that slightly crooked, charming smile crept over his perfect features.

"Why, hello, old boy. Nice of you and your friend to drop by. Shirley," he said, turning to the lady and nudging her. Still lost in her erotic dream, she groggily lifted her head and with some difficulty focused her eyes on me, "Shirley, my love, I'd like you to make the acquaintance of a good friend of mine, Mr. Iron Eyes Cody."

Shirley's eyes, finally getting the message through to her otherwise occupied brain, suddenly opened wide in horrified recognition. There, standing before her with blood dripping down his face and some horned beast draped over his shoulder, was a savage Indian, no doubt about to use her for some strange sexual rite. She fainted dead away without a word.

Flynn gave her another nudge.

"Shirley? Shirley, c'mon now, girl. Is this any way to act with a guest . . . or guests?"

He turned to me and, shrugging his shoulders, said, "Well, it seems the bitch was so overcome by the presence of a star like you she's passed out. Say, why don't you unload that deer somewhere and take a round with her yourself. That'll wake her, sure enough. But get yourself cleaned up a bit first, old boy. You look like hell with that blood on your face."

I said he seemed to be doing okay by himself, and left him to resume arousing her through his own efforts. Not for any moral reasons, but somehow playing seconds never did interest me. I was also convinced by this time that Flynn must have picked up a dose or two from one of the many waitresses, secretaries, and streetwalkers he entertained at my brother's house. I spread some newspaper out on the kitchen table and unburdened myself of the deer. Washing up in the bathroom, I shouted down the hallway, asking Flynn where Silvermoon had disappeared to.

"Oh, I don't know," he yelled back, still vigorously occupied with his guest. "Expect he went out to . . . (groan) . . . find a few birds for himself."

No sooner had I emerged from the bathroom than my brother appeared at the front door with three girls, all of them barely eighteen.

"Hi, Iron. Where's Errol?"

"Where you usually find him—in your bedroom."

They found Flynn easily enough. Sitting there on the couch with a drink in my hand, listening to the racket they were making, what could I do but join in?

Okay, I know what you're saying—I didn't *have* to. But sex

[158]

permeates everything that goes on here, on and off working hours. It's what makes the stars glow. It's what people do who are blessed with physical beauty and great charm, and cursed with the need to constantly prove it to themselves.

Which isn't to say I had anything to prove to myself, not having beauty or much charm, but I was mesmerized by all the star power around me. Actually the entire decade of the thirties—especially the first half—is a kind of blur, a fade-in and fade-out of one wild party after another, coupled with the grind of making movies. During the day I was falling off horses, raiding forts, and plugging hats with arrows. At night I tried to catch as many fallen starlets as I could.

So did Errol Flynn.

Errol met my brother, and then me, while filming his first super hit, *Captain Blood*. (It was Silvermoon who whips him in that scene after he's caught by the Spanish). I was in every Western he made after *Blood*, most of them forgettable affairs Errol hated making, plus a number of general action films like *The Charge of the Light Brigade*. We hung out quite a bit, and I came to know him well, if it was possible to say that about Errol Flynn. When he wasn't working hard, he spent most of his time drinking, fighting, and wenching through the bedrooms and barrooms of Hollywood, hardly pausing to wind his watch. There were complexities to his character, to be sure, but he tried his damndest to keep them hidden behind a macho facade. We called him the "cocksman," an image he often complained about ("I'm just a goddamn phallic symbol to the world!") and yet pursued with a single-mindedness, energy, and talent you could really marvel at.

But I don't know. With Errol Flynn it may have just been a helluva sex drive and the equipment to put it to constant use. He was so well hung that he was famous for it all over Hollywood. In fact, such was his reputation, I know of several otherwise perfectly sane (well, that's all relative out here) directors who actually asked to *see* it, right there on the set. Only too happy to settle any lingering doubts as to his masculine dimensions, Errol would unzip and proceed to set the record straight. Regardless of who was present. And if you find this silly, there was another fellow named Freddie Frank who the casting directors used to keep on the lot solely for the purpose of servicing the more needy of their female leads. His piece, which I understand he charged a good penny for, was colossal. Amazing. He and Errol, when the latter was drunk enough (which was most of the time), used to have "stretch and measure" contests. Always an inch or two short, Errol never conceded defeat but blamed his drinking—that is, not being sober enough to match Frank's stretching capabilities.

Ah, Hollywood!

Another adolescent masculinity contest came in the form of holding, at arm's length, a sledgehammer upright by the end of its handle, slowly tilting it back towards the face till it touched the nose, then, without at any time bending your arm, returning it to its upright position. There was many a bloodied nose—even a few broken noses—on the set when Flynn got out the old hammer. I still have it in my basement, a gift from him, although I never got in the act myself. My nose looks broken enough as it is.

While some could match Errol's strength, I don't know of anybody who came close to his callousness. He had just about everybody either hating or fearing him, always picking fights and making corny, insulting jokes at your expense. It's solid testimony to the sheer force of his personality that most people, while hating him, still liked him very much. Suckers all, he probably thought. Including myself.

We had been on location for days shooting action sequences for *They Died With Their Boots On*. This is the Civil War/Little Big Horn Battle opus tracing the life of General George Custer with much liberality regarding factual matters. The final battle scene, showing Custer rallying his troops and waving his big saber (actually, Custer never carried a saber into the fray), was a tricky and complex second-unit job. And I really had my work cut out for me with the hundreds of Indians used.

In one of the final moments, I was to come charging up, let out a war whoop, and leap from my horse onto Errol's back. He was then supposed to fling me off and, with me lying on my back, shoot me with his pistol. Fine, we'd done this kind of stunt dozens of times. And Errol was a true athlete. He'd know how to move, how to gracefully and harmlessly perform this kind of stunt. The only problem was that during our entire time in the desert he had been drinking. I think this was his gin period, and he'd guzzle the stuff like orange juice first thing in the morning, continuing throughout the day. Every day. By the time we got to this last crucial scene, he was staggering about, bleary-eyed and dazed, waving his saber recklessly. He was the perfect Custer, half-crazy from battle fatigue, rallying non-existent troops in a hoarse, gin-soaked voice.

So there I was charging up behind him, whooping, my tomahawk in hand. I yanked back on the reins, at the same time lifting my right leg up and behind, the combined movements catapulting me onto Errol's back. Now I'm not sure at this point if he even remembered this was to occur, since he flung me off with such violence. Then he swung about and, before I even hit the ground, stuck his gun in my back and fired point blank. I had no shirt on and felt a hot, searing pain.

It must be a miracle I'm alive. That pistol, loaded with what had to be an extra couple portions of blank charge, tore a half-inch hole, narrowly missing my spinal column. Now I know how Tim McCoy must have felt back in the twenties when he was blown off his horse with a blank charge. I let out a groan and rolled like a dead man over on my back, clutching the wound with one hand. Blood was pouring out and it stung a good deal, the powder having burned the skin around the "bullet hole."

"Help, I'm shot," I yelled feebly. "I'm shot, I'm shot!"

"All right, boys, hold that line there!" cried Flynn, still waving the saber and firing his pistol into the mass of steadily encroaching Indians. "We've got 'em on the run!"

I lay there on the ground, bleeding like a hog with its throat cut, while the entire Second Cavalry was wiped out. Finally, Custer got his fatal wound, dropped to his knees and heroically let off a few more rounds, and the battle ended. Cut! Raoul Walsh, our director, came running all excited.

"Beautiful, Errol, beautiful. Great stuff. We can put that one in the can for sure. And Iron Eyes, that was a nice piece of stunting there. Iron Eyes? Hey, what's the matter with him?"

"Ughhhhhhhhh," I moaned.

"Somebody get the doc. I think Iron Eyes here's been hurt."

The doc, another heartless jerk, rolled me over and saw the bloody wound in my back. "Errol, Raoul, get a load of this. Ever see a blank do that kind of damage before?"

Errol peered at me with saddened, alcohol-soaked eyes.

"Hey, old boy, I'm really sorry . . . Oh God . . ."

I'll say this much. He seemed genuinely contrite.

"You fired point blank," I hissed. "Where does it call for that in the script?"

"Now, now," said the doc in that irritating "don't-talk-it'll-only-make-it-worse" tone. "Better let me patch you up and . . . Lord, just look at that laceration, will you!"

"Humph," said Walsh, shaking his head and admiring the gore with the doc and Errol. "I thought he was just using a blood bag. Iron Eyes, you're a real trouper. Yessir, they should re-name you Iron Balls."

"Ughhhh. Ohhhhh."

While these characters chortled over my bravery, and Flynn staggered off to change, I was stuffed with cotton dressing, shoved into an ambulance, and sent to the nearest hospital about ten miles away, at Sunset and Vermont. I was there three days, lying on my stomach, when Flynn finally came around for a visit. No one in the hospital recognized him. For some reason he didn't look as Errol Flynn-like in his street clothes. Just another Hollywood smoothie in an ascot and thin mustache.

"Hello, old boy," he said cheerfully, bounding into the room. "Looks like I got you on the wing."

"Yeah, that you did. Fine shooting. Congratulations."

He sat down beside me, put his hand gently on my arm, and spoke in a quiet, soothing voice.

"It was an accident, that gun going off like that. You know it, don't you old boy?"

"Okay, so it was an accident."

"So. I'm sorry."

"Fine. Thanks."

"C'mon, don't be like that. Cheer up. I'll make it up to you, you'll see."

"What'll you do, use smaller blanks next time?"

"Why, no, real bullets of course."

"Don't make me laugh. Hurts too much. Listen, Errol, there is something you can do for me, now that I think of it."

"What's that, old boy?" he said, squeezing my arm in reassurance. "You name it."

"Come closer, it's hard for me to talk."

He leaned closer to the bed.

"No, closer, closer. That's it."

"What, are you deaf now, too?

His ear was about an inch from me when I yelled at the top of my lungs—and I've got a voice that can break a whiskey bottle from all the whooping and singing over the years—"STOP CALLING ME 'OLD BOY!'"

I don't know as Flynn actually did ever "make it up to me," although he did once show a side of his character not often demonstrated, at least in public.

An old Osage Indian friend of mine who did some acting in the movies, Bibs Brave, had been on a drunk and almost killed somebody in a car accident. While it wasn't clearly established whose fault it was, because he'd been drinking (and probably because he was Indian) he was immediately thrown in jail. When Flynn found out, he decided to raise bail money by throwing a combination party/fund-raising event. All his Hollywood cronies showed up, and the money flowed as freely as the champagne and it wasn't long before Bibs was a free man. And while he was convicted, deservedly, of the drunk driving charge, it was established in court the other party had been in error.

Speaking of courts, Flynn, as you probably know, was charged with the statutory rape of two fifteen-year-old girls named Betty Hanson and Peggy Saterlee. For the record, he did know these two charmers in the biblical sense. Paul McWilliams is a good friend of mine who's a dead ringer for Flynn. He played his double and sometime stuntman in films, and even lived with him in the years before his death from booze. Both Paul and Errol enjoyed the girls' company to the fullest on many occasions—on the beach (the truth be known, I was with them on the beach), at my brother's house, on board Flynn's boat, Sirocco. In fact, everybody knew them. It turns out the little hookers had plotted the whole thing from the start with a boyfriend, the idea being to sue the pants off Flynn once they had "gathered enough evidence," so to speak.

The defense attorneys called me into court a couple of times in case I was needed as a witness, and I got to see Flynn operate under real pressure. He was all grace and cool as ice. When the prosecuting attorneys asked if he had had sexual relations with the "young ladies" in question, he shrugged his shoulders and, gazing at his accuser with twinkling eyes, said, "You bet, old boy. Fine little bodies. And they were mighty willing, at that."

Charges were dropped when a score of men all stood ready to give evidence of same carnal knowledge.

While we're playing "fact or fiction" regarding the myths surrounding Errol Flynn, there's a few I think we can safely clear up here.

First, this ridiculous rumor circulating that Flynn was some kind of latent homosexual. With this gay rights movement and the women's movement, coupled with what must be a large dose of sheer jealousy, it's fashionable nowadays to try and make he-men types into either closet homosexuals or muscle-bound fools. Errol Flynn was neither. I know of no man who loved women more than he. I haven't any psychological evidence; I'm just telling you what I know from what I observed and felt. He may have been a complete ass at times (and he'd have been the first to admit it), but he was super-straight. I'm not denying the possibility of latent homosexuality for a number of other super-macho types—particularly a few around today. But not Flynn.

Next, there's this business of him being a Nazi. The rumor probably got started when Flynn began hanging around with a few Nazis in the thirties. I'm convinced, though, that it had nothing to do with his ideas of what the world should look like politically. He never gave me, or people I know who were close to him, any indication that he gave a damn about politics. He was fascinated with brawlers, criminal types, and womanizers. Stands to reason he'd associate with folks who qualified in one or more of these departments. Same goes for Flynn's friendship with Batista. He often spent time in Cuba partying on the dictator's yacht, sleeping with his mistresses, and listening to his war stories. That doesn't qualify him as a fascist, just somebody with bad taste in friends.

Then there's the story that a bunch of Flynn's friends stole John Barrymore's corpse from a morgue and dragged it up to Flynn's place for one last party. Actually, that's all true. Complete with booze and ladies. It was a royal sendoff, one I'm sure Barrymore would have heartily appreciated and chosen over the standard

Christian variety. Barrymore often talked about death in a cheery fashion, like it was a big vacation he was planning. His peculiar view was shared by another character with equal measures of death-love and misanthropy, W.C. Fields. Fields, in fact, was in on the invasion of the Barrymore body snatchers. He helped pay off a couple stuntmen: one of whom, now dead, was a good friend of mine. An attendant of the mortuary, who was also given money, let the two in through a window. They took the body right off the slab, hoisted it out the same window, and drove up to Errol's place in the North Hollywood Hills.

"We sat Barrymore up in a lounge chair," said my stuntman friend, "stuck a drink in his hand, and waited for Errol. When he came home—Jesus, you should have seen the look on his face! For a minute we all got scared and thought he was gonna kill us. Then he just laughed and said, 'Old Barrymore should be here to see *this*!' He poured us all a drink and we toasted the 'greatest actor in the world, past and present.' "

Errol always appreciated a good laugh. In fact, I'd say he ranked right up there with Coop as a practical joker. Once, Errol, Paul McWilliams, and I were on location for a picture directed by Michael Curtiz. It happened that, while shooting a particular scene, there were no toilet facilities on the set and Michael had sneaked around to the back of a tent. Errol, Paul, and I decided this was too good an opportunity to pass up. We persuaded one of the extras, an amiable guy named Sailor Vincent, to enter the tent, slip a shovel under the back flap and under a squatting Michael, and catch his business. Without Michael noticing, Sailor then managed to spirit the whole load into the tent, leaving the ground under Michael without a trace of his being there.

Now, I'm sure there's some animal instinct buried deep in us compelling a quick, self-assuring look when we've finished adding our natural fertilizer to the earth. Might have something to do with making sure our territorial markings are all in order, or staking out a good hunting ground. Whatever, I'm sure something very different entered Michael's mind when he pulled up and fastened his pants, turned to survey his accomplishment, and saw . . . nothing!

"What's the matter," said Errol to Michael back at the set. "You look a little pale."

"Do I?" he replied vaguely. "That's funny, because I don't feel too well, either. Very strange things have been happening to me since we arrived in this place."

"That so?"

"Yeah, uh, just a few minutes ago I was—oh, never mind. You wouldn't understand."

For the likes of Errol Flynn—actually any recognizable movie actor, including myself at times—the streets of Hollywood were filled with legions of women stalking their prey. They wanted no courting ceremony and were ready for action at a moment's notice, in broad daylight and in full view of the public. They came from all walks of life, all social backgrounds, all ages. One particular female desperado, married to a wealthy man highly placed in society, once spotted Clark Gable sitting on a couch at a party. She actually ran across the room, jumped on the couch, hiked up her skirts, and tried straddling his face. Poor Clark, always the gentleman, managed to tip the couch over backwards, making it appear like she accidentally "fell" on him.

Another such ready-for-action beauty was among the "bevy of beavers," as Flynn called them, at the fund-raising party for Bibs Brave. She was very blonde with cute, sharp little features and big, roaming, anxiety-ridden eyes. She wore a tight-fitting blouse, a loose skirt, and, sitting with one leg propped up like a signal flag, it was obvious to all who ventured a look that she wore no underwear.

She was indeed noticed by a portly gentleman with a bulbous red nose who talked out of the side of his mouth like an educated gangster. He waddled up to where she was seated, leaned over, and took a long, hard look up her dress. The lady didn't flinch, but wore a "So, whaddya lookin' at, fats?" expression. He shook his head gravely and tipped his hat.

"Pardon me, madame," he said, "but you haven't been blonde for long, have you?"

Pure W.C. Fields. And that was when he was stone sober.

Actually, despite what you may have heard, Fields was at his comic best when he hadn't had a drop of the stuff. Let him loose in front of the camera when his wit and sense of balance weren't

blurred by the juice and he was a genius. He didn't lose his cool—
or his comic sense—even when an earthquake hit, which is when
I first glimpsed the master in action. I had been on a lot adjacent
to Field's at Paramount filming *Wagon Train* with Gary Cooper,
and during a break went next door to watch the proceedings there
for a while. Fields had a habit of tipping his hat frequently. I've
always thought it had something to do with his inner sense of
timing. With the camera rolling, he touched the brim as usual,
stretched out both arms, and leaned over a pool table with cue in
hand, about to line up a shot. Suddenly the ceiling lights started
swinging back and forth, and back and forth like pendulums. Fields
peered up and frowned.

"Would somebody kindly tell the elephants up there to forage
elsewhere?"

When it became apparent it was an earthquake and the floor
started doing the rumba, people poured out of that place in a
second, while others dived under the big tables used to support
heavy equipment like kleig lights. Everybody scrambled except
Fields. With the camera still on him (the cameraman and director
stayed, too), he just shuffled-walked to one side, saying, "Don't
worry, folks, it'll pass, it'll pass." And, of course, it did.

But when Fields was drinking—even one or two glasses of
wine—he'd turn into this kind of bumbling Humpty Dumpty,
continuously crashing into props or an inconveniently placed wall.
When I next saw him we were on the set of *My Little Chickadee*,
about to film the train-chase scene. In it, I come charging up on my
horse and shoot an arrow through Field's oversized hat. Actually,
this is filmed two ways—one shot taken while actually "chasing"
the train and firing the arrow into a window, the other taken in a
studio where we set up the arrow-through-the-hat shot. Fields,
who had already slugged down a few, actually had to be led about
and steered in the right direction.

"My dear man," he said to me, "you don't actually propose to fire
that contraption in my direction, do you?"

"It's no problem, W.C. With a hat that size, how can I miss?
Besides, you'll be wearing this."

I showed him a steel skull cap all my "victims" wear whenever
I'm about to skewer anybody's head gear, a pretty common stunt in

the Westerns. Fields did one of his famous doubletakes but, mumbling something about the revenge of the Red man, put it on and went through the take okay. Only a few minutes later, though, he felt the top of his head with a worried look on his face.

"Where's my hat, where's my hat?"

"It was shot off, Fields," said the director, "remember?"

"Don't talk nonsense, man," he barked. Then, glaring at all of us through eyes narrowed to slits, he said, "One of you pilfered it, that's what happened . . . Ah *ha! There* it is."

He walked over to a hat rack, bumped into it, took an imaginary hat off, and delicately placed it on his head.

You may not believe this, but I don't think one of us knew whether the whole routine was meant as a joke. He could get a little weird when on the sauce. This was especially so when it came to his relations with women.

Field's lust for the opposite sex is legendary, but when it got down to it I think he just preferred having women around to having them carnally. When we had finished shooting *My Little Chick-adee*, I asked if he intended going to the cast party.

"Party, hell," he snorted, "I know of a fine little establishment of ill repute in Sonora. What say you and I forgo this party foolery and head yonder for more sensuous grazing."

So I went to a whorehouse in Sonora with W.C. Fields in my new Kaiser Frazer. When we got there, everything was reserved for us. We had only to walk in and the madame, a sumptuous woman of almost exact same proportions as her guest, was effusive.

"Ah, Mr. Fields, Mr. Fields," she said, joining her hands at her ample bosom. Come to think of it, she even sounded a little like him. "So nice to see you again. The girls will be delighted."

Beaming, Fields tipped his hat.

"And your friend, Mr . . ."

"Ah, Cody," replied Fields, "Mr. Cody." He turned to me and whispered out of the side of his mouth. "Blondes okay with you? They're all knockouts!"

I shrugged my shoulders. "Sure."

We were escorted to a finely appointed set of rooms done in red velvet, brassy fixtures, and antique lamps like you see in the finest hotels in San Francisco. Presently, three blondes walked in. Fields hadn't steered me wrong. They *were* beautiful—not a trace of the life they were living was etched into their fine, creamy complexions, no sags or lumps in the wrong places from excessive handling. Fields, who had just poured himself a brandy from a crystal bottle, raised his glass to me and nodded in the direction of the ladies.

"Iron Eyes, here's to the real thing."

He threw the brandy back with one gulp and the effect was immediate. His head gave a violent lurch, like he'd been bopped with a rubber night stick. He started navigating in the direction of the women, but his port side began listing dangerously, which he'd correct by applying the brakes, then his starboard—all the while singing a tuneless jingle.

"Bum bum dee dum—whoops!—ta tum dee dum."

Two of the girls grabbed under each arm and guided him to the calm waters of the couch.

"Oooooh," cooed one of them, "I love your nose!" She gave it a little tweek, which Fields seemed to enjoy.

"Careful, my dear, careful. That fine instrument you just woman-handled is insured for one million dollars, American."

"A million? Well, honey, let's put it to some *real* use, then."

"And you shall, my kumquat. But be gentle."

"Now you just relax, uncle," said the other, apparently the more business-minded of the two. She started unbuttoning his shirt in a no-nonsense fashion. "We have to get you out of these here clothes, nose or no nose."

"Ah, your voice is like an angel's harp to me," he said, reaching in turn for the front of her dress. "If you'll just let me pluck a few strings, what heavenly music we can make together."

"Yeah, yeah, now raise your arm, that's it. Lordyloo! Look at that gut. Shame on you, uncle. How you gonna do anything *except* with that nose, luggin' around a belly like that!"

Meanwhile, the remaining girl took my hand and led me to the bedroom, whereupon we proceeded to have a fine time, indeed. They were expert, those girls, and particularly well acquainted with all the various weaknesses and insecurities of men. After about half an hour, though, I couldn't help noticing things had not appeared much progressed in the other room. Field's voice would occasionally rise above the girl's chatter and giggles with a pronouncement or two, all indicating nothing much else was taking place.

"What's going on in there?" I asked my partner. "Doesn't he ever get down to business?"

"Who, Fields?" she laughed. "Nah. He just likes to take off his clothes and talk. That's why all the girls like him so much."

I guess we all have our little secret ambitions.

Hollywood's public ambitions were on display at parties. The place doesn't need too much by the way of an excuse to throw one—signing a new contract, getting out of an old one, finishing a day's shooting without a major catastrophe. One actress I know even had a party, a simple gathering of close friends—maybe a thousand—to celebrate her cat's birth of kittens. There were the "traditional" parties, Christmas, Halloween, New Year's, and so on. They were extravaganzas, each put on with the same attention to detail and expense you would think is reserved for entertaining royalty, and each intended to out-do the other. I liked the Halloween parties the most, what with all these people doing what they do best—dressing up and playing a role. Birdie and I once went to one as a cowboy and a cowgirl. Nice twist, I thought.

Then there were just plain old parties, for no reason other than to either have a blast or make important connections. I don't think anybody could beat Errol Flynn in the blast department, but there were a few runners-up. One was Tyrone Power.

Tyrone's parties always stressed imagination and attention to detail. Coop's ex-girlfriend, Lupe Velez, was another of the women in Hollywood who prowled the streets sans any underwear. In her case, though, I think it was just that she liked the freedom. I don't suppose she had in mind straddling Clark Gable, but you never know. She used to sit with her legs casually spread apart, and everybody who walked past would, to her amusement, take a peek and say, "Beaver?" Even Cecil B. DeMille. Once, she had a scene at Fox Studios with Cesar Romero in *Springtime in the Rockies* where they were doing some Spanish dance number. And, of course, with her twirling about, her skirt blew up around her waist—just in time for a handy publicity photographer to snap it, catching everything. It wasn't long before the new rage in certain

Hollywood circles was having an eight-by-ten glossy of Lupe baring her all for the dance. Had a few myself, but Birdie made me burn 'em. Tyrone, being in a somewhat freer domestic position at the time, had one blown up life-size and hung next to his front door.

Actually, Tyrone Power, along with Cesar Romero, was a perfect gentleman most of the time. At least outside of parties. Birdie, for instance, got along with both of them very well, often going off together with the more sophisticated folks to places like Bomars. Bomars was a ballroom, very nice, very tame. It presented a suitable front for movie stars, or would-be stars, to be seen and photographed with other national dignitaries for the columnists. But there are two sides to everything in this town: the side you present to the public through publicity agents and managers, and the side you live privately. Those people finding the scene at Bomars and the like a little on the bland side would slip across to the Zarape Club at the corner of Alvarado and Sunset. Here the tempo picked up a bit, and you could spend the night grinding your hips against a charming Hispanic senorita to the bump of a marimba band. Errol Flynn, Paul McWilliams, and I were regulars there for a while, with Errol doing most of the successful scoring. Which was fine with me, because after a few months I'd decided I'd had enough of the Hollywood life. I felt I had to run away from it all—and I did. I joined the circus.

11

SEEING AS I WAS offered a well-paying job, my decision to "run away" to the circus was not exactly like bundling up a few things in a handkerchief and hitchhiking to Madison Square Garden. Tim McCoy had been asked to tour his Wild West Show with the Ringling Brothers and Barnum and Bailey Circus by Samuel Gumperts, a one-time Coney Island entrepreneur who was then head of operations for "The Greatest Show on Earth." Tim called me in the winter of 1934 and explained he was leaving Columbia to tour with the circus.

"This won't just be Indians either this time, Iron Eyes."

"Yeah, I know. We've always included cowboys."

"No, no. What I have in mind is a presentation of the Snake Dancers. Authentic."

"You mean the *Hopi* Snake Dancers? Real rattlesnakes and kilts and everything?"

"Yeah! Won't it be great? You can be the chief dancer, find me all the other dancers, and run the whole show. I'll pay you anything you want over expenses, put you up in the best hotels. Whaddya say?"

"Look, Tim. Sounds like a good idea except for two things. One, you'll never get any Indian today to dance with real rattlesnakes except some drunk. Two, I can't go with you the full nine months. Birdie'll have my skin."

"Well, how about if you help us get started for a few weeks beginning with Madison Square Garden, then Boston and back to Brooklyn. From there I think we can handle it ourselves. As for the drunks, if you can handle those damn snakes and keep them from biting, you can keep the bottle away from the dancers for a while."

"Mmmm, maybe, maybe. Snake venom, alcohol, it's all the same poison."

In truth I had plenty of experience with snakes and drunken Indians already. On the set of a crazy movie called *Green Hell* with Douglas Fairbanks, Jr., I did a kind of voodoo medicine man who wraps snakes around himself and dances to African music. I wasn't playing an American Indian but a "native," a sort of stock Hollywood primitive that came in handy for confrontations with explorers in imaginary jungles. You'll notice they were rarely Blacks or authentic Indians. Too ethnic, I suppose. Anyway, in this film I was also extracting the poison from the snakes to use on spears and arrows. My "native" cohorts had to carry the snakes to me in ritualistic fashion, and I had to get them all drunk before they'd even touch the vipers. These were just bull snakes—big enough (actually bigger than rattlers—up to seven or eight feet and sometimes ten inches around) but not poisonous. They *do* bite though. A bull snake can get a hold on you and it's like a bull dog's grip. You might have to literally kill it before prying those jaws loose. They're strong enough to bring down a full-grown cow—or an Indian Snake Dancer, as we'll see later.

I'm also well acquainted with rattlesnakes. Had one for a pet, in fact. Found him on a hunting trip in the hills near where I live. Actually he had found me while I was sleeping and curled up near me for the warmth. Incidentally, you may have seen in a Western movie where a cowboy will circle his bedding with a rope to keep the snakes away? It's true, it works. Snakes don't like their bellies tickled by the fibers in a rope. I just didn't happen to have one on this trip. In the morning, after carefully sliding out of my bag, I picked him up by the tail and chucked him in a game bag. He found himself an agreeable abode in a gopher hole in a lot I owned next to my home. I named him Pete and promptly proceeded to de-fang him. An old Indian on the reservation taught me the trick. What you do is take a silk handkerchief, wave it in front of the snake's nose till he strikes, then give it a good yank. The fangs, which are hinged and fold back in the jaw when not in use, will usually pop right out. This accomplished, you can then teach a snake not to strike you at all by holding your open hand up to his face and bopping him on the nose with your palm when he tries to strike. He'll just eventually get sick of it and not bother you anymore.

Little Pete would help me train the Indians I had in mind to snake dance for the circus. The only problem was getting Birdie to agree to let me go. Somehow *that* prospect seemed less feasible than convincing Pete, my pet rattler, of the fun he'd have dancing with Indians.

"Call him up," she bellowed, pointing at the phone, "call up that Tim McCoy right now and tell him you can't make it."

It was worse than I thought, requiring careful strategy.

"Now, Birdie," I said reassuringly, "it's only for four or five weeks. And we can stay at the Waldorf Astoria in New York. A whole suite, just to ourselves. You, me, and little Wilma."

"You and *who*? You don't think for a minute you'd get Wilma and I anywhere near those snakes, do you? Isn't it bad enough you keep one next door? Almost scared all of us to death, it creeping up here like that. Makes me shudder to think of it. And those mice you feed it, the way they're swallowed whole. How horrible."

With it "creeping up here" Birdie was referring to the time Pete had ventured out of its pit, climbed the back steps, and sucked up the milk she had set out in the sun to "clobber," or turn to cheese. The woman next door spotted it first and screamed, "Rattlesnake, rattlesnake!" Never knew a rattler that liked milk like that little one. All snakes are deaf but can sense sound vibrations through the bones in their skull. This one must have felt an earthquake rattling his match-head-sized brain with all the shrieking and commotion, but calmly went on sipping his snack. Birdie was yelling at the top of her lungs to "get that disgusting thing off her porch" and how could I be so irresponsible and it should be killed and so on. Snakes and mice are two things women don't seem to warm up to, that's for sure.

"Aw, c'mon," I persisted. "He's just a little one, just as afraid of you as you are of it."

"What does his size or disposition have to do with it? A snake's a snake. What if Wilma should wander over there and get bit by it someday?"

"Well, that's the reason I put those cactus all around his hole. To keep kids away. Besides, you know I de-fanged him. He's perfectly harmless."

"You're not getting me to go on any circus tour when you're handling those filthy snakes. If you're crazy enough to get near the devils, that's your business. Wilma and I will manage fine right here, thank you."

Works every time. Overplay your cards a bit and they'll always think they won something in the bargain. I was free to go off to the circus, provided I went alone. The only thing I had to do before leaving was sew up the mouth of poor Pete, at Birdie's insistence, or she said she'd have him "properly disposed of" while I was gone. So that's what I did. Snakes only have to eat once or twice a year—he'd be all right till I got back. And his biting days, even if he were so inclined, were at least postponed.

Which was fine with my would-be snake dancing Indian friends. After I had managed to woo fifteen movie actor Indians—all of them heavy drinkers—away from the studios (and a couple of them out of jail) with the promise of $50 per week (which, of course, was big money in those days) I got them all lined up in the lot next door and explained what was required of them. Then I pulled out little Pete, his rattler buzzing in warning, and held him aloft.

"Okay, boys, you all know we're gonna handle snakes like this. Which one of you'll be first."

Complete silence.

"Look, he can't hurt you. His mouth has been sewn up. Now who's going first?"

Nobody would go near it. Finally one guy stepped forward and asked if I had any beer. Well, I wasn't getting anywhere with the snake dancing so I had Birdie bring us over a case of beer, which they all proceeded to demolish in about two minutes. Then a big Indian named Lee Roebuck stepped up and said, "I'll hold him if you make me the chief dancer."

"If you hold him, I'll let you join us. That's all I can promise."

Now Pete must have been feeling pretty bad since I'd sewn his mouth. Didn't have any pep left and hardly moved as that big guy first gingerly held him at arm's length, then, reassured he wouldn't drop dead, started heaving Pete about and stroking him, all the while laughing and dancing about like a crazy man. The rest got courage from this display and handled him likewise. It was a start, but I could see these guys were going to need lots of work before becoming Snake Dancers. Finally after weeks of drilling them on the steps and chants, all the while trying desperately to keep them sober, I felt they were ready. I had them all outfitted with authentic Pueblo costumes (Hopis are a religious sect of the Pueblos), boarded them on a chartered Trailways bus, hired a security guard to keep the fights to a minimum during the four-day trip, and off we went to the circus.

It wasn't long before there was trouble. At each stop most of the Snake Dancers would find their way to the nearest bar, get soused, and start fighting. We lost two or three along the way to brawls, or they'd just get so drunk they'd wander off and miss the bus. The fights got so bad the security guard couldn't take it anymore and quit. Finally, the skyline of Manhattan came into view just as I was also about to quit, along with the bus driver, who threatened to walk off if another empty beer bottle whizzed by his head. With stone drunk Indians hanging out the windows, waving bottles and catcalling to amused New Yorkers, we lurched into the Garden.

I got the Indians settled into a modest hotel, someplace tolerant of the racket they were bound to make, and checked myself into the Waldorf. The next day, I arranged to have my shipment of rattlesnakes from Brownsville, Texas, set up in a tent pitched especially for them in a lot outside the Garden. They were huge Western diamondbacks. Not as long as the Eastern diamondback but thicker and just as deadly. Most of them were at least six feet and there were a few babies thrown in, maybe a foot long. Rattlers, unlike most snakes, give birth to live young, and the little devils come into the world with a full set of fangs and lethal venom. Within seconds after the damn things emerge, they can strike with lightning speed and inject enough poison to kill you. That is, you'll be dead if you panic and run around pumping the poison through your system.

All these snakes were supposed to have been defanged, so I reached in for the biggest to see what kind of life he had in him. That flat, triangle-shaped head darted at my hand and sank two very much present fangs three-quarters of an inch into the back of my hand. The bastards in Texas had either missed this one or the fangs, being regenerative, had grown back! I wrenched my hand back in horror, my first instinct being, of course, the wrong one. Panic. Run to find help, a doctor. Finally getting hold of myself, I simply sat down in the dirt where I was, took off my shirt, and fashioned a tourniquet above the elbow. My hand swelled up to the size of a softball, normal for a snake bite. I let the blood pulse through the tourniquet just enough to keep it from going numb.

"Nice little snake," I hissed, holding back my rage. "We'll see about you later, got it? Don't think you're gonna get away with this."

He was unimpressed.

I hollered to some passersby until somebody tending the elephants stopped, came into the tent, took one look at what was in the crates, and said, "Jesus, and I thought you was just some kinda crazy guy. I was gonna give it to you with the shovel if you was to try anything."

"Yeah? Great. Now do you think you could go and find a doctor? Be sure and tell him to bring an antitoxin for rattlesnake bite."

The circus doctor finally arrived, gave me a shot, and had me carted off to the clinic. I spent the night with a fever and retched a few times, but the next day was fit enough. When Tim McCoy saw my hand, which was still swollen, he wasn't amused. In fact, he was terrified of snakes and wouldn't go anywhere near them.

"Christ, Iron Eyes, will you be more careful? What the hell you doing with those snakes anyway? I thought they had their fangs taken out or something."

"So did I, Tim, so did I."

Then I did something I knew I had no business doing. That big rattler was only acting out his role in nature, but somehow my affection for the latter was overwhelmed by a keen sense of revenge. I got out the old silk handkerchief, and waved it tauntingly in front of the serpent's nose till he'd go for it. Then I'd yank it away. He really was unusually vicious, the bastard. Climbing impolitely over his neighbors to attack his prey, he'd strike with terrific speed.

"C'mon ya sonavabitch. That's it. You'd like to get at it wouldn't you?"

After teasing him a while, I finally let him hit it and pulled the thing right out of the crate, dangling and twisting. Grabbing him behind the skull, I pulled so hard on that handkerchief that his jaw broke. Then, throwing him down, I crushed his skull with the heel of my boot. Had his jaw been intact, that would have been a mistake as a rattler can bite right through boot leather, no sweat. Later, when I was skinning him, a whole pile of tiny rattlers came pouring from his belly, all alive and snapping. "He" was a female. I still have her skin on the wall in my basement, almost seven feet.

Meanwhile, in Manhattan's West Forties where the Snake Dancers were "settled" into their hotel, quite a commotion was underway. The hotel's owner and manager was an Hassidic Jew, a kindly man who shared with many of his fellow Jews a fascination with American Indians. The man's patience had apparently been tested to the limit when, in a drunken craze, the biggest, meanest of the Snake Dancers, an Apache, had chased our poor host around the hotel lobby with knife in hand, threatening to cut off the long curls Hassidics wear over their ears. Good thing he eventually tripped harmlessly over a coffee table, crashed to the floor, and passed out. His name, incidentally, was Frank Hill. Remember Frank Hill? He's the Apache who almost blew Tim McCoy's head off way back in the twenties when we were filming *War Paint*. I would have to try and keep Frank's enthusiasm for realistic action under control.

"Mr. Iron Eyes," the manager said to me later, his voice shaking, "You must try to control these men. At this rate I'll lose my hotel the way I lost my *payis* (the curls over the ears)."

"I'm sorry, sir. It won't happen again. I'll go up and have a few words with them right now."

I was furious. Something happened since that snake bite: maybe some of the venom still coursing through my veins affected my brain. Ordinarily I don't get mad enough to flatten a snake's head just because I happen to be in his (or her) way, or harbor similar ideas for the likes of Frank Hill. But I'd had enough of these drunks and was going to put a stop to their craziness right now. Frank had once beat the hell out of my brother when he was too sick to properly defend himself and his meanness still stuck in my memory. I stomped up the steps and flung open the door to the room that seemed to have the most noise coming from it—coarse laughter, loud music. Through the darkness, I could make out a couple on the bed, naked.

"Hey, what *is* this?" came a deep voice, understandably irritated.

"Sorry, sorry, wrong room. You really should lock your door, you know."

I quietly closed the door, mumbling something about how this was just like in the movies, and went on to the room with the *next* loudest noise coming from it. I knocked.

"Yeah, come in."

That was a recognizable voice. I tried flinging the door open, but only crashed into it with my shoulder.

"Goddamnit, Frank," I screamed, pounding on it with my fists. "*Open* it, it's locked."

I was met at the door by Frank's wide face wearing a sardonic grin.

"Hail, Iron Balls," he said, waving a gin bottle in mock salute, "Here, have a drink, chief."

I pushed him in the chest, hard, knocking the wind out. The bottle fell to the floor as he stumbled backwards across the room. I followed, kicking the door closed, and grabbed him by the collar so he could hardly breathe. Six or seven other Dancers lay sprawled about in various attitudes of inebriation. The place was a total wreck—furniture upturned, everything reeking of booze. I knew the only way you could take a big guy like Frank was to get him by surprise and keep up the momentum before he catches his breath. At the moment, he was turning blue as I squeezed his collar.

"You ever pull a stupid stunt like that again, chasing that poor old man around who's shown nothing but kindness to you, and I'll kill you, Frank. I'll hit you just once, and you'll be a dead man."

I threw him in a chair before he'd a chance to react, and turned to the rest of them.

"You're slobs, and a disgrace to your people."

Then I walked out and slammed the door. Not a bad performance, if I do say so. I knew I wouldn't put an end to the drinking, but thought maybe I'd shamed them into quieting down a bit. It's also important to let them know who's boss. Frank Hill could pick me up and snap my back like a pretzel if he wanted, but now I didn't think he would.

The next day I had the Snake Dancers lined up, ready to start rehearsing.

"All right, boys," I barked with military ruthlessness. "I want you each to take up one of these here snakes and get to know him like you know your wife. Never mind giggling. You'll see they're all a lot bigger than the one we had in Hollywood, and they weigh a ton. Don't let that scare you. They can't bite because I outfitted each with a little leather hood. See?"

I decided not to take any chances since I was bitten. From a big piece of rawhide, I cut a sort of mask for each snake, including holes for the eyes and mouth, and tied it around the base of their skull. They looked even more sinister with the masks on, their tongues darting out of the leather like a little pink devil's fork, their eyes gleaming through tiny slits.

"Holy *shit*," said one of the Dancers. "You expect me to handle one of them?"

"No, I expect *us* to. C'mon, look, they're harmless now."

I grabbed one up and tossed him to Frank, who caught it gingerly and held it at arm's length.

"Frank here's not scared of him, are you, Frank?"

"Huh? Naw, naw. Ha ha."

"Okay, so let's get started," I said, passing one out to each Dancer. In a few hours I had them ready for full dress rehearsal before Tim McCoy and Samuel Gumperts. In their authentic costumes, they looked really terrific. They had on white-fringed moccasins and beautiful, hand-embroidered kilts depicting the dance with symbols of dancers, the snakes, and nature. Different kinds of paint on their chests and faces showed whether they represented the day or night. The dance itself is for fertility, rain, good hunting—for a happy life in communion with nature. We also added a few twists and turns to make it more dramatic.

In full costume, we paraded ourselves into the vast arena, where Tim and Mr. Gumperts sat by themselves up in the seats. We began the dance and everything went without a hitch, except at midpoint one of the snakes had somehow slipped its face mask! Maybe it hadn't been tied correctly, I don't know. At that instant, the dancer flung it to the ground, and it took off for the other dancers, trying to hit each one. So they were all hopping around screaming, everything disorganized and out of tempo with the music. I thought for sure that was the end of my circus career. But Tim and Mr. Gumperts, thinking it was part of the act, loved it.

"Wonderful, Iron Eyes," he said, clapping enthusiastically.

"We'll really pack 'em in with *that* routine, I'll tell you. How on earth did you get the snake to perform on cue like that?"

This gave me an idea for improving the act, adding a touch of showmanship even P.T. Barnum himself might have been proud of.

Opening night for the circus is perhaps even more nerve-racking for the performers than for the actors of a Broadway play. Many of the acts are new and untried before a live audience of thousands. A Broadway show critic may figuratively dip his pen in blood before doing a review, but the sawdust rings of the circus have been known to actually absorb the real stuff after a disastrous first-time performance. A horse, grown skittish from the crowds, falls and breaks a leg, and the rider breaks his neck. Or maybe a lion, fascinated by its newfound glory, will just sit there and stare off in the stands with a look of disinterested nobility in his eyes. It's a risky business, the circus. A lot of unknowns.

But somehow on opening night in Madison Square Garden, it all unfolds more or less as planned, and "people of all ages" get to see The Greatest Show on Earth. In those days, there were six rings instead of the three used today—sometimes six acts being performed at the same time, all with amazing precision and grace. At midpoint, after the Wallendas had finished balancing their human pyramid on a wire strung a hundred feet above the ground, we made our entrance. Tim mounted a big, white palomino, which he called the "dumbest beast on earth," clopped-clopped out to the center ring, and, mike in hand, told something of the Wild West spectacle about to "unfold before your very eyes." Then all of us galloped out—cowboys, Indians, Cossacks, trick ropers, impalement artists, whip crackers, and crack shots. Tim, in fact, was one of the best shots in the business. As part of his own act he would glue a postage stamp on a one-inch washer, throw it in the air, and neatly drill a bullet right through the center. Then, in rapid fire, he'd blast an image of an Indian in a block of wood seventy-five feet away. The whip cracker swatted cigarettes from the lips of pretty girls and popped the caps off soda bottles. Another performer blindfolded himself and casually tossed axes into apples resting on top the heads of his two nieces (mixing a little Robin Hood in the old American West, I guess). The two Cossacks flipped and bounced around on the bare backs of horses as though on trampolines. All this to the tune of hee-hawin', shit-kickin' country music and six-shooters going off continuously like strings of fireworks.

Then, causing a considerable gasp to arise from the folks, we fifteen Indians charged in brandishing those big snakes. Quite a sight, with as many thirty-pound, nasty-looking serpents without any visible constraints. I don't think you could see the masks from even the front rows. The traditional drums, flute, and singing began, and we passed the snakes around, keeping them calm by stroking their mouths with an eagle feather. This doesn't massage or tickle them into submission, but I had trained the snakes earlier that striking a feather, like hitting the palm of my hand, is a useless activity. At the sight of one, they just become indifferent and passive, like a cat bored with a rubber mouse. We then put the snakes in our mouths and, with the audience positively squirming, ran around the ring. (Rattlers aren't too bad; they're something of an acquired taste.)

Frank Hill had decided to ignore my warning not to dance with the one eight-foot, unmasked bull snake we had. I suppose, being a kind of surly, independent type and not too well liked, he wanted to stand out from the crowd. He started running around with the snake, and before you know it that bull's iron jaw had clamped itself around Frank's forearm like a vise, spraying the sawdust floor with blood like a lawn sprinkler. But the damn fool continued his performance which added to the gore and was pretty spectacular. Finally he just collapsed near the end and the audience stood and roared its approval. It took three of us—one to hold the snake's body, one to pry its mouth from Frank's arm, and one to hold Frank—before we finally managed to get the damn thing off him. Wouldn't you know, but no sooner had we accomplished this feat than Frank grabbed the snake by its head, held him up, and proclaimed proudly, "This snake is my friend. I dance with him from now on."

Crazy Apache. That bit of grandstanding, incidentally, left a scar on his arm the size of a big lemon.

As a grand finale I used the innovation I had thought of during rehearsal. Instead of having the dancers run out of the ring with the snakes, they pointed them in the direction of the audience and let 'em go. The thrill certainly gave everyone their money's worth, what with the screeching, standing up on chairs, and general commotion the act caused. Not until the last minute did we run after the snakes and scoop them up, saving dozens of folks from certain death.

After the show it seemed that the entire New York press took close-ups of the Snake Dancers with their terrible rattlesnakes. With about twenty of those old-fashioned light bulbs popping at the same time, the snakes were getting jumpy, their rattles buzzing nervously.

"Hold on fellas, careful with those lights," I warned. "Rattlers are particular about getting their picture taken."

"Aw, I knew it," said one of the reporters. "They've got masks on. No big deal dancing with them when they've got masks on."

At that moment, a snake that Frank Hill was displaying happened to somehow squirm loose from his grasp, making a beeline towards our reporter friends. Never saw a room empty so quickly. Gathering up his escaped dancing partner and stuffing it back in its crate, Frank mumbled something about half-assed reporters and chuckled to himself.

In *The New York Times* the next day there was no mention of the masks, but another complaint was registered. Apparently New York's weather had been warm and sunny till we came to town, at which time the skies turned grey-black and it rained continuously. The *Times* piece read:

"Will Tim McCoy and his Snake Dancers please leave our city? We believe their dance can bring rain, but can't they practice their religion elsewhere?"

They couldn't have been more flattering to our troupe.

The catchphrase "Under the Big Top" doesn't become relevant to the Ringling Brothers and Barnum and Bailey Circus till after the show opens in Madison Square Garden and makes a similar appearance in the Boston Garden. Then, at some point during the Boston performance, a small city packed with military precision into four trains departs from winter quarters in Sarasota, Florida. This is the circus that goes on the road for nine months and brings its own portable amphitheater with it, the great "Big Top." It also has a school, teachers, doctors, police, even detectives. Among the four trains there are one hundred cars, providing quarters for 1,400 people and 600 animals, including elephants, rhinoceroses, horses, apes, camels, lions, tigers, zebras, and llamas.

When I toured with it, each morning at dawn, or earlier, the circus chugged into town and pitched its huge tents. The help included elephants lugging around poles of various sizes and highly skilled workers. The black workers sang wonderful songs to the rhythm of pounding stakes and pulling slack out of the thousands of feet of canvas. After feeding all the people and animals, an afternoon and evening performance is given regardless of the weather. Then, in the middle of the night, the tents are struck, every last piece of equipment is methodically packed up, and the circus is underway again. Loading everything on and off the trains without missing a beat is the key to this operation. Each flatbed railroad car is fitted at one end with a metal plate, joining it with the other and effectively making a kind of continuous roadway. Then the horse-drawn wagons are pulled by ropes up a ramp on the rear car and along the row of cars up to the front. When the train arrives in town, the engine is disconnected and the first wagon on the cars is the first one off. It contains the last equipment packed and the first needed for setting up a new encampment.

German Nazi generals paid us a visit one year. Impressed by this operation, they sent emissaries over to learn how to quickly transport large numbers of troops and equipment for massive surprise attacks on neighboring countries. They called it a "blitzkrieg."

I had promised Birdie I'd be back home at the end of a month, so I went to Tim McCoy and told him I'd be leaving soon. Incidentally, he had a whole train car to himself, complete with living room, bedroom, kitchen, bath, and canopied porch at the rear. It had once been an observation car.

"But, Iron Eyes, you can't leave now. We're just getting warmed up. Do you realize because of our Wild West Show—in particular because of your Snake Dancers—this circus is packed to capacity every performance? The press has gone wild over this thing. People love you."

"I realize only one thing. If I don't get my ass back to California pronto I won't have a wife to return to."

"How about if I double your salary?"

"No, no, you could offer me . . . *double*? Did you say you'd pay me twice what I'm getting now?"

"That's right. That's how much it means to me having you aboard."

"I don't get it. I'm not really crucial to the Dancers. You could run them yourself. That's what we agreed on."

"That was before I saw what one of those damn rattlers did to your hand. Besides, you're the only one who can handle these guys, Iron Eyes. With all their drinking and carrying on, I'd probably lose my temper and blast one of 'em."

"I'll tell you what. You've got a deal if *you* convince Birdie that I should stay on."

We found a phone and Tim called her, pretending I was busy with the show. I knew if she got me on the phone it would be all over.

"Hello, Mrs. Cody? Tim McCoy here. Fine, fine, yourself? Good. Mrs. Cody, let me get straight to the point—Well, er . . . yes, that, uh, is what I was calling about in fact. He really is necessary to the performance, and because you've been so patient, I've decided to give him a substantial raise, yessir, a substantial raise, indeed. And, because I do appreciate how understanding you've been, especially since you're a working woman yourself, I'll be sending you a check on a monthly basis from here on in . . . How much? . . . Oh, well, yes, I suppose that can be arranged . . . Fine, well, good talking to you, Mrs. Cody, and again, thank you."

"Well, what did she say? What was that about a check?"

"Whew, she's some woman, Iron Eyes. Knows what you're gonna say before you say it."

"The check, Tim?"

"Oh, it's okay with her if I send her a portion of it every month."

"How big a portion?"

"Uh, half."

It should come as no surprise that I came to love circus life. What could be closer to me, descended from Plains Indians, than living in tents, traveling around the country with fun-loving gypsies, sharing their tribe-like sense of family and togetherness? Full of adventure and excitement, the circus is a romantic's dream. There was nothing better to cure me of the Hollywood crazies than my stay with these wonderful people.

I especially liked the clowns, and spent a good deal of time on "Clown Row," where they had their dressing rooms. A circus clown comes from a peculiar breed, I'll tell you. They're very insular, preferring the company of their own to mixing with the circus folk at large. They have their own set of rules and sense of decorum: one of them being never speak about the past. I have no doubt that many of them came from tragic backgrounds. Another rule is, provided nobody is seriously hurt, any kind of practical joke is perfectly okay to play on your neighbor, who must bear the brunt of it with a certain degree of clown-like dignity and appreciation of a good gag. They were always hiding each other's costumes just before show time, or literally pulling the rug out from under one another. One guy, who also doubled as the circus postman, carried a razor strap and at the least provocation—usually an infringement of their code of ethics—could haul off and belt you with it. Of course, performers from other sectors of the circus were always fair game for tricks. One of the clown's favorites was sending false messages to, say, an equestrian (in the circus, you can never call such an illustrious character a mere "horse rider"). It might say that the President of the United States will be attending this evening's show and asks for a private audience. Once a clown dressed up as a secret service agent and attempted to have somebody arrested for statutory rape. Then there are the standards, the time-honored tricks. Throwing a foot out to trip up an innocent passerby. Pouring ice water down somebody's back. The victims usually share one thing in common: an excess of dignity.

Another unwritten rule among the clowns is: Always help thy neighbor. I guess that's what I liked about them most, their impishness on the one hand, and on the other their sincere, child-like devotion to each other. A clown will practically do anything for a fellow clown if the need is genuine. No amount of money is too much to ask, no favor too troublesome to grant. And if they give an outsider like myself their trust, they extend their generosity as well.

Every clown I ever talked to was well versed in the psychology of humor and pathos. They know that laughing is just this side of crying, and understand both. Each act is carefully conceived and rehearsed, with constant attention given to new ideas and gimmicks. Every clown follows set standards for costumes, makeup, and mannerisms. They are all descended from three basic types: the Joey, the Auguste, and the Charlie. The Joey is the athlete, performing on the tight rope or horseback and providing comic relief against the serious artists at work around him. The Auguste is a whiteface, traditionally with the red putty nose, giant shoes, and bald dome, and specializing in slapstick. The best-known example of the Auguste is Lou Jacobs, still the most popular clown today and a great personal friend of mine. The Charlie, familiar to most of us through the late great Emmett Kelly, has a sad expression, a charcoal beard, white lips, derby hat, baggy pants, and tattered coat.

The midgets were another favorite of mine. They were frisky little devils who did quite a lot of drinking and more than their share of pranks. Midgets are perfectly proportioned little people who can mate with regular-sized folks and produce "normal" children. One pretty female three-footer one day announced her betrothal to a performer who billed himself as "The Biggest Man in the World"—circus folks always thinking in the superlative. He stood about seven feet six, and called himself Texas Jack. They made a fine looking couple, those two. And, this being a gathering of people used to all kinds of arrangements of nature, not too many eyebrows were raised in astonishment. Well, except maybe in one department. The two of them strolling together might occasion a harmless inquiry or two. Like, "Hey, you two gettin' any these days?" Gazing up at her man of more than twice her size, she'd reply, "Hell, what do *you* think?" You're probably just as curious as I how they went about this, but I never had the nerve to ask.

One day, a huge white Rolls-Royce came roaring through the circus gates and screeched to a halt in front of me. I was rehearsing a new bit with the Snake Dancers, and we were outside. A middle-aged man dressed in white eased himself out of the front seat, plunked a huge peaked sombrero, also white, on his head, and stretched. It was Tom Mix.

"We-e-e-e-ll! Look here, will you. Injuns!"

"Hello, Tom," I said. We shook hands.

"Iron, you haven't changed any. Still as mean lookin' as you were ten years ago."

"I work at it. Pays the rent."

"Yeah, ha ha."

Mix looked as though he'd been drinking a little. Well, I shouldn't say "a little"—frankly, he was plastered.

"Say, Iron, where's that Irish bastard, Tim McCoy?"

"Right over there in that tent. But I don't think he'd like it if you walked in on him now. He's occupied with a lady."

[187]

"Ha! That right? I wouldn't think 'a walkin' in on him at a delicate time like this. No sir."

With that, Mix jumped into that Rolls, revved up the engine, and tore off across the field in the direction of Tim's tent. It looked like he was headed straight for it, doing at least fifty miles an hour, but at the last second he swerved the car into all the supporting ropes. The stakes popped out of the ground in succession and the tent collapsed.

"Ya-hoo!" yelled Mix, waving that big hat of his out the window and skillfully swerving the Rolls around in a neat circle. "Tim McCoy, that you in there? Ha ha. Ya-hoo!"

Two heads became apparent under the canvas, working their way towards the edge. I thought Tim would kill Mix for a stunt like that, but as he emerged he was smiling.

"Tom Mix, you sonavabitch!"

He introduced Mix to his lady friend, and couldn't seem happier to see him. Tim was pretty hard to figure at times. With his arm on Mix's shoulder, he called to me.

"Iron Eyes, c'mon over. Let's have a drink with our old friend here."

While Tom Mix had retired from the movies by this time—he was in his fifties—he was doing okay for himself. It happened, he explained over beers, that he'd joined the Sells Floto Circus and was knocking down ten grand per week. That was back in '31. Then his last movie, *The Miracle Rider*, didn't do so hot, so he quit the film business for good and went on the road with the Tom Mix Wild Animal Circus. He and his beloved horse, Tony. I never thought that Tim was all that friendly with Tom Mix, but apparently he'd heard of his circus adventures. They were kindred souls, now. And I'll be damned if, every time we were in the same area, Mix wouldn't pull the same stunt again and again, knocking down either Tim's tent or somebody else's. Each time, Tim never lost his temper.

A few years later, Mix drove his car through a detour sign at about ninety miles an hour. The car careened down a steep embankment and he broke his neck as it flipped over. The story has it that a metal box he always carried with him flew off the back shelf, struck the back of his head, and killed him instantly. I bet Tom Mix's white suit wasn't wrinkled a bit.

The impossible task of keeping the Snake Dancers sober from one performance to the next kept me pretty busy. Of course, getting lubed up a bit on the juice didn't hurt their dancing any and may have improved the taste of the snakes. But it was when they'd start fights or pass out cold from hooch that things really got out of hand. It was especially bad on the long rides from one town to another. Almost every night I'd have to break up a brawl by busting heads and getting my own cracked in the process. In the morning there was a routine water-dunking to bring two or three out of their drunken stupor. A pretty grisly business. A few times, one or two of the dancers would climb between the cars for some air, lose their footing, and fall off the train while it was going full speed! Then, still dressed in their outfits from an evening's performance, they'd wander into farming communities and terrorize the folks.

It was Frank Hill that topped them all, though.

Near the end of the tour he had been getting even ornerier and ornerier, fighting half the time and then drinking till he'd pass out. One day, after the afternoon show, he found some marijuana growing wild in a field in Kansas City and stuffed some in his pockets. He rolled a bunch of joints later that evening and on the train he smoked one or two, then tore into a quart of gin. At one point he staggered out to the rear of the car, mumbling something about taking a leak, and that was the last anybody had heard of him. I was in the middle of breaking up two or three fights, and never got a chance to take the usual head count before turning in. At our stop in the morning we got a call from a mortician in a small town, saying some farmers had found a dead man dressed in a wild Indian's outfit lying by the tracks in a snow bank. I jumped in a car and drove fifty miles to the place. I had come to like Frank, despite his craziness, and was very upset.

I roared up to the mortuary, ran in, and who do I see sitting in the outer office sipping coffee but Frank Hill. He *looked* like he was dead, his normal copper skin a greyish mud-brown. But corpses don't sit up drinking coffee. Before I could ask him anything, the mortician bustled up to me, all in a fluster.

"I never saw anything like it," he stammered. "In my twenty years in this business, never, never."

"Okay, take it easy. What happened!"

He pointed a shaking finger at Frank. "He was dead, that's what

[189]

happened! He was cold, stiff. I took his pulse and there was nothing. No need to call a doctor, right? The man was *dead*. We carried him in here, put him in a coffin, and, just as I was about to nail it shut, he-he-he sits up and asks where the circus is!"

During the drive back, Frank assured me he was going to lay off the sauce for a while. It "had a funny effect" on him, he said.

12

I TOURED WITH the circus three seasons—'35, '37, and '38. In the fall of '35 I knocked off over a year to join Cecil B. DeMille at Paramount for his first major Western since the advent of talkies, *The Plainsman*. Although my father had worked for C.B. on a number of occasions, I had never met the man and was looking forward to teaming up with the old master of the Hollywood extravaganza. Most actors, though, found the prospect of being directed by DeMille unsettling. His tough-guy reputation wasn't helped by the gun he wore strapped to his side in his early days in films. Even the pros were scared of him. Including my friend Gary Cooper, chosen for the lead part of Wild Bill Hickok.

"You know anything about this DeMille?" he asked me on the phone a week before filming was scheduled to start.

"Well, I've never worked with the man, but I understand he's a real bastard."

"C'mon, heh heh . . . really?"

"Yep."

"Listen, it says here in the script I've got to do some Cheyenne sign language, and I've heard DeMille is a stickler for authenticity. Suppose you could drop by and give me a few lessons this week?"

Coop had nothing to worry about, as he was C.B.'s ideal image of masculine virtue—tall, strong, quiet, and physically brave. He also didn't talk back to or argue with his directors too much. C.B. would stand for none of that. Coop was at this point a very big box office draw, being fresh from the great success of *Mr. Deeds Goes to Town*, and also an independent, under no long-range contract to a particular studio. There were already signs that the director respected his leading man a good deal, having agreed to name the film *The Plainsman*, when his writers were working under the title *Buffalo Bill*. The story was as much about Buffalo Bill as about

Wild Bill Hickok, but Coop's agent insisted his man would never appear in a movie named for a character which he wasn't playing.

So, I was finally going to meet the great C.B. DeMille. Of course, this wasn't C.B.'s first Western, but his first *talking* Western. I mentioned earlier it was DeMille who, in 1912, came out West to shoot his first picture, a Western called *The Squaw Man*. In 1912, Hollywood was already eyed as a desirable place to while away your time, mostly by retirees, and several luxury homes were popping up along its dusty roads and in the sand dunes of adjacent Beverly Hills, some worth as much as $10-15,000. But with the success of *The Squaw Man*, the place was well on its way to becoming the film capital of America, and C.B. DeMille, the most powerful man in town. Well, not exactly. He had his ups and downs. For the next fifteen years, he would finish making one blockbuster, like *The Ten Commandments*, but always manage to follow it with a string of failures. Some of them were a little ahead of their time, like *The Golden Bed*, where we find young men, abstractly representing the theme of decadence, licking the chocolate off living female candybars. Pretty sticky material for the twenties. The censors, wasting no time letting him know their feelings were hurt, banned the film wherever they could. C.B. had his own strong notions about art that weren't shared by either his financial backers or the general public. They liked his extravagance, his big sets and crowd scenes, but only when he kept it simple and aimed towards the gut. It was a lesson he learned only after seeing his own film company go bankrupt and having his option dropped by MGM in the early thirties. He was finally reduced to speaking in the only language understood by producers, the language of profit. He arrived at the door of the company he helped found, Paramount, and, with hat in hand, asked for another chance from his old bosses. I guess it's comforting to know even the great among us are occasionally humbled.

After sixty films, at the age of fifty-nine, DeMille had lost none of his characteristic swagger and toughness when he came to directing *The Plainsman*. Or his extravagance. When I arrived on the Paramount lot, DeMille had commandeered six acres and erected a perfect replica of Fort Leavenworth, Texas, a Mississippi River boat (including the river, of course), a wharf, and a number of authentic period buildings. For the dozens of journalists who always followed the doings of a DeMille picture, he built an exact replica of a nineteenth-century telegraph office just so they could cable their stories to the world "in the right frame of mind." C.B. always had an eye for publicity.

I was ushered into DeMille's office for one of his many formal planning sessions. It was luxurious and masculine. Paintings of key scenes from many of his pictures hung on the walls, together with dozens of antique pistols and flintlocks. Many of the guns used in the picture were from DeMille's own private collection of antiques, about seventy or eighty of them. The hundreds of others he would have built in the prop shop to exacting historical standards. The "grail" used in the Last Supper scene of *King of Kings* rested in a special cabinet, spears from *The Ten Commandments* arched over a doorway, broadswords over the fireplace, and animal skin rugs were thrown everywhere. His desk was massive. I sat at a big Spanish-style table with DeMille's various assistant producers and directors until The Man marched in. Everyone promptly jumped to his feet. He looked in very good shape for a man almost 60. A great believer in the physical life, he swam and exercized daily. His bald dome had a pink glow to it and his somewhat roundish face contrasted—almost conflicted—with his features. Many believed that DeMille's penetrating eyes were capable of X-ray vision for, no matter where you were in a DeMille picture, even a thousand miles away on location, he always seemed to know what you were doing. He wore a colorful sports shirt and his characteristic riding pants and puttees, the knee-high boots that laced up the front which he popularized for other directors (although by 1936 nobody else was wearing them). Actually, DeMille wore puttees to help support his weak ankles and because, while on location, he was deathly afraid of snakes. I never had the nerve to tell him leather was no protection against snakes, but for all I know he may have had the boots lined with steel.

We all stood at attention till DeMille sat down at the head of the table. No one ever sat down until The Great Man did.

"Good morning, gentlemen," he began. "We have a new member of the staff with us who will be very important to this production, as he'll be helping direct the thousands of Indians we're using on location. Say hello to Iron Eyes Cody."

We exchanged polite greetings around the table and everything went along as expected for a few minutes, with each giving a brief presentation of what we were to be doing. The wardrobe department chief then showed us a few sketches of costumes. DeMille sat listening while this nervous man talked in a tremulous voice for about sixty seconds, then slammed his fist on the table.

"I don't like it!" he bellowed. He jumped up from his chair, grabbed the sketches, and ripped them to shreds. "I told you exactly what I wanted and this isn't it! Now get back to your office and do them again, and again, and *again*, till you get them *right*!"

"Yes, Mr. DeMille," he said, trying to pick up the scraps.

"*Leave* them!"

"Yes, yes, of course."

And with that he stumbled out of the office, knocking into a corner of an end table as he passed.

"Idiot," mumbled DeMille to himself. "Don't know why I don't fire the man. All right, let's see how the set is progressing, gentlemen."

We all filed out with DeMille in the lead, walking by himself. He always walked by himself, with his underlings following. Actually, I should say we marched, each of us falling in step behind the Generalissimo.

We had our little tour of the set, which pleased DeMille immensely. He got up on a platform and, speaking into a megaphone which could be heard for about a half mile, congratulated the staff on its superb efforts, for having truly captured the spirit of the American frontier, and so on. While he spoke a few women extras were talking under their breath to each other. DeMille stopped in the middle of a sentence and said, "You women can continue your discussion outside the gates of Paramount Studios. You're fired!" He fired people left and right, that DeMille. I would say on the average at least one person got canned each day we were filming.

I decided early on that the only way to deal with C.B. was not to let him push you around. If he fires you, so what, but I wasn't going to be another head wardrobe man. I was shortly able to put my integrity to the test. When my brother and I had assembled the thirty or so Indians in full costume, and white men dressed as Indians, for the scenes to be shot in the lot, DeMille had them line up so he could make his inspection—again, military style. Everybody stood at attention while he walked up and down the ranks.

"Okay, take that off," he said, stopping at one end, pointing to a beaded vest. He stopped again. "Take that off, and that, and—"

"Wait, *wait* a minute, C.B. You can't take those things off. He's gonna be a chief. Cheyenne chiefs *wore* vests like that. And he's a warrior, they always wore leggings. That's a medicine pouch on him. It stays."

"You've got too much clothes on them."

"Not for these Indians, C.B. We either do an authentic picture or I'll walk off and the Indians will come with us. That's the way it's gonna be."

He looked at me hard, but with a smile creeping in the corner of his mouth. "You're sincere, aren't you."

"That's right," I said, setting my jaw and crossing my arms. I thought any minute he'd kick me in the ass.

"Your father, did you know he worked for me?"

"Yeah, I know that."

"Then you know we didn't have any trouble with him."

"Well, you're not talking to my father now. I know what these Indians should wear for this picture, and if you can build an authentic telegraph office for a bunch of reporters, you can keep the Indians in your picture authentic."

"Ha!" he exploded, slapping my back. "You've got guts, Iron Eyes. I can see where you got your name from. Okay, they stay dressed like Eskimos. But if I hear any complaints about the Indians being *un*authentic, from anyone, I'll have your hide. Got it?"

"Right."

"Okay, ladies and gentlemen! Let's break for lunch!"

And off we'd march in step to the commissary, where writers, directors, actors, and actresses, all of us would stand around the table at our appointed chairs till the general was seated.

"All right," he growled, slamming the script down in front of him and not bothering to look up, "who's blessing the food today?"

DeMille always insisted on the food being blessed before a meal, being a devout Episcopalian. Woe be to anyone who touched a crumb on his plate before the blessing. Once somebody did, but before he got a morsel to his mouth, DeMille demanded he leave the table. The offender scurried off, carrying his food with him.

There were three or four volunteers for food blessing—I suppose it being an attempt to garner favor with His Highness—but DeMille ran his finger down a list and chose the name of an elegantly dressed Arab sitting a few seats from me. The Arab, a set visitor whose name I can only remember sounding something like Dr. Abusan, positively jumped when his name was called.

"We haven't heard from you in a while," said DeMille quietly, not looking up. "Would you do us the honors?"

The Arab began reciting something in his native tongue, but I'll be damned if before he was finished DeMille didn't interrupt him.

"Humph," he muttered, flipping a page on the script under his nose. Then, still not looking up, he pointed to one of his assistants and said he wanted some changes in the lighting of a particular scene. Even God could never completely take DeMille's mind off his pictures!

You can imagine the pressure on a DeMille set was at any time close to the boiling point, and one of the ways of cooling off was through drink. And any kind of drinking on a DeMille picture was strictly forbidden, unless he didn't catch you at it. Roy Burns, a long-time production manager for DeMille, fooled the old man for years, or so he thought. He was simply plastered all the time, and finally DeMille took me aside one day and clasped my arm.

"Iron Eyes, where the hell does Burns hide his whiskey?"

"What do you mean?"

"C'mon. You know as well as I do he's drunk all the time. He smells like a cheap gin mill. He's good, I'm not gonna fire him. I just think if we can locate his source and dry him out, we'd be doing him a favor."

"I'll keep my eye out for you, C.B."

"Good man."

It appeared as though I'd been taken into C.B.'s trust, something which I wasn't so sure was good for me. It was probably through other "trustees" that he kept such close tabs on everything and everybody. Anyway, one day I was in Roy's office waiting for him and, sure enough, I felt something hard and lumpy in my chair seat. I stood up and felt the outline of three pint flasks in the pillow stuffing. Just then Roy breezed in, leaving his customary aroma of bourbon hanging in the air. Unfortunately he was followed by C.B., the wardrobe man, and a couple of assistants. They gathered around a table and spread some drawings out.

"Oh, hello, Iron Eyes," grunted DeMille. "Here, have a look at these new sketches. Some are of Indian costumes which I suppose we'll need your approval of from now on."

C.B. liked some of the drawings, but lit into his wardrobe man once again for the rest of them, sending him out in tears.

"Hey, C.B.," I said, "Why don't you take it easy on that guy."

"What did you say?"

"I said, take it easy on him. He's got a heart condition and can't stand too much pressure. I feel sorry for him."

"Iron Eyes," he snorted, "you'd feel sorry for a dead rat. You're too soft."

The subject abruptly went back to business, and as DeMille talked he strode about the room, tossing out ideas in rapid fire and gesticulating with his hands. He stopped in front of the chair with the whiskey in it, and I looked at Roy, who seemed about to faint dead away. DeMille slowly lowered himself on the booze-implanted pillow, but continued talking till he finished his point. Then he got up and looked Roy dead in the eye. Sweat glistened on Roy's forehead.

"That chair's very uncomfortable, Roy. What do you have, rocks for stuffing?" Turning to leave, he snapped, "See you all on the set at seven sharp."

He marched out and slammed the door. Roy, visibly shaken, collapsed at his desk and mopped his brow. "God," he said in a shaking voice, "that chair he was sitting on is loaded with whiskey. I thought it was in another pillow."

I reached in and took out one of the flasks.

"Well then, I think this calls for a drink."

Shooting for *The Plainsman* began in earnest, but it wasn't long before there were problems. Right off, DeMille wasn't at all pleased with Coop's style. He grumbled and mumbled to everyone on the sound stage that there was nothing to the man, that he was "too wooden." He didn't offer any direction, though, as Coop was the sort you had to just leave alone to his own resources. But after DeMille saw the day's rushes he seemed pleased enough. Whatever

Coop did, as understated as it always was, seemed magically intensified on film, actually drawing attention to himself. This was especially so when opposite more flamboyant types like Jean Arthur, who played Calamity Jane.

It should be mentioned here that if you always suspected *The Plainsman* was complete nonsense from a historical standpoint, you're right. The real Calamity Jane was a vulgar, tobacco-chewing, raw-boned kid who resembled nothing more alluring than an oversized Huckleberry Finn, minus the charm of innocence. She was a great shot and horsewoman, but Wild Bill Hickok certainly did no romancing with her. Hickok was also shown in the Battle of Arickaree, which he never set eyes on. There's no historical hint of him ever attempting to warn anyone of the impending Custer battle. It's interesting, because this was the first time DeMille ever strayed from the facts.

There was also occasional grumbling from various quarters about the clichéd lines the actors had to work with. At one point James Ellison threw up his hands and cried, "Jesus, have I got to say *this* crap?" Good thing DeMille wasn't around. Coop is said to have once told Howard Hawks, when asked how he could deliver "those goddamn lines" of DeMille's: "Well, when DeMille finished talking to you, they don't seem so bad. But when you see the picture, then you kind of hang your head."

I didn't see too much head-hanging on the set, as there was never any time. But once, when Coop was delivered a fresh set of lines, he read them silently, then raised his eyebrows and whistled softly, shaking his head.

You may recall a scene where Coop runs into a Cheyenne warrior on the trail after Custer's battle, and the Indian sings a Cheyenne song signaling defeat of General Long Hair. That was Anthony Quinn with his movie debut. He kind of botched it, though, as DeMille actually thought he *was* a Cheyenne and didn't prepare him for any Indian singing with my instruction. Tony ended up sounding like a hillbilly yodler.

"Cut, cut, *cut!*" DeMille boomed. "Who hired this man? Get him out of here!"

"Now wait a minute, Mr. DeMille," said Coop. "Maybe he's just a little confused or something."

"Yeah, like he doesn't know we're making a movie. Get rid of him, I don't want to waste time."

I thought this was part of my responsibility, so I volunteered to teach Tony some Cheyenne right there on the spot.

"Good, let's give the boy a chance," Coop piped up. "He seems like a real nice kid."

Grumbling, C.B. agreed and I taught Tony a quick Cheyenne song appropriate for the occasion, which he pulled off pretty convincingly. Ironically, Tony later married DeMille's daughter, and even directed a film under his guidance, *The Buccaneer*, which I understand he botched so badly that he never was in his father-in-law's good graces again.

For my own part, I played a young Cheyenne chief. A memorable scene is when we come upon the cabin of Buffalo Bill's wife, done beautifully by eighteen-year-old Helen Burgess. The fear in her eyes was so real it almost scared *me*—maybe that's why we seemed so "savage" in this scene. It's another ironic and sad note to *The Plainsman* that Helen died of pneumonia shortly after the filming. She would have become one of the greats.

In mid-March we loaded our equipment into buses and arranged for a rendezvous with 2,500 Sioux and Cheyenne, plus a number of hand-picked squads of the 115th Cavalry and the Wyoming National Guard. DeMille's usual thousands. We were to meet in the Tongue River country near Lame Deer, Montana—virtually a raw wilderness with only, at this time, a dirt access road. DeMille sent his assistant director, Art Rossen, to handle the job, with C.B. directing some of the scenes by remote control with a ten-foot model of the terrain back in Hollywood, and a specially rigged-up telephone. We had some classic Western action scenes to shoot. A wagon train siege, various battles and skirmishes, plus the Custer disaster itself. All told, we would be in the wilderness for four long months.

The buses pulled up to the lodge where Coop, James Ellison, Jean Arthur, and all the technical crew, including myself, would be staying. And there, covering the whole side of a mountain, was a sight not seen on the earth for probably seventy years. Hundreds and hundreds of tepees—well over a thousand, in fact. There were tepees of both canvas and hide, some with colorful paintings on the sides. They were set against magnificent terrain—tall, stately pine trees, hills and crags lightly covered with snow. Each tent had a fire crackling in front. A woman would often be seen bending over a big black iron pot, which was all very comforting because it was getting colder and colder. Well below freezing. Then it started snowing.

It snowed most of that night, with about a two-foot accumulation, and we postponed shooting the next day. It gave me a feeling something like the rare occasions it would snow in Oklahoma when I was a boy, and there would be no school. Coop brought along a tall, very warm-blooded blonde—and was settled in nicely with her. The cowboy extras, in their own cabins next to the main lodge, were content, for the time being, drinking a popular rotgut booze called "rock 'n rye." I thought it a good time to get acquainted with some folks on the hill. I met a number of families, most of them bearing up cheerfully enough. Each male was making fifteen dollars a day, a small fortune for these people. Many of the men were off hunting for meat to add to the stew pots bubbling in front of their tepees. Some of the others were off visiting girl friends in other tepees. I was invited into the tepee of a tall but bouncy woman, half Cheyenne and Shoshoni. Her name was Louise Little Crow.

"Watch this," she said, picking up one leg at the ankle and, standing like a lovely, graceful swan on the other, twisting it up over her head. "I'm a contortionist."

"Well, I'll be damned, so you are. Ever think of taking up ballet?"

"Naw," she said, her eyes gleaming, "I want to be in the movies."

"Oh. Well, you are, aren't you? We're not here to play Parchesi."

"Look at this one." She stretched and arched herself backwards till her hands touched the ground, then she walked on them till she touched her feet, looking like an upside down U pinched at the bottom. She managed to spring herself back in an upright position, flat against me.

"How's *that*?" she cooed, breathing a little heavy.

"Er, fine, fine. We'll see what we can do about . . . finding a proper vehicle for you."

We tumbled down onto her bed. I wish I could tell you it was a buffalo robe on the bed, but in those days they were rare. (You see more buffalo on reservations now than in the thirties, having enjoyed something of a comeback with government protection. We had plenty of patchwork quilts to snuggle under though.) I tell you, this woman (as you might expect) had some moves! With the way she was flipping me around, twisting, and, well, contorting, it's damn lucky I managed to even crawl out several hours later. My back felt like it had been used for a trampoline, but I was happy.

I trudged back up to the lodge and was greeted by Coop.

"Well, how was it, tepee creeper."

"Tepee *what?*" I said, straightening out my spine.

"Tepee creeper. That's what you've been doing, right? Tepee creeping? Bet they're wild, huh? Will you take me along next time?"

"Sure, sure. What's the latest word on the weather?"

"More snow. How many were you with?"

"*More snow?*"

"Yeah, looks like we'll be holed up here for a few days." He clasped my arm tightly and spoke softly out of the side of his mouth. "Listen, this Mormon gal says she likes you. Whaddya say we, you know, kinda swap cultures," he said kiddingly.

Any kind of holdup in a massive production like *The Plainsman* is extremely expensive. With almost 3,000 salaries to meet daily, you can imagine that DeMille wasn't letting Art Rossen forget his budget constraints. Art didn't look all too happy at supper that evening, having just gotten off the phone with the boss.

"DeMille thinks we're up here having a goddamned picnic," he mumbled into his wine glass. "You know, when I told him about the snow, he actually just chuckled and started regaling me with the good old days? Something about a time when his crew was snowed in in the Rockies. Says they had to burn the camera tripods for firewood and eat roots. Then he blasted me and said we begin shooting tomorrow without fail, even if we have ten feet of snow." He looked about the table and, with a sardonic grin, said, "Are we all prepared to start eating roots?"

C.B. wasn't to have his way on this one. While it didn't snow quite ten feet, by early morning it had almost topped the lodge's window sills. At least six feet! We not only cancelled filming, but were trapped, with no food other than present stocks. There were no special flights bringing in frozen TV dinners. No interstate highways nearby. We settled in for a long siege.

Now it is ordinarily very boring on location shooting. Nothing could be further from the truth than any notion of glamour and excitement in regards to moviemaking. From the stars all the way down to the extras, most of the time is spent sitting around waiting for your moment in front of the camera, waiting for the director and technicians to prepare a shot. And then you might have to do it again, and again, and again. This is especially true with the big budget films, where so much care is put into each take. And, of course, the technology has gotten more and more complicated over the years. The "good old days" of the not-so-fussy two-reelers were long over. No more sticking a relatively small camera on a wooden tripod, the second unit director shouting "Okay ya bastards, *action!*," shooting it, canning it, period. Especially with this, the biggest DeMille picture yet. We hadn't even started shooting yet, but the snow was just another routine wait between takes. At least for the time being. We all took it pretty much in stride and found suitable diversions to quietly pass the time.

Which is to say we all discovered rock 'n rye whiskey. And, for some, "tepee creeping."

This latter activity was limited because, for the most part, the Indians camped out in the hills were part of solid, traditional families, and any thought of sexual relationships with the movie people would have been unthinkable. But, as with any large group, there were a few wild individuals.

As the snow fell, tepees were dug out and re-entered on top of packed-down snow. Three layers of skins and quilts were thrown on the frozen floor, leaving a spot in the middle for a small fire, not these huge bonfires you see in the movies. That would smoke up the place.

In the meantime, a serious food shortage was developing. With the roads closed to the nearest town, there was no way to replenish our dwindling stock, so we were all put on rations. The staple in these Indians' diet was fried bread, and whatever could be hunted up for stew. But they loved white bread, especially French, and cherished the loaves that were handed out at the kitchen each day. On rations, each was given two slices. Since those in the lodge didn't seem to be suffering the same lot, this caused a lot of anger. Powwows were held and war parties formed. But on the seventh day of our entombment, the snow started giving way to slush and mud.

I got wind of some trouble brewing over the bread issue and, as the more cantankerous of the Indians were making alcohol a permanent high percentage of their bloodstream, thought it wise to lift the rationing. I told Rossen how I felt over dinner one night.

"I know they don't like it," he snapped. "DeMille likes the fact that we're sitting here on our asses even less. You don't know the hell I've been getting from him."

"We should be filming in a day or two, and the roads will be clear to get more food through. What the hell difference does it make to start giving out more bread now?"

"No difference at all. You tell that to DeMille."

The upshot was that the Indians stayed on their rations. After dinner, I was sitting in front of the fireplace with Coop, who regarded this whole situation with seemingly great interest. We had been drinking a little.

"Jesus," he said. "What do you think will happen?"

"Well, I didn't mention this to Rossen because frankly I don't give a damn now. They're planning on a raid of the food store."

"Gee, really? War paint and everything?"

"Yeah, I guess so. War paint would be appropriate."

"Hey, real war paint . . ." he said, his voice trailing off.

"Uh oh. You've got that crazy glint in your eyes again. You're not thinking of—?"

"Yep! Joining 'em! It's been a long time since I had on war paint. C'mon, think of how much fun it'll be. We'll be really slamming one up the old man's behind with this one, huh?"

I thought about this for two seconds, and said, "Okay, you're on, Wild Bill. Meet me in my room in ten minutes and I'll fix you up with an outfit."

"Why don't I just come up with you right now?"

"Because, dummy. We have to use separate trails. Indian style."

"Oh, sure."

When Coop knocked, I opened the door, looked up and down the hall to see if anybody noticed us, and let him in with a somber headturn. He was grinning.

"This jacket," I said, helping him slip into a fringed buckskin, "was one worn by Chief Joseph of the Nez Percé. The beaded belt here has real scalp locks on it."

"Real ... scalps?" he said, gingerly touching the little tufts of hair. "Aren't they kind of small?"

"Yeah, they're the small, variety size. You could take a bunch of them with a slight twist of the scalping knife after somebody else got the full scalp, which includes the whole center of the head."

He took a deep breath. "Oh."

I mixed up a small batch of bole armenia after helping him climb into his outfit, spread it on his face, and added some war-paint streaks across his forehead and down his cheeks. He looked great, like a Nordic chief with his brown hair. No longer was he the skinny, twenty-three-year-old of more than ten years ago, when I first outfitted him in a G-string. I placed a headdress over his hair, and he looked like a perfect Indian chief.

"Great! Have a look in the mirror."

He walked regally to my dresser mirror, looked at himself, gave an approving nod, and raised his right hand.

"How," he said.

We climbed out the window, jumped down two feet onto the snow, which hurt a little because it was packed so hard. Then, with a half moon following us over the tops of pine trees like an old friend, we stole off into the night towards the sound of the tom tom.

At a more permanent camp in the middle of the winter, there might be a big lodge, about the size of twenty tepees, for dancing and other ceremonies. The walls would be built from logs with a circus-style, "big top" tent roof. This dance was taking place out in the open, sort of makeshift. When Coop and I arrived, it had already begun. There was a huge bonfire, with groups of people sitting in clusters around it. Six men beat out a slow, steady rhythm on a huge drum, and sang songs about good times in high-pitched voices. Incidentally, this type of Indian singing has no words, but expresses what the singer is thinking and feeling. Words just get in the way. The women sat separately from the men and danced with themselves, although nowadays women dance right among the men. They had on their best flannel dresses under buckskins, which were sometimes white. They were adorned with beads and elk tooths, and when they weren't dancing they sat among each other showing off their finery and giggling about which men were the most handsome, who were the best lovers, and so on. Indian women will never speak like this when there are men around, but you get them together in ceremony and they loosen up like drunken sailors. Make up for their puritanism, I guess. The men looked wonderful and fierce, some of them carrying war clubs and wearing ceremonial buckskin shirts painted in bright colors. They wore feather outcroppings on their behinds, also brightly painted, and little rings of sleigh bells around their ankles. Their dress moccasins were covered with beautiful beadwork, as good as anything Birdie could make, which was the best in the whole perfect world, as far as I was concerned. And the idea of the dance *is* to draw attention to the perfection of the world, its Great Mystery needing no explanation other than everything having a place and purpose in nature. You don't actually think this; you *feel* it through the drum.

As we made our way through the camp, Coop drew the attention of the men, who regarded him with either a cool indifference or a quiet, friendly welcome. But the women, well, they positively screeched with delight. And to this day I don't know if, as they dragged him off to their circle and swarmed over him like happy bees, they knew he wasn't just any white man but Gary Cooper. The men got a great kick out of this and laughed, saying the women have a new dancing partner. All the while Coop was being his aw-shucks, yes-ma'am self as the women touched him and pulled at his clothing and giggled and whispered, holding him prisoner by his two arms. He would occasionally look helplessly over his shoulder at me, silently mouthing "What should I do?" and I shrugged.

"Don't worry, they won't hurt you," I yelled in Cheyenne for everybody's ears, and the men laughed once more. When I thought he'd had enough, I said in English, "Start dancing when I do. They'll let you go then."

"I don't know how."

"Just do what I do."

The drum had begun to pick up its beat and the dancing got a little more complicated. A bottle or two of rock 'n rye appeared on the sidelines, and was passed among the men. One or two of the men would take a long pull, throw his head back, and howl with great delight, then leap into the line of dancers with much abandon. Every part of the body moved with the rhythm of the drums, each dancer experiencing his own personal ecstasy and yelping and whooping louder as the dance got faster. The women backed away from Coop as he started a kind of tap dancing shuffle, blushing so much you could see it through his makeup.

"Let loose, Coop. Feel the power of the drum."

"I'm trying, I'm trying. This is a tough dance."

Well, it wasn't long before he got the hang of it and was whooping and gyrating around that fire like the rest of us. Several of the older men sitting out the fun didn't laugh anymore but nodded in approval, saying in their native tongue, "Hey, not bad for a white Indian," and, "He got fierce blood, must be part human being." We danced and danced and danced, working up a tremendous passion. The women watched and felt the excitement building, and occasionally one would let herself be led away to a tepee by a brave. Other dancers had visions and would wander off into the night, speaking and gesturing to spirits, or maybe the soul of a nearby tree. Finally, long about four or five in the morning, dancers began leaving the circle and, their ankle bells jingling happily, would trail off to their homes. That left a hard core group of thirty or so raiders.

"It is time," said Big Man as the drum got softer and slower again. Rightly named, he stood about six and a half feet and had a big hook nose with a scar trickling down the length of it. Big Man's eyes were lit up like hot coals, a little bloodshot from drinking, and it was hard to tell how seriously he was taking this thing. All I know is the scalp locks dangling from his war club, which was topped with a grizzly bear tooth at a mean angle, may not have been passed down from previous generations. Or at least not from distant generations.

"Yeah, let's go," piped Coop, guzzling whiskey and slamming the bottle into my chest. "Yahoo!"

Several of the braves picked up a log cut into a battering ram and, with Big Man leading, we slipped along the outskirts of camp and down the hill towards the food warehouse and kitchen. We stopped in a little clump of trees about thirty feet from our target. I don't imagine we pesented the most efficient example of warriors to ever stage a raid, as two or three had already fallen out owing to excess drink. A number of others staggered instead of stealthed, and as we gathered in the trees there was a fair amount of giggling and arguing about the best method of approach and who should go first and who's hogging the bottle.

"Quiet!" admonished Big Man under his breath. "You sound like a bunch of coyotes. Don't forget, after we break in and load up with white bread, we meet on the south side of the stream, where it bends around the opening."

I'm sure different people react in different ways to nervous excitement. Some can't speak, some stutter, others hiccup. In Coop's case, when Big Man gave the signal and we all charged behind the battering ram carriers, whooping and hollering for the sheer joy of it, he started laughing hysterically. Sounded like a goddamned hyena. As the battering ram crashed open the double doors to the warehouse, he came staggering behind us, holding his gut with one hand and seeming about ready to wet his pants. Some warrior chief.

"Wait for me," he cried, his other hand raised, an imploring finger outstretched.

Inside, on rows of metal shelves, were hundreds of loaves of French bread, ready for the day's dispensing. There were big hams hanging alongside sides of beef. On other shelves were huge cans of peaches, fruit cocktail, string beans, and the like. The Indians gazed on this splendor for a couple of seconds, staring about wide-eyed and taking in the rich smells in a sort of silent reverie. Coop held back a giggle. Suddenly, someone—I don't know who, maybe a cook—appeared in the doorway to the kitchen. He was dressed in long johns and, after rubbing one of his eyes, the first thing he saw was Big Man towering over him. Then his gaze took in the whole room, filled with some twenty Indians painted for combat.

"*Jee*-zus!" he said, running his eyes up to the beartoothed club of Big Man. Big Man raised the club an inch and stomped his foot. Terrified, the man ran back into the kitchen. At that, everybody whooped and yipped and jumped to, grabbing up armfuls of goodies, having pillow fights with the French loaves and creating a kind of general mayhem. Coop pointed at the proceedings, roaring helplessly with laughter. It was getting pretty contagious, and I joined in.

From listening to snatches of conversation for several days after, I learned that the Indians got away clean with their loot and had one hell of a good feast down by the stream. Apparently only a few cowboys, curious about all the racket, had thrown on their pants and wandered over to the food warehouse. They encountered the Indians pouring out, some carrying sides of beef and large cans of food, on which they were pounding like drums, some with arms full of French bread. A handful of cowboys followed and joined in the feast. With the idea of avoiding later detection, Coop and I went through the kitchen and up the back stairs to our rooms. He was staggering a bit at this point, from the long night of dancing and drinking, and we walked arm in arm, still giggling and flushed with victory. Only a housemaid saw us as we stumbled down the hall. She didn't think anything of it. After all, we *were* movie people!

Shooting began on *The Plainsman* as the temperature rose above forty degrees and the sun shown brightly. The snow melted, small animals scampered about the yawning blades of grass, birds began assembling homes for their soon-to-arrive young. And, unfortunately, the ground under hundreds of horse's hooves and thousands of people's feet quickly turned into an ocean of ankle-deep muck. Everybody proceeded to slip and slide through each take, and before half of each day's shooting was completed, we were covered from head to toe in mud. Not only that, it became dangerous. A number of mounts had slipped and fallen, injuring their riders. A day didn't go by without two or three people in first aid, having heads looked at for concussions or broken bones set. One scene required the Indians to charge up a particularly steep grade, and they flat out refused. Not many of them were experienced horsemen. I was singled out as "the best rider in camp," and I was never able to resist a challenge laced with flattery. I proceeded to charge my steed up the slippery incline. The damn beast reared, threw me backwards, and I landed on my head. "Lucky it wasn't a vital organ," laughed Coop, standing over me at the base of the hill as I regained consciousness. So much for the camp's best rider.

The shooting slogged on for the next two months pretty much on schedule. DeMille never found out about the food raid—in fact, I'm really not sure who among the top people knew of it. Rossen must have, but probably declined telling his boss for fear of the Almighty's wrath descending on all of us, together with a week's ration of crackers and water. But tension among the Indians and cowboy extras persisted, together with a continued flow of rock 'n rye. The Indians, a little high from downing a few good slugs before mounting their ponies for shooting the wagon train siege, might have actually bopped a few settlers' heads with war clubs instead of pretending.

The Plainsman opened to great reviews and enjoyed tremendous box office success. It's thought by many that the Paramount studio execs were finally satisfied that, while he continued to spend lavishly, DeMille was now a safe bet. He was paying attention to what people wanted, and he was making money. But, from what I saw, he wasn't free of his hassles with Paramount yet. At least not judging from the production meetings I attended.

"Whaddya mean I can't get thirteen million?" he'd howl. "What the hell are you doing in this room, anyway?"

"To see to it you make cheaper pictures, Mr. DeMille," they would reply.

"Cheap pictures, cheap pictures! When was the last time I produced a flop for Paramount? Ten years, and I still can't get my feet out of the clay."

DeMille was referring to his only money loser for Paramount, *Feet of Clay*, back in 1928. Of course, when he lost, he lost big. Millions went down the drain as theaters across the country refused to even show it. Interestingly, the film also showed some of DeMille's peculiarities. It was common knowledge to everyone close to him that he had this thing about feet. He would never hire a leading lady without first having a good look at her feet, making sure the toes were shaped to his liking, the arch curved just so. I don't suppose he had the same regard for his leading men. In *Feet of Clay*, the hero's toes on one foot are bitten off by a shark. You figure it out.

One last note on *The Plainsman*. While the film was doing

tremendous business here in the States, it was a disaster in Germany. The little man with the Charlie Chaplin mustache, busy gearing his fatherland up for its second world takeover attempt, banned its showing. Before starting on the project, DeMille had toured the Soviet Union and met the head of the Russian film industry, Boris Shumiatsky. Hilter's propaganda honcho, Joseph Goebbels, got wind that Boris and Cecil subsequently sent Christmas greetings to each other. DeMille's work, having by this means been tainted with Communism, was not suitable for the pure ideals of the Nazis. Too bad. If the Germans had only known he would later become one of the most enthusiastic of Communist witch hunters, who knows, they too might have received Christmas cards.

After *The Plainsman* hit at the box office I officially became one of DeMille's "boys." I was installed in a permanent office in the DeMille bungalow, alongside his assistant directors, production managers, art directors, and so on. I was invited for outings on his great yacht, *The Seaward,* which were pretty tame fishing expeditions. One day a tour boat pulled up alongside as we were plying the waters just off the coast of Santa Barbara. The tour guide put a megaphone to his mouth and announced, "That, ladies and gentlemen, is the palatial yacht of the famous film mogul, Cecil B. DeMille." DeMille shouted back, "I've owned this boat since 1922 and there hasn't been an orgy on it yet!"

DeMille became fascinated with Indians and decided, after a personal tour of my collection of artifacts and props, to have the whole thing moved to the Paramount lot as a publicity stunt. Which was fine with me—no more upkeep on the warehouse. He also started an Indian museum in New York from his own collection, which was considerable. His interest in authenticity, at least as far as Indian dress went, was revived, and he listened to me with rapt attention when I'd explain what was required. He had some of my pieces copied, and then challenged me to tell them apart. I couldn't. When he wanted, his sense of detail was uncanny.

DeMille even went so far as to take a keen interest in my personal safety, something unheard of on his pictures. This concern was from the man who in the early days worked his actors 10 hours a day in the jungles of the South Sea Islands, who set up

fantastically dangerous stunts for his stars when unions didn't
allow stand-ins. One day he saw me limping about the set and
called a halt to the shooting.

"Iron Eyes, what the hell's the matter with you? Why are you
walking funny like that?"

I explained I had taken a bad fall on a bronc, so he went ahead and
had a huge back brace made up for me. I nearly died wearing the
damn thing and I'm sure it retarded my natural healing processes.
In fact, my back never really completely recovered. But I wore it for
two weeks, and not only that, DeMille insisted I now walk *beside*
him to and from the commissary. This was history in the making.
And me, a humble Indian.

While DeMille was filming *The Buccaneer* I spent my last season touring with the Ringling Brothers and Barnum and Bailey
Circus. Then, in 1938, I rejoined him for *Union Pacific*. For his
latest epic, DeMille had the cooperation of the president of the
Union Pacific Railroad, who loaned him a few perfectly restored,
period trains, mountains of historical data piled up in a warehouse,
and even first-class track-laying crews to build a railroad near the
set in Canab, Utah. There, he simply reconstructed the entire town
of Cheyenne, Wyoming, complete with banks, saloons, livery stables, hotels, and a railroad station. DeMille's office space was filled
with miniature trains and, again, little doll-house-sized sets. This
time, we brought in a thousand Navaho Indians from the Al-
buquerque, New Mexico, area, a few dozen Cheyennes from up
north, and about a hundred assorted Indian friends of mine from
Hollywood. I told them if they wanted jobs to say they were
Cheyenne—DeMille wanted "real" Indians, not "beer bellies and
Mexicans from California."

"What's the matter, " I complained, "aren't there supposed to be
any slightly overweight Cheyennes?"

"Not in my pictures," he'd snort.

"But Mr. DeMille, you've got a beer belly yourself."

"*What?*" he roared, "Never mind my beer belly! I'm on the other
side of the camera, where brains count, not stomach proportions."

As it turns out, I was able to keep a few beer bellies in the film by
hiding their paunches under thick clothing, which, incidentally,
was surely needed because no sooner did we arrive on location than

it started snowing again! This time the cold and wet, and the eventual slogging through the mud, led to an outbreak of flu. No less than 50 percent—over 500 people—were down at one time and given treatment in emergency clinics. It was terrible. There is nobody more prone to catching the various diseases associated with exposure than the Indian. To add to my worries, DeMille was a little dissatisfied with the horse falls in *The Plainsman* and decided we needed something more convincing. Fortunately the days of tripping up the horse with wires and ropes were over, and trained animals did sometimes set themselves down a little too delicately. What he did was instruct Rossen to use real wild bucking broncs. My brother and I complained bitterly, but no dice. If the Indians wanted to work and collect their fifteen bucks, they'd ride the horses provided. I'll say this much, it did make for realistic falls. And nobody ever said you *wouldn't* go through hell on a DeMille picture.

Women were no exception. Rossen had our leading lady, Barbara Stanwyck, jumping from railroad cars and allowing real arrows (shot by me), as well as bullets, to blast a canister of molasses over her head, which she then allowed to pour all over her. Despite what some say, though, she never let herself be chased by buffalo. That was accomplished with a process shot.

For the spectacular train wreck scene, DeMille used the real thing. A real trestle was built and weakened at key points, and a full-sized locomotive rode through and toppled over like some great wounded dinosaur, hissing steam. I helped Jesse Lasky, Jr., write and direct the action scenes involving the Indians, including the train-attack scene with bolts of cloth flying behind the warriors like streamers and that bit with the piano, which DeMille took a particular liking to. Actually, after the wreck I saw it standing in the dust off camera and started pounding out an Indian rhythm, like it was a drum. It caused a couple of people, including Lasky, to start, and Rossen cried, "Good! We'll use it!"

DeMille must have gotten so exhausted from just thinking of all the difficulties he could heap on us—from his safe vantage point back in Hollywood—that he collapsed. His prostate gland had apparently flared up, which required an immediate operation. But, it's no exaggeration about him being a tough guy. The next *day* he was on the sound stage directing on his back, from a stretcher, with a temperature of 102°. I guess that meant that the guy who was always there to put a chair under C.B. when it looked like His Majesty was about to sit was now out of work. Or maybe had a new job helping to carry DeMille on his stretcher in and out of the ambulance, which is how the director was conveyed to various parts of the Paramount studio for the rest of the filming.

The final scene in *Union Pacific* showed the driving of the golden spike which joined the track-laying teams and completed the transcontinental railroad. It was a beaut, a fine example of what the epic master did best. Shot in Canoga Park, near Hollywood, the scene had C.B. himself at the helm. The golden spike used was the real thing: the actual one from the 1869 ceremony, spirited down from a special vault in the Wells Fargo Bank in San Francisco (the one actually driven with hammers in the film, of course, was a copy). The two trains—again, perfect replicas in every detail—touched cowcatchers, and a full brass band struck up. Officials and businessmen stood about radiating an air of self-congratulation, the Chinese and Irish laborers flung their hats to the wind and cheered to the tune of the locomotives' whistles.

As we were setting up the shot, DeMille said to me: "All right, Iron Eyes, have your Indians line up along the tracks here. Remember, their lands have just been sequestered, progress and civilization are triumphant, and this scene is symbolic of their plight."

"So?"

"Well, so they look *sad*," he snapped, but with a hint of conflict in his voice. DeMille always played tough on a set, no matter how delicate the situation or what he actually felt. I'm convinced he felt a good deal, though.

"Okay. Sad Indians. That shouldn't be too difficult."

The scene was shot, and the Indians sat quietly by the side of the tracks amidst all the hoopla. They looked sad, indeed, the pain in their eyes not requiring any acting. Two steel rails lay across the breadth of their once holy hunting grounds like dead black snakes, and the fire-breathing "iron horse" which slithered noisily along them would soon chase away the buffalo forever.

Union Pacific was another triumph for C.B. DeMille. It was rousing Americana, great adventure, and, with the war gods brewing up an evil stew abroad, pretty much suited to the American mood in 1939. And, for the first time really, DeMille now had no problems asking—or rather, demanding—what he wanted from the studio bosses. DeMille knew what the hell he was doing now, they thought. The production meetings were more cordial, polite. He was asked to sign a new contract giving him more money than ever, and he signed me up for four more years. In fact, he was so pleased with me that I was awarded the DeMille equivalent of Knights of the Round Table—a silver Virginia Dare coin commemorating the 250th anniversary of the founding of Roanoke Island.

In March of 1940, DeMille began shooting *Northwest Mounted Police* in an authentic reconstruction of Fort Carlton in the Paramount lot, and on location at Pendleton, Oregon. For once everything went smoothly. No extremes in weather, no major injuries or sickness, no extremes in temperament as the leading stars—Coop, Robert Preston, and Madeleine Carroll—all got along fine. DeMille's only difficulty was coming up with an actress for the role of Loupette, a half-breed slave, which he envisioned as having "fiery sexuality, tempered by a soft heart." He despaired, thinking that a woman of that nature didn't exist anymore. Then, an extremely beautiful woman I met years earlier when she was married to Charlie Chaplin stormed into his office one afternoon dressed up as a gypsy—complete with the old bole armenia (compliments of yours truly) to darken her face.

"So-o-o-o!" she said, throwing herself down in one of his leather upholstered chairs and hoisting a leg baring a *naked* foot up on his desk. "You theenk you're one beeg shot director, eh? Well, I am Loupette!"

C.B. took one look at Paulette Goddard's perfectly shaped arch and, gasping, signed her up immediately.

"He even gave me the pen," she told me later, laughing.

Not long after the release of *Northwest Mounted Police* on December 7, 1941, the world fell to pieces.

VVVVVVVVVVVVVVVVVVVVVVVV

13

"The most dangerous of the American
soldiers is the Indian. He is brave above
all else. He knows far more about camouflage, inherited from his ancestors,
than any modern soldier that has had the
benefit of science and great laboratories.
He is a dead shot. He needs no orders
when he advances. He is an army within
himself. He is the one American soldier
Germany must fear."
— GENERAL CARL VON PRUTCH
June 6, 1944, addressing
a Hitler Youth gathering

GERMAN COMMANDERS like Rommel, Von Rundstedt, and von
Prutch knew a great deal about Indians. They read about the American Indian Wars, studied the Indians' battle tactics, and learned
the various tribal names. They also liked Western movies, along
with Germans of lesser rank. Probably the average German
schoolboy knew more about Indians that his American counter-
part. The Germans had always been fascinated and, now that they
were fighting Americans, they were fearful. After all, it was the
Indians who invented commando warfare, which was fundamental
to the Nazi's glorious campaign. Commando warfare means you
fight in hiding rather than en masse. Either you hide behind a tree
or bush, camouflaged to resemble nature as much as possible, or
you "sneak attack" (blitzkrieg). Camouflage, commando raids,
scouting and spying, foxholes for cover—all were originated
by Indians centuries before World War II and first used by
white men under the command of George Washington. (The
British had never before encountered an army casually dressed

in practical, outdoor work clothes, not facing them in a formal attack but hiding behind trees and picking off their seasoned but exposed troops like turkeys.) The Germans, after careful scrutiny, thought that no race could have made such a profound contribution to the Third Reich without having come from their own bloodline, so at the outbreak of the war the Reich Courts officially declared American Indians to be of the Aryan race. Our friend Goebbels picked up on this and did his best to get Injuns teamed up on their side. He began trying to foment a "Red Rebellion," issuing statements saying Indians were "slaves awaiting liberation from their oppressors."

Well, maybe the Indians were repressed, but they weren't about to be tricked a *second* time. Join the Nazis and be "liberated" along with the other German minorities? Hah! Besides, Indians didn't like the looks of Hitler and called him "Mustard Eater," probably having something to do with what they perceived running from his nose and nestling on his upper lip.

Then the Japanese got into the act. On the day of the attack on Pearl Harbor Roosevelt made his rallying speech to the American people, and the Indians decided they'd hit the warpath again. This time, it would be alongside the same army they fought so bitterly only seventy years before. Understandably, a handful of tribal leaders snorted in disgust at this prospect, saying the war was the white man's problem, let him fight it alone. They organized a draft resistance (Congress had granted full citizenship to Indians in 1924, and they were subject to the draft like everybody else) but it never really had much effect. The vast majority of Indians felt outrage that their homeland had been attacked. Word spread quickly to the most remote reservations and there was a general call to arms by the chiefs. Old Henry One Bull—then a spry ninety-seven and one of the Little Big Horn veterans—led the first Sun Dance in the Dakota country in fifty years, to pray for the 2,000 braves the Sioux nation was sending into battle. Characteristically, the young warriors were put off by the idea of a draft, not because they were going to war but because they were *told* to. "No government has to tell *me* to fight for my country," said one recruit. A tribe of Navajos, literally within hours of getting the word, donned the warpaint, tied their bedrolls to their horses, and galloped to town, guns in hand and whooping fiercely. They were disappointed when told there weren't any Japs hereabout yet and the only requirement at this point was to sign up. Those on their way to the Pacific "theater" (that word always kills me—what, is war, some kind of song and dance?) took a vow not to return until they did a war dance on the streets of Tokyo (I answered my own question). The Winnebagos elected General MacArthur as Chief of all American Indians. Per capita, more Indians joined the service in 1941 than whites, blacks, yellow, or any ethnic group. Over 15,000 were in uniform, almost half of all males between the ages of eighteen and thirty-five. The great majority were volunteers.

Indians even gave money. Despite the rampant poverty among the nation's poorest minority, dirt-scratching tribes who, individually, would not see the far side of a hundred dollars in a year, geared up their moneymaking crafts and actually donated to Uncle Sam as much each *week*. Cheyenne, Arapahoe, and Nez Percé tribes voted to suspend their claims against the government for the duration of the war. The Indians lent the United States government over $5 million through the Indian Office.

Once they were in the service, Indians became fairly typical troopers, which is to say they did their share of griping about regulations forbidding contact with commissioned nurses, the rotten food, and long marches. But many soon distinguished themselves as brave and selfless soldiers, especially against the Japanese.

A flyer named Ralph Sam, a Paiute, was a gunner on a plane which was dive-bombing a Japanese convoy off New Guinea. Suddenly they were attacked by a squad of Zeros, and Ralph was hit bad. His entire right arm was blown away. Now the ordinary procedure, of course, would be to radio the pilot you are hit and request first aid. But Ralph, described by his fellow crew members as "quiet and uncomplaining," preferred staying on the job. No longer able to operate his big twin machine guns, he used his left hand to pull out his revolver and spent the last few moments of his life blasting away at enemy planes with a pistol before bleeding to death. He was awarded the Silver Star posthumously.

Another Indian named Lester Reymus, also a Paiute, was a member of the Army Air Corps, 77th Pursuit Squadron. When a P-37 crash landed on an air field, without waiting for an asbestos suit, he ran up to the plane and jumped through sixty-foot flames which had already spread to a dangerous gasoline can dump. Lester, badly burned himself, yanked the unconscious pilot out of the wreckage and dragged him to safety. There are dozens of stories like these.

It was in this atmosphere of patriotism—a love of country felt deeply even by a people long neglected and oppressed—that I decided to quit the movie business and go to war. The sense of obligation felt by us all at this time was overwhelming. I just *had* to go. I don't know as Birdie felt this same sense of self-sacrifice and devotion to country as most of the rest of us, being, I guess, a little more sophisticated. When I told her I was joining up without waiting for my draft papers to come in, she said just one thing:

"You're crazy."

That was it. Of course she was right. Wxre all crazy. And I went down to the recruiting station, filled out the preliminary forms, went back for a physical, was poked and probed and told to cough in the usual manner. After bending over and straightening up, I was asked if I had back trouble. I told them about my horse fall on DeMille's *The Plainsmen*. They took some X-rays, then said I couldn't join active service.

"You've got a slipped vertebra, Iron Eyes," said the doctor. "You can take a desk job, but you'll never carry a gun into battle."

"Can't it be operated on?"

"Not a chance. I'm afraid you'll have it for life. You're not 4-F, however, so you'll be put on a waiting list."

"Oh, I see. And if they really get desperate . . . "

"Something like that."

Well, I waited around and waited around, but the army apparently wasn't too desperate yet. Then one evening I ran into an old friend of mine at a party named Ed Weyland, an FBI agent who did some community work with me. I thought he might have some kind of in with the Selective Service, and asked if he could do anything. After thinking a minute, he poked his finger in my shoulder, FBI style, and told me to stop by his office in the morning.

"You mean spying?" I said the next day in Ed's office, when he asked if I'd like to do undercover work. The room was appropriately spartan—on the wall a steel-framed photo of J. Edgar, family photos on the desk next to a miniature American flag.

"We call it intelligence surveillance. Since it's domestic, it's handled by the Bureau. We have reason to believe there's sabotage occurring in our shipyards."

"Where would I fit in? I'm an Indian, I'd stick out like a red thumb."

"That's the idea!" he exclaimed. "You'll be the last one to be thought of as an agent. We'll get you a job in the yards, you just keep your eyes and ears open."

"I don't know, Ed. This spying business isn't exactly what I had in mind for serving my country."

"Iron Eyes, I don't have to tell you how important building ships is to this war. We need them by the thousands, and we're starting from scratch. The Japs," he said, stabbing the air for emphasis, "would like us to stay at scratch. Fighting them at home is just as important as fighting them overseas."

"Yeah, but I've always thought how you fought is as important as why."

"Ever try your hand at welding?"

And so I was placed in the shipyards as a welder. My life as a spy for the U.S. government had begun. I got pretty good at welding because, at least at the outset, the spying business seemed dull stuff. The new war industry signaled the end of the Great Depression as thousands of men and women flocked to the factories and shipyards. Most of these people were good, honest working types just down on their luck throughout the Depression. My job seemed about as important as being a riot control cop at a stamp collectors' convention. But there were plenty of shiftless types among them, people I guess damaged enough by years of bread lines and no-work signs to accept a bribe and accidentally dump over a can of gasoline in a fire-risk zone. Or even plant explosives. Just watching for this sort of thing, though, still left me with a lot of energy so I decided to become an air raid warden at night. Each night after nine, I patrolled the neighborhood where I lived, making sure that everybody had their lights out. During actual air raid warnings, with the sirens yowling, I would drop whatever I was doing, run out, and help people find shelter. They scared the hell out of us, those damn air raid warnings. You never knew if this was when the Japanese had decided to make their Pearl Harbor encore.

My life began developing a rhythm to it, a sense of anxious purpose. Each morning I donned my khakis, leather apron, hard hat and gloves, and headed for the yards. I worked diligently and kept all my senses tuned into what was going on around me. I heard mostly talk of hard times, of the war, complaints and locker room humor. Each evening I patrolled the streets, flashlight in hand. Sometimes I'd come across a late-night poker game, and after getting them to switch out the lights and light candles, I might join them. Even my life with Birdie was doing tolerably well, with open, if somewhat strained, lines of communication. We watched our baby growing up into a young, pretty girl, and worried about her future. We watched and listened and waited: for developments overseas with "our boys," for the next siren wailing, for radio and newspaper announcements.

That's how we fought the enemy at home.

As I began serving the war cause in this manner, there was a boy of seventeen, a full-blooded Pima Indian from Bapchele, Arizona, who had the same notion I first did. He wanted to go in the worst way. I first met Ira Hamilton Hayes in August, 1942, just after he had signed up for training as a paratrooper with the Marines. He had a few weeks to kill before shipping out and decided to look up his sister Mablette, who was friends with Birdie and worked at the Indian Center. He was about a foot under sized, with soft, childlike features and a porcupine hair cut. To this unimpressive appearance he lent a smoldering temper, stubborn fearlessness, and an air of dead serious self-importance. In short, you couldn't help wise-cracking on him.

"So, you're gonna be a Marine, huh?" I said as we were introduced. He had just marched into the Center and, regarding me with a challenging glint in his eyes, squeezed my hand a bit too hard. "I didn't think they took little-bitty guys like you."

He rolled his tiny shoulders into a ball and I thought I noticed that bristly hair of his standing straight up on his head.

"Yeah, I'm gonna be a Marine. I'm gonna be a *good* Marine."

I patted him on the shoulder and told him, yep, he was gonna be a Marine all right.

So Ira Hayes joined up with the American forces leapfrogging their way from island to island across the Pacific. A good Marine he was, slithering on his belly through steaming jungles, becoming part of the land, using guerrilla tactics his forefathers would use on pony raids. He was quick, in a war where split seconds separated you from a sniper's bullet, and his size made him a less convenient target. He was brave and resourceful in battle, but scared to death about himself. He was still wondering who he was and, even after distinguishing himself at Bougainville, doubting if he was good enough to be a Marine. He grew strange and sullen, began drinking—even while out there in the jungle under fire. He also became obsessed with death, and thought he could see it in his friends' faces before going into battle.

"Death comes on a guy like a glow," he said to me one day during one of his visits to the museum while on leave. "Just before it turns out the light."

Finally, on Christmas Day, 1944, he set sail for Iwo Jima, the last imperial stronghold guarding the "Gateway to Japan." On "Dog Day," February 19, Ira was waiting offshore of the island, sweating it out with over 70,000 assault troops, the largest Marine operation in history. He took a slug from his canteen of whiskey, looked about, and spotted something funny about the face of one private first class, Franklin Sousely, a green recruit.

"You're gonna get it, Sousely," he said sardonically, "and in case I'm not there, this is for you."

Ira took out his harmonica and played taps. Sousely, already frightened enough to wet his pants, was very shaken.

"What's he mean," he cried, "what's he mean?"

A sergeant waved off Ira's evil eye. "Ah, don't pay him no mind. He's just a drunken Indian."

Ira laughed.

Now you've probably seen Duke Wayne play Sergeant Striker in *The Sands of Iwo Jima* and from time to time read something about this particular fight. It was gruesome, all right, and I don't have to embelish on it any here. Besides, who the hell am I to be playing war historian? There is one point to be cleared up, though, one that Ira told me about at least half a dozen times. When a platoon of Marines finally trudged to the top of Mt. Suribachi and planted the American flag, there wasn't any battle raging about in the immediate vicinity. The mountain had technically been taken before one Marine set foot on its slopes, the carnage occurring during the approach.

"We came up against one pill box after another," said Ira. "We burned and blasted them out with grenades and flame throwers, then picked off the survivors as they ran out the back door."

As the Stars and Stripes fluttered on the mountain's summit, tears streamed down the cheeks of the Marines still battling for their lives on other parts of the island. This first flag was not the subject of photographer Joe Rosenthal's famous shot, and Ira, standing guard, played no part in raising it. As I understand it, a Navy colonel, fearing the original flag would be stolen by a Marine souvenir hunter, ordered it taken aboard one of the ships off shore and a new one hoisted in its place. A few Marines accomplished the switch and, as Rosenthal stood precariously on a couple rocks for height, six men hoisted the pole up a second time. Ira was on the extreme left (to this day, there's some question about where he actually was in relation to the others), his fingers as though providing a frame for what was to become the most famous war photograph of all time.

As the picture was flashed worldwide, Ira Hayes became an overnight national hero. He and two others taking part in the Iwo Jima flag raising were ordered home by Roosevelt to help sell war bonds. The other three weren't so lucky. The battle for the island stronghold took another three weeks—and 26,000 casualties—before being won by the Allies. The three other participants were killed, along with the man who stood directly to the right of Ira in the photo. He was Franklin Sousely, the raw recruit who earlier bore on his face what Ira had recognized as the sign of death.

So Ira Hayes came home, but he wasn't too happy about it. He didn't give a damn about meeting the president or members of the U.S. Senate and spent most of the time sweating and fidgeting. His friends were still over there "getting their heads blown off," he said. What was he doing here? He traveled all around the country as part of the war bond effort. He was photographed, written about, and cheered by tens of thousands. He appeared in newsreels. He recited his lines about the flag raising, given to him by public relations officers. With a trembling finger, he'd point to his own position on a blow-up of the Rosenthal photograph. When asked why he didn't accept an offer to lead his own platoon, he said: "I'd have to tell other men to go and get killed. I'd rather do it myself, because I know who's gonna get it." He gave brief speeches of his exploits. When he was sober it went okay, but most of the time he wasn't. Sometimes, barely able to stand, he'd tell people the flag raising was "baloney," and that he preferred to be back with his friends in the 28th Regiment. People would stir uncomfortably in their seats. After a few weeks, he was sent back to his regiment overseas.

Throughout the war I made no movies. I kept busy in the ship-yards and dutifully reported each week on whatever suspicious goings-on might happen to cross my path. This meant people skulking about and whispering in groups and anyone talking in a foreign language. I had my work cut out for me, as this included about half the laborers. Just as the whole thing was beginning to seem really silly to me, one morning I did see a worker, a tall, skinny guy I'd never seen before, talking with a sweating, over-weight, middle-aged man in a crumpled, dark suit. The fat man kept glancing about and mopping his forehead and the top of his balding head with a hanky. Then they exchanged something— slips of paper, money, I don't know. I reported the incident that evening in one of our secret meetings. Incidentally, the reporting was done kind of "deep throat" style, and I never learned any names, had to promise not to reveal where we met, and so on. The two agents I talked to—or at least I assumed they were agents— acted as though it was all routine as I gave them the descriptions, but I felt a certain intense interest on their part. Maybe it was the way they exchanged glances as I started talking. A week later, there was an explosion in the yard, killing a few workers and severely damaging one of the ships. I wasn't on the scene, but I was told a tall man was seized immediately by about five or six guys that came out of nowhere. He was shoved into an unmarked car and they sped off. To this day I don't know if I actually had a hand in breaking up a sabotage ring, or if this was even the same guy. The FBI never told us anything about it.

Birdie and I also had our hands full with our one child, Wilma (Tomato Soup). In her early teens now, she was becoming a true beauty: bright eyes like her mother, a perky, insolent little nose (good thing it wasn't my beak!), radiant, black hair which she wore long and straight, and willowy, nicely shaped limbs. She took to wearing makeup, listening to the new swing music, drinking a little (we suspected), and cultivating a string of boyfriends which would have rivaled any movie star. In short, she was getting wild, and Birdie would have none of it. Birdie was a very traditional woman, you'll remember, and with Indians that means modesty, above all else. With me taking a back seat (how could I complain about our offspring being wild?), battles ensued about proper attire for young women, the right time to be in at night, who she was seeing. All the usual adolescent stuff. Indian or white, kids are always the same.

Finally, with Birdie admonishing me for "not taking a stronger stand," we agreed to send her to a government Indian school in Riverside. The discipline there, we thought, together with teaching traditional Indian culture and life styles, would be perfect for calming our wild filly down a mite.

The war finally dragged to an end in Europe. In Japan the A-bombs performed their grisly task and the empire was forced to surrender without the need for an invasion. On Iwo Jima, only 26,000 American bomber crews ever had the chance to even use the island airstrip—less than the number of casualties it cost actually taking the place. In no time, outcroppings of foot-high Johnson grass sprang up out of the volcanic ash at the base of Mt. Suribachi and extended into the island, the same ash Ira Hayes and his buddy Marines struggled through months earlier.

Our little girl visited every other weekend, and in the two years filled out into a beautiful young woman. Knocked me out every time I saw her. "She's too beautiful," said Birdie. "Too headstrong. She'll be in trouble even in the new school." Sure enough, bad reports trailed Wilma as frequently as her visits. She was not studying enough and fooling around with the boys. She argued with her teachers. She stayed out late and drank. Finally, when she came home one weekend Birdie lit into her like I've never seen her light into anyone. (Well, save myself on several occasions when I thought she'd as soon kill me.) Birdie called Wilma a tramp, said she'd wind up on the streets, and they screamed and yelled at each other till I thought the house would fall down from the noise, and I told them so. They kept at it anyway. Wilma finally stomped out of the house and ran up the street, tears streaming down her cheeks. I ran after her and grabbed her elbow.

"Whoa, slow up there. Your old man can't run like you anymore."

"Lemme go," she cried, taking a roundhouse swing at me, "lemme go."

I gave her a shake, letting her know I wasn't about to let loose. She quieted a little.

"Hold on to yourself, Wilma. Try to tell me what's bothering you these days. I know we haven't talked much, but I've always thought you didn't like me."

"What?"

"You know, because I haven't been around all that much. And your mother and I, us not getting along like we could."

"Well, you pick a fine time to get into that, Dad. I don't really feel that way about you. It's Mom, she just doesn't understand me."

"That's probably true. She don't understand me, either. But her intentions are good, believe that, Wilma. Hell, she's got more sense than the two of us put together."

She didn't answer, but studied the sidewalk, as if thinking it over.

"You still want to take off, I won't stop you. Just remember we both love you."

She turned, without speaking, and walked slowly down the street, her head still down. I watched her a few seconds, then trotted after her.

"I thought you said I could go if I wanted," she said, trotting also. She ran just like a young colt.

"Well, sure, (pant, pant) but where are you going? Girl of fifteen can't get too far."

"You and Mom were married at my age."

"Yeah, and look where it got us."

"Don't worry, Dad," she said, picking up the tempo. "I'm just gonna visit some friends."

"Fine, fine, but don't be home late, okay? Your mother'll have a fit."

"Don't worry, Dad," she said, calling over her shoulder, having broken into a full run. Standing there catching my breath on the walk, I watched her as she disappeared around the corner, her hair streaming behind her. Our children cause us such heartache.

She didn't come home that night, nor all the next day. Of course, Birdie was furious with me for letting her go. There's nothing worse than being caught in the middle of two headstrong women, I'll tell you. Finally, late that night, I got a call from the police. (How we parents dread calls in the middle of the night!) My heart jumped crazily as he told me they'd picked up Wilma. I was afraid to ask the important question.

"Is she all right?"

"Yeah, she's okay. Found her talking to some drunks on Sunset Boulevard. You'd better come down and pick her up, Mr. Cody."

We dashed down to the station, and there was poor Wilma, looking a little dog-faced. We glanced at each other, and her eyes fell to the floor. I felt a curious mixture of guilt, shame, and anger. The cops, being naturally suspicious I suppose, asked us why the kid had run away. I explained her mother and her had a spat, and they just nodded. Sign here, one of them said, and we were all on our way.

We hardly said anything to each other the next day. I didn't ask what she was doing talking to drunks and I'm sure she'd nothing to say about it. That evening she was on her way back to school.

The semester would be over in a few weeks and we expected her home as usual. Instead, she called and asked if she could stay with her grandmother, Birdie's mother, Bula. You'll recall she tipped the bottle quite a lot, and I had bought her a house up in Oregon just to put distance between her and my family. But we couldn't see any harm in Wilma spending a week or so with her grandma. Maybe the old gal would come through for us and try to set the girl straight. Children will often listen to a relative with a suspected reputation more than their parents, right? Parents are always square. We arranged a flight, and she was off.

A week later we got another call. This one in the middle of the day. It was from a forest ranger. Your daughter's been killed in a hunting accident, the ranger said.

"How . . . what. . . . " I couldn't talk. He said he was sorry and to come up and claim the body as soon as possible.

Bula, still very attractive in middle age (she was actually beautiful when she was young) had remarried. The man's name was Tom Filson, a half Swede and half Indian, harmless enough but not too smart. He had given Wilma and her friend each a 22-caliber rifle to shoot rabbits. Excitedly, the girls ran out in the fields, gleefully shooting after a rabbit and missing. Tom Filson enjoyed the show for a while, laughed as he watched the pretty girls. Then he left them alone. Wilma always liked running, but nobody should be running with a loaded gun. She tripped, fell on her gun, and it went off.

On the plane trip up Birdie sat quietly sobbing to herself, muttering and clenching her fists. I sat there numb. We didn't say anything to each other. We arrived at Bula's and the dam burst. Birdie screamed at her mother, said she'd kill her if she ever laid eyes on her again. Her mother sat and cried and begged her not to say these terrible things. Then Birdie turned on Tom Filson.

"And *you!*" she hissed, slowly walking towards him. "How could you be so stupid you . . . you idiot!"

She picked up a miniature stone totem pole on the fireplace mantle and went after the poor man. I knew if she got within reach she'd try to kill him, so I grabbed her from behind. Terrified, he ran out the door and as far as I know was never heard from again.

"Birdie, don't, don't," I said, struggling to hold her. It was like trying to hold an angry mountain lioness, but I managed. The stone totem pole fell to the floor and she burst into tears. I carried her upstairs and put her to bed. When I came down, Bula was still wailing and sniffling. I went out on the porch and sat down feeling more weary than I think I'd ever felt in my life. I stared into the dark, moonless Oregon night.

The war was over for us. It wasn't over for everybody, though. Wars don't just end and everybody cheerfully goes back to business as usual. Things were different now, you could just feel it. It was the end of an era. There were millions of veterans returning from the battlefield. There were the wounded and the maimed. Indian vets in particular were concerned about their future. They had fought for their country and had seen the world. They asked the government to help develop reservation resources, diversified industries to create jobs. They were largely ignored.

After Wilma died, the best way to describe the life Birdie and I led was empty. We had something holding us together in our only child, and now she was gone. We went through the motions of daily living, we tried comforting each other, but it just didn't seem to work like it should. It would take time, we knew.

Then one afternoon, I got one more call from a sheriff. This time, it was an officer I knew from my work with the Los Angeles Indian Center.

"Iron Eyes, I've got somebody down here says he knows you. He's drunk in a bad way."

"Yeah? Who?"

"Ira Hayes."

When he was discharged from the service, Ira, one of the men who raised the flag at Iwo Jima, had come home to a hero's welcome in his hometown of Bapshule. More than a thousand Pimas threw a big barbeque feast under a traditional canopy of brush and sage. Of course, Birdie and I were there to welcome him and help with the festivities. He seemed okay at the time—still drinking, but not too unhappy. You could never tell with Ira, though, he was always so stone-faced. Taking advantage of his national prominence, the Pima tribal leaders petitioned the Arizona and New Mexico legislators to provide for an amendment in the state's constitution guaranteeing Indians the right to vote (denied in these two states at this time—even while citizenry for Indians was enacted in 1924—but voted through years later). After a few weeks in Bapchele, it was off to Chicago for Ira, where the National Congress of American Indians gave a luncheon in his honor and voted him first commander of the American Indian Veterans' Association. But Ira wasn't cut out for administrative work. He began hitting the bottle hard, got into fights with association members, got thrown out of bars dead drunk, and wound up in jail a few times. Finally, he abandoned his post and wandered back to Los Angeles where he had some old friends.

When he was arrested, he was so drunk he barely knew where he was. He had been taking a leak on the rear bumper of a police car, which is probably worse than knocking off the corner liquor store with gun in hand. Lucky I knew the offended officers. He'd have been up on fifty separate charges had I not managed to persuade them I could dry him out at home.

Ira looked like he'd been lying in some sewer for about a week. His complexion was blemished and grey, his once prickly, shining hair now all matted and greasy-dull. His clothes were filthy, his fly was open, and he stank. When I first saw him, half sprawled on his jail-cell cot, I almost burst into tears. What the hell is it this country does to its heroes that so many of them end up bums? Ira was lying on his back, feet on the floor, with his head propped against the damp wall, like a lifeless dummy. His eyes were shut tight, but he was mumbling, as though having a bad dream. I swallowed, put on a big buddy act, and slapped him gently on the shoulder.

"H-hey, Ira, whaddya say? Been drinking a little, huh?"

His hands sprang in front of him in defense and his eyes opened wide in terror. I took a step backward, scared.

"Ira? It's me, Iron Eyes."

He then squinted, adjusting to the light.

"Whozat?"

"Iron Eyes, ya galoot."

"Iron? Oh." He relaxed and just looked at me dully.

"So whaddya been up to? Drinking up all the wine in the San Fernando valley? You don't look so good, you know that?"

"Zatso. Got a few bucks you can spare?"

"Sure, sure. Hey, know what you were doing when they arrested you?"

"Who's they?" He looked about the cell, only now, it seemed, recognizing where he was.

"The cops, dummy. You were pissing on the bumper of their car. Ha! Boy, that's a good one. Pissing on the bumper"—he wasn't listening—"Look, Ira. We gotta get going now, okay? Let's go home."

"Did you say you had a few spare bucks you could lend me?"

I shoved some bills in his hand.

"Thanks. I gotta go now," he said, struggling to his feet. I made a gesture to help, but he pushed me away, took two steps, and started falling towards the cell door. I grabbed him, threw an arm over my shoulder, and zipped up his fly.

"We're going home, Ira," I said.

Half dragging, half supporting him, I teetered past the officers and gave them a small wave of thanks. They nodded sadly, watching us leave.

For a while it was pretty touch and go. I stayed with him for two days, not letting him out of my sight. He seemed on the verge of the DTs for a while, hardly recognizing Birdie or me. Finally we managed to stuff some decent food in him, got him exercising and talking again. I couldn't stay with him forever, of course—I'd begun working at Paramount again—but we couldn't leave him alone, afraid he'd wander off into some tavern and that would be that. Birdie finally came up with the idea of Ira staying with her at the Southwest Museum. They had an extra room that could be fixed up nice, like an apartment. She wouldn't find him any trouble—in fact, Birdie cheered up considerably while taking care of Ira. He was, after all, just a boy in need of mothering, even after all he'd been through in war. I saw it as a tonic for both of them.

The museum was just the thing for Ira. Every day he assisted Birdie and the anthropologists in preparing specimens, setting up exhibits, organizing expeditions which he'd go along on. I gave Dr. Harrington some money, which I told him to give to Ira periodically, like a salary. As far as I knew he fell for it okay. As word got around to my closer friends in Hollywood that Ira Hayes was staying with me, he had regular visits from fans, which seemed to please him. When they asked about his fighting, he only talked in general terms, though. Usually he just said, "It was hell," and that was it.

One of Ira's biggest fans pulled me aside one day on the studio lot and spoke with me in a palsy-walsy tone.

"Iron Eyes, you people all seem to know each other, right?"

"I'm not sure what you mean, C.B. You mean, us Indians?"

"Yes, you, er, Indians. Do you happen to know Ira Hayes? I'd certainly enjoy meeting him, and I understand from the papers he's somewhere in the Los Angeles area."

"In fact, I might be able to arrange that. He's staying with me."

C.B. did a double take.

"*What*? Staying with you? That's *great*. When can you bring him around? I'll have the entire studio out, the press, producers, the stars, the—"

"No, hold on, C.B. Keep it simple. He's had a tough time of it, and I think crowds make him uneasy."

"Whatever you say. Incidentally, what's Ira Hayes doing with you? Visiting?"

"You could call it that."

There's probably no man who ever worshiped war heroes more than DeMille. I honestly never saw him enjoy the company of someone more than when I brought Ira to his office with another Indian vet, a Sergeant Windlow.

Things seemed to be going fine for a few months, but eventually it occurred to Ira he'd have to do more with his life than help Birdie out around the museum.

"Hell, I gotta do more than paste labels on old bones and stuff," he said after dinner one night. "You and Birdie have been great, and I appreciate it. I also know you been doling out that money to me—it's okay, don't feel bad. I appreciate it, really."

"So what do you want to do, Ira?"

"I think I'd like to go home. Work with my people again. Help my parents. The only thing is, I don't have the money for busfare, but I don't want to ask you for it—"

"Say no more," I said, holding up my hand. "You'll be on your own soon, you can pay me back."

We took him to the station, I bought a ticket and stuffed it in his jacket pocket, we said our goodbyes, and left him there. I thought he got on the bus and was safely off to Arizona. The next day, a friend from the Indian Center pulled up in a car with Ira sprawled out in the back seat.

"He was drinking in a bar downtown," he said. "Lucky one of us was there. We were able to hustle him out before he busted up the joint."

Ira had cashed in his ticket and gone on a quick binge. Good thing a bus ticket won't take you too far at the booze counter. Birdie and I poured coffee in him, cleaned him up, and took him right down there to the bus station again. This time I bought two tickets: one for Ira and one for another friend at the Center, about six-foot-four, who said he'd make sure Ira got there okay.

For a while Ira did fine. He was working outdoors, involved with the community, and, as far as I know, staying away from booze. He even met a girl. Then, as the story goes, one night he got to playing pool with some rowdy friends. One of them had a pint, which he passed around, and that was all it took. They went out and got a few more bottles, Ira wandered off into a field with one for himself, and they found him there the next day, dead. He was lying face down in three inches of water. With the parched land his parents had attempted scratching a living from all around him, Ira Hayes, one of the most celebrated heroes of World War II, drowned in a puddle.

VVVVVVVVVVVVVVVVVVVVVVVVV

14

"YOU GET ANY closer and I'll kick you in the nuts!"

Paulette Goddard was screaming at me, and for good reason. I was approaching her with a red hot spear and she was tied to the stake. As I burned the bark of a tree with the spear, I demonstrated for the cameras of *Unconquered* that it was now hot enough to set fire to Paulette's hair. She twisted and thrashed about in her wrist bonds, throwing her head back in exaggerated agony and screeching at the top of her lungs. I stepped in closer, crouching low and baring my teeth, trying to look as fierce as possible. I got within the kicking range, the spear inches from her hair, and thwop! Her foot, the gorgeous foot that DeMille was so in love with, landed right between my legs. I gasped and crumpled over.

"Goddamnit, Paulette! Did you have to do *that*?"

"That's right. And if you get any closer to me with that thing I'll kick 'em again."

"*Cut!*" roared DeMille. "Cut, cut! What the hell's going on here?" He strode up to me and jammed his fists on his hips.

"Well," I said, feebly, "it's Paulette, C.B. She doesn't want to be burned at the stake."

"Oh, she doesn't, does she?"

He helped me up and walked me back to the fire. An assistant had already picked up my spear and stuck it back in the flames, heating it for Paulette's head again. DeMille put his hand on my shoulder and spoke in a stage whisper so everybody, including Paulette, could hear.

"All right, Iron Eyes, this time get in there and burn the hell out of her. And if she kicks you, kick her back!"

"Kick her back? How's that gonna look, me kick a defenseless woman?

"You think she's defenseless?"

He had a point. The cameras rolled for take two and I carefully stalked my prey as she once again bellowed and cursed. Sure enough, when I got within range she lashed out again, but this time I was ready with an artful dodge. I set her hair on fire—her wig, actually—and she screamed.

"Cut!"

C.B.'s voice had a mocking patience to it.

"Ladies and gentlemen, while most of you have endured great hardships on this picture, braving physical hazards without thought of personal safety, there are those on the staff who have done otherwise. They are a cowardly lot, refusing to take any chances for the sake of creating a work of artistic merit, and they indulge their weakness by appearing on the set drunk. This won't be tolerated! We are going to shoot this scene right if we have to do it a hundred times before certain individuals sober up. Now, whenever Miss Goddard is ready."

Gary Cooper, who was also tied up, and who had been sipping a little of the same cognac Paulette was, began chortling to himself. C.B. didn't like it.

"What are *you* laughing at?"

"Nothing, Mr. DeMille, nothing, nothing."

We did another take. It still wasn't to DeMille's satisfaction. Paulette was exaggerating her emotions and postures, and still kicking, making me look more like a ballet dancer than a fierce warrior. DeMille decided on a different tactic. He walked up to her with a pleasant smile on his face and lifted her drooping head with a tender finger under the chin.

"You know, Paulette," he said, soothingly, "you're a great little woman, and you're a beautiful woman. But you're getting uglier and uglier every day. Look at yourself. It's getting difficult to cover those lines under your eyes, Paulette. You're not taking care of yourself. Cut out this drinking and take up acting again. I know you can do it."

"I only drink a little cognac to relax me," she said, on the verge of tears. *"You* drink cognac, Mr. DeMille."

"Only for my heart (ahem). Now we're going to do this scene again, and this time I want it right. No theatrics."

We did another take, and another, and another. Sixteen in all.

And DeMille still wasn't satisfied. He had broken down Paulette, to the point where she was just letting people put a new wig on her head and not even raising her head. Finally he dismissed the entire cast and crew and told Paulette we would "start fresh tomorrow."

And that was the whole idea, I think: starting fresh. DeMille would never waste an entire day like that without good reason. His star was drinking and, as far as he was concerned, screwing up the picture. He was putting her through hell to try and snap her out of it. But it didn't quite work. The next day she showed up somewhat rested looking and sober. We did the hair burning scene in one take, although she still postured too much, and she hit the bottle promptly after.

It was 1947, and *Unconquered* was another massive DeMille epic, this one about indentured servants in the American colonies. Paulette had a pretty tough role to play, requiring her to be tortured by yours truly, whipped, chased in a canoe over a waterfall, sold as an indentured servant on an auction block, and to scrub a tavern floor while scruffy men made lurid advances. She would have none of it, being fearful of damaging her most important asset, her fantastic beauty. And DeMille would have none of *that*, being inclined to despise anybody who didn't measure up to his standards for physical bravery. With his usual sense of perfection, DeMille had the script reworked several times, till in the end it closely resembled the story of *The Perils of Pauline*. But with our leading lady's problems, we called it *The Perils of Paulette.* I chased Coop and her throughout half the picture—in the canoe over the rapids (actually, the waterfall was trick photography), I shot a flaming arrow into her skirt, and threw fireballs at her during the siege of Fort Pitt—or somebody who looked like her. DeMille constantly tried to shame her into submitting to these dangers, but she held fast to her own safety measures, and to her cognac. I love Paulette, but her performance was less than professional in this one. She was never to work on a DeMille picture again.

It was another matter with some of the other cast members, whom DeMille was delighted with. He had his eye on one of them back in the planning stages of the film, in early 1946.

"Iron Eyes, how would Boris Karloff be in the role as Giasuta." Giasuta was the Seneca chief in *Unconquered,* a major part.

"I think he'd be perfect," I said. "He's played an Indian before, a crippled Cherokee professor called Tishamingo. It was back when he was making those horror movies for Universal."

"Let's call his agent, then. And make sure he understands he's going to be speaking actual Seneca dialect in this picture. I don't want to just hear a lot of gibberish."

It happens that some time before filming got underway Boris had undergone a spinal operation to remove an entire vertibra. Seems he had damaged his back somehow while playing professional tennis years before, then aggravated it further doing the Frankenstein monster for so many years.

"It was those bloody boots I had to wear," he said. "They were lead-weight, twenty-five pounds each, and the way they were elevated twisted my back all out of shape."

Through the filming of *Unconquered*, Boris was in constant pain. Each day before making him up, we had to strap him into a metal brace that fit around him like a girdle, then went up his back. He was practically naked, and we covered this contraption with a loincloth and feathers. He never complained once. And incidentally, there was no need for the old bole armenia with Boris. He had an equal portion of Egyptian mixed in with his English blood, and that dark coloring you see on film is his own. When it came time for him to learn Seneca, he spoke it perfectly, with just the right inflection. He was a fine actor, and it's too bad he's not thought of for doing anything beyond monsters. In fact, setting aside the back problem, he said he deeply regretted the day he first put those goddamned Frankenstein boots on.

There was another career start on *Unconquered*. DeMille needed an especially rugged and tall Indian to push Coop around when he first attempts his compass trick to escape from our war party. My brother chose one of the extras we hired, a big, handsome Mohawk Indian named Jay Silverheels. You may know that Jay went on to become America's first really bigtime Indian star, playing Tonto in "The Lone Ranger." Jay was from back East, where he was a champion lacrosse player and a very good boxer till he got one of his eyes bopped out. Had himself fitted with a glass eye and, with some vague notion of becoming a professional gambler, he packed up his lacrosse stick and headed West. He began hanging around Gower Gulch, which is where my brother and I spotted him as potential movie material. I mentioned he got his start in *Unconquered* because that's the first time anybody singled him out for any close camera shots. Actually, he had been playing bit parts since we took him to Canab, Utah, years earlier for some riding sequences in *Western Union*. He distinguished himself by not being able to ride at all. But like Jim Thorpe, Jay had raw guts and a high pain threshold. Without knowing what the hell he was doing, he managed to keep up with the rest of us riders of the purple sage, falling off his horse both on cue and off.

After his appearance in *Unconquered*, Jay and I became good friends. He moved in with my brother on McCadden Place and we continued to see that he got decent parts in the movies. He also began hanging out a little with Errol Flynn and Tyrone Power. When Tyrone went down to Mexico with Cesar Romero to do *Captain of Castile*, Jay went along and did a very good job as a pivotal character in the story, causing Tyrone Power to risk his life in the beginning by helping him escape from a cruel Spanish master, then saving his life in the end. From there he landed a screen test along with Lee Powell in "The Lone Ranger," playing Tonto. He was an "overnight" star. He moved out of my brother's place, never bothering to pick up his lacrosse stick or his one suitcase. He bought up a bunch of race horses and realized his dream of big-time gambling, losing money by the thousands. When the series began fading, they made two successful *Lone Ranger* feature films, and he was back on TV, stronger than ever. For whatever reason, though, he and Lee Powell never got along too well. When "The Lone Ranger" did finally exhaust its popularity, Jay made lone personal appearances and was very popular. No longer in demand as an actor, he took up buggy racing, actually driving the horses by himself—and this was when he was in his late forties.

Then Russel Means of the American Indian Movement (AIM) began publicly ridiculing Jay. They called Indians like him—that is, any Indian who tried to make it by working within the system—a "Tonto." I should mention here that "tonto" is Spanish for "crazy" or "idiot." And you remember in the series that Tonto always called the Lone Ranger "Kimasabe"? "Kima" is Pueblo

Indian for "hello" and "sabe?" means "understand?" in Spanish.
Anyway, not long after, Jay suffered a terrible stroke, leaving him
completely paralyzed down his right side. He was first confined to
a hospital, then to an actor's nursing home, remaining forgotten for
a while till his friend Jonathan Winters proposed to have him
elected to the Sidewalk Hall of Fame along Hollywood Boulevard.
And he was. At the ceremony, Jay was honored by singing and
dancing performed by members of the Little Big Horn Association,
of which I'm president. Later, at a party, Jay struggled out of his
chair and, supporting his now wispy frame on one foot, sang
"Home on the Range" with the Sons of the Mountaineers and Roy
Rogers. There wasn't a dry eye in that group.

It was bound to happen that sex would begin bubbling up in
Westerns. Before the war, the sexiest you got was Mae West and
W.C. Fields in *My Little Chickadee.* But that was just a lot of silly
fun. Then came *Destry Rides Again,* a remake of the old Tom Mix
picture, this one starring Marlene Dietrich and my friend Jimmy
Stewart. Marlene did her best to introduce sexiness into the wild
frontier, but Jimmy's presence added a soft, apple-pie touch. And
you have to keep in mind that, in both these movies, sex was
secondary to the story. Action, adventure, and heroism were still
the central themes. It took a new kind of moviemaker to come
along after the war and say, "Hey fellers, I think the Western is old
enough for some adult sex," somebody with a lot of money to blow
on a gamble and who would just as soon shove a cactus up the
public's rear end as heed its cries of outrage. What better "somebody" than Howard Hughes?

Hughes' *The Outlaw* was the first Western, to my knowledge,
sold solely on the basis of sex. It featured ads and posters showing
Billy the Kid dragging into a cabin one Jane Russell, a ripe bosomy
teenager at the time *The Outlaw* was filmed, and a "discovery" of
Hughes. Recognizing her potential, he personally invented a kind
of "heaving" breast harness for her. The first cross-your-heart bra.
She was already extremely well-endowed, but this thing made her
look like a couple of footballs were stuffed under her blouse. It
drove all the men on the set crazy, including Ben Johnson. This was
his screen debut, too, having just come out from Oklahoma with

his own horses for use in the production. Taking one look at her walk on the set for the first time, he whistled and spoke for all the wide-eyed wranglers present.

"Damn! Will you look at those tits!"

It's to Hughes' credit, I suppose, that he promptly threw all the men not necessary to the scene off the set. That's the way the rest of the shooting of *The Outlaw* went, with only a skeleton crew and essential actors on hand. You can be sure he did it more out of jealousy than any consideration for Jane's feelings, though.

Actually, I first ran into Hughes in the thirties, back when he bought up RKO Studios. I was on a Western—the name escapes me—and we were on location doing a scene where I was to ride by a stagecoach and shoot an arrow in the driver's back. The driver, a stuntman I'd never met before, had on one of my balsam and steel vests, but didn't like the idea of me drilling him anyhow. In fact, he got outright nasty and kept calling me "Blanket Ass." I can take this kind of thing from the likes of Gary Cooper, who you always knew was kidding, but this character? I knew he was uncomfortable in that vest, bouncing along like a marionette on the hard buckboard seat. When it came time to plug him, I missed. Ditto on the second take, and so on. It was great! He grew more exhausted, sweaty, and dirty, and more abusive with each try. Finally he threatened to call in his "friend" Hughes, and left to make a phone call. Sure enough, a big car pulled up shortly and Hughes climbed out of the back, dressed in a three-piece suit. Evidently this character had worked in one of Hughes' plants as a machinist before coming to RKO. He had an "in" with The Man, and bawled his side of the story as Hughes looked on impassively. Then Hughes spoke in that reedy voice of his.

"Who'd you say this fella was?"

My tormentor pointed me out.

"What's your name, son?"

I told him. He regarded me for just a half moment, as though carefully weighing something, then made up his mind.

"You're fired."

He turned on his heels, walked to his car, and was gone.

Well, this was fine with me. I didn't need his goddamned movie anyway, but I knew they needed my costumes. Sure enough, a week later another big limo pulled up to our Indian Center in Los Angeles and two perfectly dressed, hard-looking guys stepped out. They said they "represented" Howard Hughes, as though he was an institution, and wanted to know what they could do for us. I was about to tell them what I thought they could do, but the Center's director, Joe Bascus, also a Hughes employee, blurted out that we needed $10,000. One of them smiled condescendingly, pulled out a checkbook, and wrote it, just like that. Every year we got another check, a little token from our friend Howard Hughes. I was also, as you might guess, back on his movie when he needed me.

Getting back to *The Outlaw*, because of his newly found Jane Russell toy, Hughes showed up on the set frequently. He was always immaculately dressed in sport suits, shirt, and tie. He didn't seem to take much interest in the production at first, except when it involved Jane, and spent most of his time practicing his golfing. He had a bucket of golf balls, from which a cadre of assistants nervously plucked each ball and teed it up for him. After a few shots, Hughes would go and wash his hands, come back, and have a new driving wood handed to him. He'd carefully examine the handle before touching it. Germs, you see. Then, when it appeared to be okay, he'd take it gingerly and start the process over. It was the same routine every time he showed up. One morning as I was watching this spectacle, Hughes—who was a terrific golfer, incidentally—had blasted about a quarter of his bucket of balls hundreds of yards away. He wasn't looking at me as he prepared to take another swing.

"Iron Eyes," he said after whacking the ball, watching it gently arc up in the distance, and drop. "Run down there and pick up those balls for me." He handed his club to his lackey.

"Why you sonava—"

I was about to really let him have it, but stopped short. Those checks to the Indian Center were coming in very handy—and regularly.

"Mr. Hughes, those balls are scattered all over the place. I don't know where they are. We'll just get another bucket for you, won't we, boys," I reasoned, addressing his assistants. They looked at me in horror. I had just committed the greatest sin possible. I disagreed with their boss.

"Yes," he said, almost pleasantly. "Just go down there and gather 'em up."

The crazy bastard hadn't even been listening. One of the assistants leaned over and whispered in my ear.

"Don't you know it means Mr. Hughes likes you when he asks you to do something for him?"

"Oh yeah? He must just *love* you guys, then."

Hughes went off to wash his hands again, and I grabbed a bucket and went out to pick up his goddamned golf balls. Just this once, I muttered to myself, then I'd be through with him. When I lugged the stupid thing back, Hughes was already preparing to tee off. A bucket topped with fresh balls had already been placed beside him.

Howard Hawks was directing *The Outlaw,* and as the shooting progressed Hughes showed up on the set with greater frequency, looking more disgruntled each time. Finally he called everybody together and stood before us, glaring. He cracked his knuckles, then shoved his hands in his pockets.

"I don't like the progress we're making on this picture," he said, his voice hoarse and shrill at the same time. "Don't like it at all. We're way behind schedule and running into big money here, big money."

We were seated in chairs, and Howard Hawks stood.

"Mr. Hughes, I don't think we're behind schedule at all. In fact, we—"

"Sit down!"

I'll say this much for him. Only Howard Hughes could have told the great Howard Hawks to sit down and actually have him do as he was told. Hughes created more fear in people in his lifetime than Genghis Kahn, I'll bet.

"From now on," he continued, "*I'm* directing this picture. From now on, there'll be no more goofing off. We've got a big promotion schedule to meet, and I intend to see we meet it."

And that was that. The next morning, he was out on the driving range teaching Jane Russell to play golf. Standing behind her, he wrapped his arms about her chest and "directed" her swing. After a few minutes of this, he washed his hands and had us all go to work. Hughes wasn't a bad movie director, either. What he lacked in originality and technique, he made up for with the sheer force of his personality, and he did manage to ace the thing through. For years, though, the censors kept it shelved. Their biggest objection wasn't the sex per se, but that Jane played "Rio" as a woman who was capable of nothing but. She was the first Western sex object and, despite official objections, it made her a star.

For a few years, Hughes' donations to the Indian Center actually increased. He also had about fifty acres of land behind one of his airports set aside for us, promising to build a new Center and fund it permanently. Then one day The Man himself showed up at the Center, I suppose to check out how his investment was coming along. He stepped out of the limo, being careful not to touch anything, and walked stiffly into the reception room. Several administrators offered their hands to him, but I knew better than to do that. He would just look at the proffered hand as though it were some curious obstacle, sidestep a little, and continue looking about. He never said a word to anybody, and his eyes were noticeably distant and strange. After a few minutes he'd had enough, and was whisked away. Not long after that, he dropped all his support, including his plans to build us a new facility.

"Too messy," was the word from his staff. "Mr. Hughes likes things tidy, and you people are too messy."

To think I had bothered picking up the bastard's golf balls.

After *The Outlaw*, Jane Russell was in the big time, and I went with her and Clark Gable down to Mexico to film *The Tall Texan*. Then it was on to the two Bob Hope Westerns, *The Paleface* and *Son of Paleface*. Now, Bob is a pretty funny guy, although I'm not the type to crack up over one-liners. Like a lot of comedians I've known, he never turns it off. Just naturally funny, all the time. When I met him on the set, he raised his hand in Indian greeting. He had been out in the sun and his nose was peeling.

"How."

"Hail, Paleface," I said.

"No, me Peel Face."

Not hilarious, as I said, but he kept it up all the time. He did have Jane laughing continuously, though. In fact, she got so flustered she couldn't remember her lines. But then he always did have a way with the ladies. I first met Bob on the "Road" pictures, of which I was in four. There was always a flock of adoring women fluttering around him and Bing Crosby. Especially Bing, believe it or not. It wasn't unusual for him to disappear into his dressing room with three or four beautiful women at the same time. And you thought he sat around singing "White Christmas" and played priests all the time!

With the success of *The Outlaw,* sex was also in for good with Westerns. *Duel in the Sun,* which had some really torrid scenes between Gregory Peck and Jennifer Jones, was nicknamed *Lust in the Dust.* If there was going to be some romance in the old Western potboiler, there would also have to be an equal serving of sensuality. The "good" girl would have to be contrasted with the "bad" girl. In John Ford's *My Darling Clementine,* Kathy Downs played the pure school teacher, who remains unscathed by lust. Linda Darnell was cast as "the other woman," a barroom girl who falls hard for Doc Holliday (Victor Mature), takes up with another man to make the Doc jealous, and gets herself killed—after being shot at the O.K. Corral and being operated on by Doc! It was Linda, incidentally, who played in that famous scene with Henry Fonda (as Wyatt Earp) as he balances himself on one foot, then the other, all the while tipped back on a porch chair. This was supposed to be symbolic of Earp's risky, tenuous life in Tombstone, at least according to the critics. But if you told Jack Ford that he'd have punched you in the nose. He didn't like symbolism, no way, and just wanted to have Henry Fonda doing something.

VVVVVVVVVVVVVVVVVVVVVVVVVVVVV

15

AFTER THE TWO *Paleface* movies, I teamed up for ten years with a man who, while he wasn't a particularly good cartoonist, could render a decent mouse. The "golden years" of Walt Disney were the fifties, when Disney Productions was doing just about everything from Westerns to space exploration. The Disney studios in Burbank stretched over sixteen city blocks, with over 3,000 employees cranking out feature and short cartoons, the Disneyland TV series, the "Mickey Mouse Club" TV series, and full-length feature films. In addition, Walt was planning his multimillion-dollar gamble at this time. He was going to call it "Disneyland." Everybody thought he'd finally cracked. You couldn't pump that much money into a giant amusement park that required 40,000 visitors a day just to break even and expect to remain in business for long. They thought any day he'd been seen skipping merrily down Hollywood Boulevard wearing a pair of Mickey Mouse ears and singing the theme song from that goddamned TV show. (A full-grown man doing the same thing down Hollywood Boulevard nowadays wouldn't be given a second glance.) Walt did, in fact, have just about everything around him "Mousketeered," big posters of the rodent on his studio trucks, on the walls of his office, stationery, calendars, clocks, and, yep, wristwatches. But Disneyland made—and continues to make—millions. I never saw him wearing mouse ears.

Actually, I had met Walt years earlier in the thirties through his mother. I was hunting up in the hills with bow and arrow with my friend, the great Western artist Clarence Ellsworth, when we came upon a big, grey-black modern house. There was a delicious aroma of baking coming from the place. As we got closer, we saw a woman out back with a bunch of pies lined up on a picnic table. The woman was Mrs. Disney. The pies were coconut cream, my favorite. A few weeks later I was at the old Disney studio at Hyperion

[244]

and Riverpark, doing some minor function, and Walt strode in, discussing something with a group of assistants. I introduced myself, saying I had the opportunity to enjoy his mother's pies. That was good for half an hour's conversation. Walt loved homey things like baking.

Then, in the late forties, Tim McCoy and I were doing our own TV show on KTLA. Birdie joined me again, as she enjoyed telling the same Indian stories we used on our radio show. The show was very popular for a long time, as it was the first chance people had to see an accurate, documentary-type image of the Indian on the screen, I think, outside of a few scattered movies. Walt saw the shows and called me up.

"How would you like to come up and star in a series I'm doing?" he said. "It's gonna be called *The First Americans.*"

This was my first starring movie role, and it led to a lot of good things for me. I don't know what the people at Disney expected when they knew they were getting an authentic Indian to be their leading man. I think most people have the notion that Indians have trouble being anything other than, well, Indians. Maybe it's the same with all minorities. I wore my buckskin outfit even during the planning sessions, and they seemed delighted, although I noticed a certain "delicate" handling of me. As though I'd never seen a movie camera before. I was huddled together with writers and directors in a story conference, being asked if I understood this and felt okay about that. Then we began on a few technical matters for dramatic effect. I decided to offer a suggestion.

"Tell you what you ought to do. Open with a wide-angle lens on a long shot of me entering upstage. You dolly in with the Mitchell and I'll be lit with a couple of juniors. Then do an over-the-shoulder shot of me, and I turn into the camera for a big close-up with Rembrandt lighting."

There was silence around the table for a minute, then somebody spoke.

"Er . . . that sounds fine, fine. What do you think, Charlie?"

"Fine (ahem). Fine with me, too."

I didn't have too much problem in the condescension department from there on in. They're all good folks there at Disney, really.

The First Americans was also a first in that the Indians were depicted as being systematically stomped on by the whites. Walt's usual policy was that he approved of a story, entrusted his writers and directors to produce it, then, if he had the time—which was usually—he saw the final movie and gave his final approval. We were all pretty nervous that he'd take one look at this thing and tell us to go open a pizza parlor somewhere. As it happens, he never got around to formally reviewing *The First Americans*, and he didn't fire anybody after it was aired. Maybe he never saw it at all.

To describe Walt (incidentally, he insisted everybody call him Walt, never Mr. Disney) as conservative is like describing Buffalo winters as chilly. I never heard of him chasing after women or drinking or being other than a successful, family-oriented, dull businessman. He did have a few quirks, though. One was his language. I've been around some rough-language characters in my time, and Walt swore right up there along with them. It was a most peculiar feeling, listening to the creator of *Snow White* spew out something like, "I don't give a damn what he says, no sonavabitch asshole is gonna tell me how to run my business!" I should add he ran Disney Productions like a true dictator. He never tolerated dissent of any kind. If you drank, got involved in any scandals, or expressed "Commie" sympathies, you were out. He was even known to fire people whose stars shone too brightly. Walt liked being able to find flaws in you.

Being with Disney seemed to contribute to, or coincide with, a calming time in my life. Birdie and I drew close together as a couple, and she gave birth to my first son Robert in '52, and Arthur in '54. We led a very domestic life, keeping the nightclubbing and partying down to a minimum. This was a very busy time for me professionally and what little free time I had we spent together at home. I even resumed making headdresses, my favorite craft hobby from boyhood. At the studios, it was hectic. I worked in countless Disney TV shows and all his frontier movies, including *Daniel Boone* and *Davy Crockett* with Fess Parker.

Leading Indian roles in other studios, formerly played by white actors, began opening up for me. I played the Medicine Man in a ten-episode television series called *The Mountain Man*, with my friend Slim Pickens. Jerome Courtland, now a producer at Walt Disney Studios, played the title character.

The Fifties saw the introduction of sex in Westerns; they also started a trend in racial consciousness. For the first time since some of those little D.W. Griffith and Thomas Ince two-reelers, Indians were being depicted with sympathy and realism. More important, in some cases they were becoming the central theme of the story. Ince and Griffith had told stories about individual Indians, but the plight of the Indian nation as a whole was largely ignored. The new Indian-as-hero trend began in 1950 with Fox's *Broken Arrow*. It starred Jimmy Stewart, Jeff Chandler, and Debra Paget, and won Jeff an Academy Award nomination for his sensitive, intelligent portrayal of Cochise. I played Tesse, Cochise's friend throughout the story. Jay Silverheels played Geronimo. Jimmy had recently married his wife, Gloria, whom he's still happily married to—one of the handful of people here in Hollywood with a stable family life. He, too, is very much as he seems on screen, shy and quiet. And those funny little Stewart mannerisms—the stutter, the breaking voice—are even more evident than when he's acting. Except when he takes a little brandy in his coffee, the only drinking he allows himself. Then he loosens up a bit. Even laughs out loud on occasion.

The success of *Broken Arrow* was followed by a torrent of Indian-centered movies. In the first half of the decade, I worked on *The Devil's Doorway*, *The Savage*, *The Half Breed*, *Broken Lance*, *The Last Wagon*, *Arrowhead*, *Tomahawk*, *Yellow Tomahawk*, and one that has become something of a cult film among Western movie buffs, *Run of the Arrow*. Tim McCoy came down from his ranch, after having retired when our TV show ran out of steam, and played an army general. Charles Bronson made his movie debut in it as a tribal chief, White Buffalo, and I got re-acquainted with an old friend, Sarita Montiel, playing an Indian maiden.

"Seen much of Coop these days?"

"Of course," she said, cheerfully. "He made me a star, didn't he?"

"Yeah, but, I thought he was . . . back with his wife. At least that's what he told me."

"Yes, he ees back with hees wife. I see them both all the time. She ees wonderful, no?"

I was glad Sarita hadn't changed any.

As the B Western began disappearing, replaced by the medioc-rities of TV, the quality of movie Westerns remained pretty high through the fifties. Coop did *High Noon* in 1952, of course, win-ning him the Oscar, and Jack Ford did his fine Duke Wayne movies—*The Searchers, She Wore a Yellow Ribbon, Fort Apache.* In 1954, I was offered a leading role as Chief Crazy Horse in a United Artists film called *Sitting Bull.* This was another Custer picture, but told almost entirely from the standpoint of the In-dians, and told authentically, too. Douglas Kennedy played Gen-eral Custer as an egomaniac Indian-hater trying his best to quash the efforts of Dale Robertson to bring about peace. J. Carroll Naish played Sitting Bull, who was the spiritual leader of the Sioux, not the military commander. That aspect was left to a handful of warrior chiefs, including the greatest Sioux warrior of them all, Crazy Horse. It was he who uttered the famous line, "This is a good day to die," before going into battle. To make things more difficult for the Sioux and their Arapahoe allies, the U.S. Army had on their side the Sioux's bitter enemies, the Crow and Shoshoni, led by the great Chief Washakie. Unity has always been a big problem with Indians, even back in the days when they were engaged in a life-and-death struggle for their homeland.

We were filming *Sitting Bull* down in Mexico, again with the Cherabusco studios. I furnished most of the Indian costumes, headdresses, and props, and also served as technical advisor. Sidney Salko was orchestrating behind the camera and my friend W.R. Frank produced it. This was to be the first Western filmed in Cinemascope, that deep-colored, widescreen look that charac-terized so many Westerns of the fifties. It almost gave you the feeling you were right there, taking part in the action.

When we eventually finished filming *Sitting Bull* a new problem arose. It seemed that everybody's favorite Mexican studio, Cherabusco, had been cheating W.R. Frank out of hundreds of thousands of dollars. We were overcharged for everything we rent-ed, even our hotel rooms. W.R. refused to pay. Or I should say we ran out of money. Only hours after W.R. had a heated exchange with our hosts, four Mexican cops showed up at the studio. We were being arrested, they informed us, for not paying our bills. The two of us were hauled off to jail where we'd probably be to this day had I not known one of the police chiefs. Over one thousand Mexican cavalry were used as extras in *Sitting Bull*, all collecting wages much higher than they made working for the Mexican government. For a large "commission," this cop had helped me go through the proper governmental channels to hire these men. I was let go on my own recognizance, promising that I wouldn't skip the country until the matter with Cherabusco was resolved. W.R. Frank was to stay put as a security measure.

The first thing I did was call W.R.'s wife (we weren't allowed phone calls in jail). I explained the situation and told her we needed $100,000 pronto. She was a cool-headed woman, I'll tell you. Not too many people would know how to come up with money like that at a moment's notice, unless it was already sitting in the bank. She sold four of W.R.'s theaters, and the money was wired to us in days. Of course, I realized that Cherabusco wouldn't be too pleased to hear this. What they were hoping for was complete control of the film. I also think the government was in on it. When money's involved, they don't mess around down there in Mexico. When I closed the deal with Cherabusco and got W.R. out of the clink, the cops were still bothering us. No explanations. They said we weren't to leave our hotel till "certain matters were looked into."

"Well, now what, Iron Eyes. You've managed to get us this far."

"You don't really plan on hanging around till they decide matters have been 'looked into,' do you? They'll come up with something else to charge us for. The film is in the can, right? On its way back home?"

"Yeah. This morning."

"So what are we waiting for?"

That night, at four A.M., we snuck out of the hotel, threw our bags in my Cadillac, and began the drive north. We drove through the night and well into the next day. The level of paranoia was pretty high, as you can imagine, and we tried to stick to the back roads as much as possible. Finally, we made it. I thought W.R. was going to have a nervous collapse at the border check, but we glided through without more than a flashlight glimpse in the back seat. Apparently, our friends the Mexican police either hadn't missed us yet or had looked into things and decided there was no more money to be made from these two suckers.

I'm getting a little ahead of my story here, because two years before *Sitting Bull* was completed, Birdie gave birth to our first son, Robert. Then two years after that Arthur came along. We were beginning a new family, and it coincided with both Birdie's and my rediscovering our Indian heritage. We weren't rejecting the white world; that, if nothing else, would be hypocritical on our part, having enjoyed so much wealth, success, and, yes, happiness. But we were finding there was something missing in our lives: the crucial link to our past, our identity as Native Americans.

And you've probably noticed something else missing, too. This book is supposed to be about a Hollywood Indian, right? So what about the *Indian* part of my life? Well, I mentioned at the outset that Hollywood Indians, including myself, became Hollywood *actors*, for better or worse, much the same way, say, an English actor became a Hollywood actor once he spent enough time out here. What we did for the cameras was act out something we once were, and usually only a part of it, namely, the warrior bit.

But America's attitude toward the Indian began changing after World War Two. It started seeing them as people rather than exotic savages, and so did the filmmakers. In the fifties I found that I could make demands on the medium and insist not only on authenticity but a well-rounded portrait of Indians. I either worked to change, or didn't appear in, movies with exaggerated scalping or other excessive violence. I worked to eliminate the typical clichéd Indian character types. The noble, childlike innocent or the vicious, bloodthirsty, brutal savage began disappearing in favor of showing the Indian as a normal human being with individual virtues as well as faults. The "Me make-um heap big money" kind of illiterate "dialect" was eliminated from screenplays. It's natural that when Indians first learned English, they spoke it haltingly. But the Hollywood "ugh" was taken from tribal songs and dance, the sound originating from the solar plexis, giving vent to feeling, not talk. Words like "squaw," which means "female slave" to an Indian, are now out. So, too, with "buck."

Now the film industry tries to show, within the confines of legitimate drama, who the Indians really were and are. It is an appreciation of a complex culture that loved and worshiped nature, one that was warring as well as peace-loving, exotic as well as prosaic. In many ways, pretty much like any other.

Hollywood's attempts to give a more balanced portrayal of Indians does not erase the fact that we were given a royal screwing by the march of white civilization a hundred years ago. Nor does appreciating our Indian heritage mean that we can turn back and readopt the tribal values we enjoyed on the open prairie. We can't live on hate. Hate just turns in on itself and poisons everything it touches. Hate is the great destroyer, and so is bitterness. The American Indian Movement (AIM) has some good people in it, and I know them. But, while the disruptions it has instigated helped put the Indians on the world map, its values and direction must change. AIM must work at encouraging Indians to work within the system if we've to really improve our lives. If that sounds "Uncle Tom," so be it. I'm a realist, damn it! The buffalo are never coming back—unless we put up fences and designate a park for them. We're never coming back either—unless we make our kids stay in school while working to preserve our heritage at the same time.

Birdie and I began the not-so-easy job of raising our two spirited boys as American Indians in a modern high-technology society. The only way to do this, we decided, was to set an example for them to follow. Kids need disciplining, of course, but we knew that eventually they were going to make their own decisions on the type of life they'd lead, regardless of our wishes.

As the years pressed on, the differences in the boys became more and more apparent. Robert, the oldest, sprang up like a beanstalk and was well over six feet by the time he was twelve. He was outgoing, handsome, charming, and already girl crazy when puberty hit him like a sledgehammer. He was an average student, and it was all I could do to keep him off his horse and into his studies. Arthur, on the other hand, was an "A" student, quiet and shy and brooding. He didn't have his brother's looks and nowhere near his height, but he made up for it with a keen intelligence and a plodding determination to succeed. What they both shared, though, was a pretty well-developed sense of mischief, inherited no doubt from yours truly. Once, I brought them to a community function where I was about to give a speech on the dangers of alcoholism to our people. There I was up at the podium, and before I opened my mouth to deliver a pious sermon, Arthur piped up so all could hear, "That's my dad and he's a chippy chaser. I want to be a chippy chaser, too!"

Don't think I made much of an impression on that group.

Weekends, we took the boys to powwows and taught them to dance in the tradition of their forefathers, and it wasn't long before Robert won all the junior championships. They participated in medicine ceremonies, learned tribal customs and manners, and tribal dress. Through it all, Robert was the enthusiastic participant while Arthur, quiet and thoughtful, seemed to be going along just for the ride. Much of the time he sat out the dancing.

What's better for boy-meets-girl fun than all-night singing and dancing festivity? Because we encouraged him to enjoy himself at these powwows, he grew to prefer them to the company of his friends on the beach. He also, incidentally, kept *growing*. Six-four, six-eight. He excelled in every sport they dished out for him in high school, especially basketball, and the races and traditional games played on the reservations. Not to be outdone, Arthur developed a passion for baseball.

Then, when both boys were in their mid-teens, I thought it time to introduce them to big medicine. Since the hippie movement of the sixties, you've probably read a lot of foolishness about Indian peyote meetings, most of it mixing Indians up with South Americans and Aztecs and what not. To set the record straight, there are no frenzied sexual relations connected with Indian peyote meetings, nor any sacrificial blood lettings on stone altars. Peyote, however, *is* used.

Peyote is a spineless cactus that produces a fist-sized, above-ground plant covered with about ten flat "buttons," some of them no bigger than your thumbnail and on up to the size of a half-dollar piece. For peyote meetings, the buttons are dried and eaten—without too much relish because they're very bitter-tasting. From the standpoint of an outsider, they appear to produce visions and "hallucinations" of colors in participants. But the reason the Indians use peyote isn't to get high. Peyote is a strange and powerful medicine that helps you unlock your soul. It's used to strengthen a sense of brotherhood and oneness among peyote men. People think that it also can cure you of physical ailments, but being cut off from your brother *is* the ailment. Quanah Parker, the great Comanche chief, came into his first peyote meeting with a bad stomachache in 1884. His pains were stopped because he found spiritual solace in his brothers and he became an enthusiastic participant.

Being the first to use peyote, the Comanches have a story about how they first discovered its powers. Once, during a raid by their rival tribe, the Apaches, a Comanche woman was captured and taken away to the enemy's camp. Over a period of time, as the tribe moved east over what is now Texas, she labored as a slave, waiting for a chance to escape. Her time came, and she made off by foot in the middle of the night. Heading west towards her homeland, she walked and walked for days, subsisting off a little dried buffalo meat and moisture she could suck from cactus. She finally collapsed at the foot of some mountains and, lying there in the dust, she thought she heard something.

She turned her head and there by her hand was a peyote cactus. "Eat me, eat me," she heard it say.

With what strength she had, she ate two or three of the buttons and fell into a deep sleep, dreaming of her former life with her people. When she woke, she found new strength in her legs, as though they worked separately from her like those of a powerful horse. She got up and continued her march, nonstop, fifty, one hundred, two hundred miles. She walked and walked, as though carried on the wind. She had taken some peyote with her, which she ate on the way, each button delivering more power to her legs. Her clothing was gradually torn to shreds from the brush and winds, and she suffered greatly, but she walked on.

Finally, having traveled over 300 miles, she walked into camp. No one could believe their eyes. How could she have traveled so far on foot? Before resting, she told them her story, and of the magic cactus she found. Several days later, a hunting party retraced the route she had taken and discovered the peyote she had told them about at the foot of the same mountains she had been at. The Indians gathered in a circle and ate the cactus, praying to the Great Spirit in thanks for delivering their sister back safely. And that was the first peyote meeting. From the Comanches it spread to other tribes in the late nineties, eventually evolving into what is now called the Native American Church.

When I announced that I wanted Robert and Arthur to attend their first peyote meeting, Birdie was dead against it. While enthusiastic about embracing our traditional customs, she drew the line at using peyote. Anything to do with drugs—in or outside of religion—is frightening to most people raised in our modern society which has people wandering the streets in a drug fog. As far as Birdie was concerned, peyote was just another step in that direction. I decided to sneak the boys out, anyway. I had been to plenty of peyote meetings and knew it was a good thing, and harmless. My boys, I was sure, were old enough to handle themselves. Robert was all for it, but Arthur balked. Said he just wasn't interested. Well, there would be another time, I thought. He was only fourteen.

Peyote meetings can be held just about anywhere—in a tent out on the plains, a cabin in the woods, or even in somebody's big living room. I've held many a meeting right here in my own front room, carried out all the furniture and had everybody sit in a circle on my buffalo robe rugs. You may be wondering how we manage to circumvent the law, seeing as how peyote is considered a hallucinogen and strictly illegal. Well, truth be known, the police usually just look the other way if it's a bonafide Indian peyote meeting, and if there is no drinking and nobody transports the stuff in a car. We have a guy in Texas supply us with a hundred buttons each meeting, and that's what we had in our buckskin-fringed pouch as I introduced my son to a gathering of fifteen peyote men seated in a circle in a tent lodge. The traditional crescent-shaped clay altar, about three feet across, was positioned in the center, symbolically representing the mountain range where the Comanches held their first meeting. The sacred gourd rattle, drum, and feather fan were placed carefully within the half-circle of the crescent. Night was falling and the eerie netherworld of dusk settled over us. Robert and two other young initiates were led outside the tent to sleep in robes on the earth till around midnight, while the experienced peyote men settled down to several hours of praying. No peyote would be touched till midnight, when the boys would be roused and brought in to take part in the ceremony. The roadman, or the head priest who serves as a guide, took his position on a slightly raised platform and told us simply to be true, not to tell any lies during the course of the evening, and everything would be all right. We chanted sacred songs and prayed as the kettledrum and gourd rattle was passed among us, each having a chance to "work out" what was inside and prepare for the peyote.

Then about one in the morning, Robert was led in with the other boys and seated next to me. The peyote was dipped in water— which would later be drunk as a sacred elixir for cleansing the body—then placed in the pouch and passed around. When Robert's turn came, he took a button and, with the roadman watching him, took a big bite. He chewed for a few seconds, then brought his hand to his mouth.

"I saw that, Robert," I whispered, "you're cheating."

"But, Dad, it's so bitter."

"Bitter or not, if you don't eat it properly, you're out."

The roadman turned his impassive gaze on the group and continued chanting. I took a button, ate it, and passed the pouch to the next participant.

It only takes minutes before the peyote begins to take effect.

You don't get the same kind of "high" you get from alcohol. Time slows down. The rhythm of the drum seeps into your bones as your senses become heightened. Your emotions bubble to the surface, and you're able to concentrate on them, on the oneness with your brothers riding along with you, on the *rightness* of everything. The sacred pouch was passed by again, and again and again. I ate three, four buttons. Soon I began to lose a sense of my self as merely a man, and this seemed funny. I giggled a little, and Robert asked what I was laughing about. I looked at my son and thought, how wonderful, how wonderful.

As the night progressed, one man began weeping. He cursed himself, flailed his chest with his fists, and cried and cried. The roadman rose from his position at the head of the crescent altar and sat beside him.

"Tell us, brother. Tell us your trouble."

"I want to die, I want to die!"

"Be true, and your soul will fly out of this dark place."

Well, we heard a sad story. It seems that this man has a daughter, and one day when she was a little girl she'd done something bad, so he took his belt off and hit her. Unfortunately he used the wrong end and knocked one of her eyes out with the buckle. All these years he had been living with the knowledge that he'd half blinded his own daughter. He wept and screamed, letting loose a decade of self-hatred, and finally the roadman helped him up and directed him outside to sit in the night and concentrate on his singing and prayers. That's what he did, and I'll tell you, it did a lot to help that man. Each meeting he's attended since, his spirit seems lighter.

Some participants say they see colors. I've had as much as ten buttons and never seen any myself. After several hours I just start to relax and feel a sense of deep ease with myself and brotherhood with those with me. It's a blessed feeling, and that's the best I can do to describe it. I'm sure people in other religions feel something like it. When Quanah Parker was asked once to describe what went on in a peyote meeting, he said, "The white man goes into his church house and talks about Jesus; the Indian goes into his teepee and talks to Jesus." In fact, a number of Catholic priests have asked me if there's any special rules about white men attending peyote meetings, and I tell them no, there's no color barriers. I've also snuck a few of them in, but I won't mention their names here because they'd probably be embarrassed if it became generally known.

Throughout the night, Robert sat there happily participating in the singing and chanting, just kind of taking things in. Then as the threads of morning sunlight began poking through the tent walls, he told me he wanted to sleep for a while before eating. So I excused him, and he went outside to snooze for a bit.

Eating breakfast together is an important and extremely enjoyable activity after an all-night peyote ceremony. Your appetite is great and you eat like a horse. It's also a time to reflect on what you've experienced, to lie around and tell stories, maybe sleep a little like Robert. Some peyote men have visions, which they relate. These can be on just about anything—from personal matters to events affecting everyone. My visions can take some pretty weird turns. I don't think it was at this particular meeting, but once I envisioned that John Tunney was going to lose the California senatorial seat to a man of eastern origin. John is a friend of mine, and when I told him he just laughed. I also caught a glimpse of a future president—a short, silver-haired man from the South. You probably won't believe it, but I swear it's true I had no idea who Jimmy Carter was at the time.

After breakfast, the meeting officially breaks up. Everybody just gets in his car and drives home. That's all there is to it. Of the countless meetings I've attended, I've never heard of anybody getting hurt or going crazy on peyote or cracking his car up because he was "high." Except if you've been drinking—which, mixed with peyote, will make you flip off the deep end in a minute— peyote is harmless if used in the right setting. Now, the police keep our peyote for us locked up, since the hippie days and well-publicized abuses on the part of white kids. But if you show your Native American Church card, you can take it out for a meeting, like using a library card to delve into the mysteries of a good book.

After the meeting, I took the roadman aside and asked if he'd make Robert an official member. He thought for a moment, then said: "I saw him put his hand to his mouth as he chewed a button. He may have taken it out. But then, he may not have. I think Robert will make a good peyote man."

And so he is. Robert, in fact, is now a roadman himself, able to conduct his own meetings. But after this first meeting, he was still a little undecided about the direction his life should take, just like any kid. I tried to help, but didn't put any pressure on him.

To give you an idea of just how completely the two worlds of white and Indian are mixed up and intertwined, one day Robert, at that time eighteen, and finished with high school, announced he was marrying. She was a traditional Hopi girl, he said. "You can't sleep with her till you're married." Then, a couple of weeks later he called from the reservation and said he was through with girls altogether.

"What happened? She up and run off on you?"

"Worse. She's going to become a nun!"

Robert swore off girls only long enough to meet a new one. After his Hopi girl, who had been raised a Catholic, was off to a nunnery, he accepted a basketball scholarship to Fort Lewis College to play center. He was now six-ten. I got a call from the owner of the Los Angeles Lakers, saying they were ready for him after a few years of college ball. But it was never to be. Robert met a five-foot-four Umatilla girl on campus, and after eight months of school they ran off to the reservation together and were married. And there he's lived ever since, raising a fine family and carrying on the traditions of his forefathers.

Arthur, in the meantime, remained somewhat aloof from Birdie and me. He kept up his grades in school, dated seldom—certainly not like Robert—and seemed indifferent to most things Indian. Again, we didn't apply any pressure one way or the other, just encouraged him to keep his options open. Then one day at dinner he announced he was joining the Marines. Just like that. Arthur's a stubborn one, and we knew it was useless trying to talk him out of it. Now he's a tank commander. His superior officers tell me he's one of the best, fierce but very quiet and uncomplaining.

16

BESIDES THE TWO clichéd types I've already mentioned—the noble innocent and brutal savage—there's another stereotype that's widely misunderstood: The humorless Indian. Indians do have a very well-developed sense of things that are funny. But when they first laid eyes on white men they were so utterly stupified by what they perceived as powerful medicine, and what they felt was very strange behavior. For instance, the very idea of putting up fences across the open prairie so that one man could own it was so far out of their range of experience it was, well, a little like people nowadays trying to imagine stepping into the fourth dimension. As we know, fences were not only "thought" of—and Indians probably would have thought that they were funny—they actually were erected. And that the Indians did not find funny. The idea of the solemn, uncomprehending Indian with a poker face came about because of the different ways the Indians and whites looked at the world around them.

What the movies did with this, of course, was again not so much inaccurate as one-sided. I suppose often the Indian reaction to things that confused or hurt him was a kind of dignified, blank expression, but he certainly wasn't like this most of the time, any more than he was warring most of the time. Indians have a light side, and sitting around cracking jokes is a favorite pastime. Granted, after the Indian wars they didn't have much to laugh about. And rituals like peyote meetings, while helpful, were a pretty weak substitute for the days when we roamed free on the open prairie and the buffalo numbered in the millions. Someone once said that courage is grace under pressure. I think Indians would add to that, "and a sense of humor." Even when they were being destroyed on the Plains, Indians didn't sit around crying about it all the time. Not even Sitting Bull, who I think is everybody's idea of the poker-faced Indian who never changes expression. When he was touring the country posing for pictures with Buffalo Bill he finally grew a little tired of his act. Just before quitting and returning to his native lands to live in a log cabin, he disappeared into his hotel room one day armed with paint brush and war paints. He created a giant mural showing Buffalo Bill's true colors for a change. Had Bill sneaking up behind Indians and shooting them, standing knee-deep in fresh buffalo shit, squatting and crapping. The humor was mixed with bitterness, of course. Sitting Bull had missed his calling as a satirist. When Sitting Bull was portrayed by Chief Thunder Bird in *Annie Get Your Gun*, he went back to being the same old stereotype. The hotel painting scene was written into the script, but Hawks said no go. He wouldn't have his hero, Buffalo Bill, treated in such an inglorious manner. The scene was rewritten to show Sitting Bull shooting out all the lights in the hotel with his six-shooters.

When Sitting Bull was dragged out of his cabin in Montana by reservation police, the shooting that ensued killed him, his son Little Crow, and wounded his adopted son, John. As a result of his injuries, John retained a slight hump back and was mute the rest of his life. He relished showmanship, though, and toured with Tim McCoy and me in some of our Wild West shows. (Tim McCoy, incidentally, never condescended to the Indians like Buffalo Bill. He always treated them with utmost respect and never had them doing anything silly or disrespectful.) John visited with Birdie and me on many occasions in the fifties and sixties and joined in a Uwipi ceremony with some other Sioux friends and myself right here in my museum. He lived well up into his nineties. Often, after dinner with us, he would light up one cigar after another, and just sit and dream about things. I didn't attempt to talk with him in signs much. Too much communication wore him out. Unfortunately, cigar smoke makes Birdie sick so, famous son or not, she shooed him out in the backyard, where he would sit on the grass in perfect contentment, smoking without fouling up the air of our house.

One day I brought him his father's buffalo horn headdress. I placed it in front of him on the grass and spoke in signs.

"John, do you know what this is?"

"Looks to me like a headdress."

"Yes. It is the headdress of your father, the headdress he wore at the Greasy Grass before his victory over Long Hair."

John pondered this a minute. He picked up the headdress, placed it on his head, and took a few puffs on his cigar. Then he took it off and carefully handed it back.

"It seems heavy on my head. Maybe it's too early. I think it might be lighter in the Happy Hunting Ground. See to it."

Less than a year later, John Sitting Bull died. The Sioux had arranged a modest funeral for him, as befitting a distinguished man who, nevertheless, wasn't chief. The traditional burial scaffolding, allowing the body's spirit to journey to the Happy Hunting Ground, had been abandoned in favor of a coffin in the ground. Too great a chance for vandalism, I suppose. The Sioux are not a rich tribe like the Navaho, and John Sitting Bull's coffin was pine, humbly crafted by hand on the reservation. And while it was a nice enough coffin, it wasn't designed wide enough to accommodate the horns on that headdress! We ended up having to take the horns off and place them alongside his face. Right there at the funeral, all the Indians laughed and laughed at this. A good joke, one I'm sure John would have appreciated. Then the Great Spirit Prayer was recited.

Oh Great Spirit whose voice in the winds I hear,
And whose breath gives life to all the world,
Hear me.
Before you I come, one of Your many children.
Small and weak am I.
Your strength and wisdom I need.
Make me walk in beauty.
Make my heart respect all You have made,
My ears to hear Your voice.
Make me wise that I may know all You have
*   taught my people,*
The lessons You have hidden in every rock.
I seek strength, not to be superior to my brother.
Make me able to fight my greatest enemy—myself.
Make me ready to stand before You with clean
*   and straight eyes.*
When life fades, as the fading sunset, may our
*   spirits stand before You without shame.*

One day in the spring of 1969, I got a call from a New York stage director who had been brought out here by Fox to direct a couple movies for them. He did such a good job they made him one of their top men. His name is Elliot Silverstein.

"Iron Eyes, we're planning a project about Indians. It's going to be authentic, based on a book by a guy up in Canada who actually lived with the Sioux and went through the sun dance ceremony. I saw you in the Disney movie, *Westward Ho the Wagons*, and a few other things, Iron Eyes. I like your work. You know Richard Harris?"

"I know who he is."

"Well, I've got him pegged as the principal character and you featured as the medicine man. It's gonna be called *A Man Called Horse*. Interested?"

"I'm interested. But when you say 'authentic,' it has to be just that, Elliot. I want to exercise authority over all aspects of the film dealing with Indians."

"Don't worry, I've got a good script writer on it now, your friend Jack DeWitt. Just get together with him and help out with all the Indian elements—most of the picture, really. And that thing you do, you know, when the medicine man dances around the fire and it goes *boom*. Will you do that?"

He was referring to some movie I did where I threw an incendiary in the fire for a minor explosion to give it that extra spooky, Merlin-the-magician touch.

"No *boom* this time, Elliot. Those days are gone. A little smoke maybe, from green grass, tree sap, and tobacco mixed together. But Indians didn't have explosives."

"Okay, so we do without the boom."

So, I was off to Mexico again. It wasn't with Cherabusco—that I'd have refused to do—but near Durango, where Duke Wayne did a lot of his pictures. We all had our own rented houses down there for eighty dollars a month, including a full-time maid. The maids, who were young and pretty, offered to sleep with you for a few pesos more. All very businesslike to these girls, I gathered. Just part of a day's cleaning house. Joining me for this trip were 150 Sioux men to play the warriors, and 150 women and children. We also hired Mexican Indians. A seventy-five-year-old artist named

Leonard Crow Dog was hired to paint the sides of the tepees. Right away there was trouble. Our producer, Sandy Howard, wanted them "colorful," but the real thing was just an outline of symbolic figures—the sun, moon, man, and so on. Nothing fancy. I sided with Leonard, and we settled on a compromise. A little dash of color was used for the film to pick up. Leonard didn't like it, though, and went out on a drinking binge. He wound up in some Mexican jail, and I had to go and bail him out.

Richard Harris is not only one of the best actors I've ever worked with, he's also a genuine tough guy. Nobody messes with him, and I was happy to learn he wanted an authentic picture as much as I. I spent three weeks hammering out a script with Jack DeWitt who wrote the script for *Sitting Bull*. We decided we were going to drag Richard all over creation and, for a grand finale, hang him up for the ritualized self-torture of the Sun Dance. Richard was delighted. And since we were away from the spying eye of union officials, he could do most of his own stunting. This, we knew, wouldn't sit well with our energetic, aggressive producer. Sandy's temperament was a carbon copy of Richard's. And we for sure had to avoid all the reporters snooping around. We decided to work out the logistics of the Sun Dance in secret.

After a few weeks, we had it. And everybody on the picture wanted to know what we were going to do. Finally, Sandy called the two of us before him, like Caesar summoning his top generals before a campaign.

"Okay, you two, I'm the producer of this movie, right?"

"Right," said Richard. He turned to me. "He's the producer."

"I wanna know how you're gonna be hung up, Richard. What the hell have you and Iron Eyes been up to for two weeks? You won't talk to me. The director won't talk to me. This is the most important scene of the picture and I wanna make sure it's done right."

"So do we," said Richard. "That's why I'm not telling you anything. You've got crazy notions about authenticity, Sandy. Iron Eyes has some good ideas how to do it, so we're going our way with this thing. And what's more, I don't want anybody snooping around." He raised that great voice of his and addressed everybody. "The first man who does will have to deal with me personally."

What we had done was locked ourselves up in one of the airplane

[263]

hangars near Durango where Richard kept his private plane. Perfect for hanging people up on hooks. If you didn't see the movie, the Sun Dance ceremony is a sacrificial rite calling upon the participants to be pierced and bled, then—often but not always—hung up by hooks under the muscles of the chest till the tissue breaks. It is, obviously, as much a display of extreme physical courage as a sacrificial offering to the spirit residing in the sun. If still conscious, the participant gazes directly into the sun and dances till he collapses in a trance-like state. Now in communion with the Great Spirit, he has visions and premonitions. Any tribal leader making claim to greatness must periodically go through this ceremony. It's still practiced by the Sioux today but only the skin is attached to the hooks now, not the muscles.

Richard Harris, wishing to gain favor with the Sioux chiefs, does the Sun Dance in *A Man Called Horse* stripped to the breechcloth, of course. There he was in our private dress rehearsal, hanging by hooks sunk deep into his chest and wired to an airplane hoist. The only people on the set who knew about it were those who helped us, the prop man, the wardrobe chief, and the special effects man sworn to secrecy lest they get a punch in the nose from Richard.

Somehow Sandy had found out where we were and gotten a key to the hangar. He appeared in the doorway just as I was about to swing Richard around and around, like we'd do later in the film.

"Oh my God. What have you done to him!"

"Sandy," roared Richard. "Get your face out of here or I'll kick your ass all over Mexico!"

"Okay, Richard. Okay, okay. Just . . . don't fall and hurt yourself. I'm going. I can see you're all right."

I don't think I've ever seen anybody as mad as Richard was. Our secret was out. It was a good thing he was still hanging or he'd have killed Sandy, who made a prompt exit.

"Iron Eyes, get me down out of this contraption. My nuts are killing me! Goddamn that Sandy!"

The "contraption" was a bicycle seat. Traditionally, the Hollywood way of suspending people in air has meant using wires and a harness. Either that or trick photography, which was the choice of Elliot Silverstein. A harness wrapped around the torso would be obviously visible on a man not wearing a shirt. So we came up with the bicycle seat idea, a very small one with wires running up through fake skin to where the hooks were "dug in" to the chest, where the wires popped through. Even with extra padding, that little saddle was mighty hard on the groin. Incidentally, Richard also subjected himself to having all his body hair shaved off for this stunt. Our plan was not to let anybody know about the bicycle seat, even through the shooting. Now that Sandy knew, the element of surprise was lost, and for Richard, that was everything.

"That's it, that's it," he roared, pacing the floor of the hangar like an angry lion after I'd let him down. "Goddamn him, how did he get in here? Wrap it up, that's it for today!"

I thought for sure Richard would go out on a drunk and start a fight with somebody. And he can get pretty mean when he's tanked up. But, as anybody who knows him will tell you, he's subject to great mood swings within the space of a few seconds. After throwing everybody out of the hangar, he looked at me and said, almost sweetly, "Iron Eyes, let's take some Mexican kids to the movies."

"Mexican kids . . . to the movies. Okay, why not?"

We gathered up about thirty kids off the set and in the neighborhood near the cinema in Durango, and with their eyes gleaming in excitement, not believing their good fortune, we took them all to the movies. The admission was a dollar, the theater one of these fifty-seater jobs with a six-foot screen and the plaster falling off the walls. We both put our feet up on the seats in front of us, and with the kids giggling and poking each other, Richard sulked while I fought a losing battle to stay awake. You'll recall I can't keep from sleeping in movies. Finally Richard nudged me awake.

"I feel like a drink."

I thought, uh oh, this is it. But he got up and returned with a Coke. Richard had sworn off booze for this picture, and he was keeping to his word, so far. Unfortunately, the Coke seemed to be having the same effect booze might and he was slipping into one of his moods, staring blankly at the the screen.

"I'm a sissy," he finally snorted, out of the blue.

"Hey, whaddya talkin' about," I said groggily, shaking off sleep. "You're a tough guy. Like Bogart."

"If I was half a man, I'd go out and get drunk, go and wake up that Sandy, drag him out of bed, and choke him a few times."

"Fine. Jus s'long as you don't hurt him."

Fortunately, Richard contented himself with grumbling for a

while and sipping the Coke. Then he settled down and watched the rest of the movie peacefully while I snored away.

The time for filming the Sun Dance "hanging" scene approached. The cameras rolled, and the symbolic enemy, a forked cottonwood tree, was struck with coup sticks by the tribe's bravest warriors. Young virgin girls helped chop the tree down, and it was carried on a set of poles into the encampment by the men. The now sacred tree was painted red on the west side, blue on the north, green on the east, and yellow on the south, and replanted in the middle of the camp. Offerings of tobacco and buffalo hide were placed atop the tree, whose outermost branches had been trimmed. Cut. Then, Richard was led in and, I thought, with much dignity he climbed onto his bicycle seat and solemnly gave the signal to the prop man to hoist away. The cameras rolled again. In this sequence, I was to dig eagle claws into his flesh in preparation for placing hooks under the chest muscles for hanging him. As I approached, Richard whispered, "Scratch me." I hesitated. "Go ahead," he hissed, "I want you to actually draw some blood."

So I did, just caught him enough with those talons to make the blood flow a little.

"*Cut!*"

Elliot Silverstein walked up to us. He looked shocked.

"What did you do, Iron Eyes? I told you just to fake it. You've *cut* him. Just look at that blood. When he gets out of that fake skin, he'll have an infection."

"For God's sake, man," cried Richard. "It's just a *scratch!*"

"I don't care, Richard. We're not taking any chances. Take him down, Iron Eyes."

We waited three days for that scratch of Richard's to heal, in the meantime dragging the poor man through the dirt again for some other scenes. The reasoning of moviemaking sometimes escapes me. Finally, after the scratch was completely closed, we strung him up again. And, incidentally, this isn't just a few inches off the ground. He was up there seven feet. Elliot gave me his directions.

"Now, Iron Eyes, when you get through going round and round him with the other Indians, singing that song, you approach Richard slowly, slowly. You have wisdom and dignity in your eyes. You put the eagle claws into him slowly—but into the *fake* skin, this time—and I'll get a nice closeup. Then you pull 'em out and put that skewer in under his chest 'muscles.' Okay? Ready . . . Action!"

We went through the dance, I skewered him in the appropriate fashion, and up he went, all the while the drums beating louder, faster, the singing growing more frenzied. Up, up, then I spun him around a few times.

"Let me down! It hurts! Let me down!"

Richard was supposed to be yelling and showing great pain. Other sounds were to be mixed in later, with his "vision" superimposed over the image of him hanging there.

"It's all right," I yelled above the drums and singing to the Indians pulling the wire. "Keep pulling, that's it."

"Please, it hurts, it hurts!"

Then, *pong!* One of the wires broke. I lunged in and tried to catch Richard, but missed by inches. He hit the hard ground, bicycle seat, wires, and all. Elliot Silverstein was furious because I had tried to intervene and stepped in front of the cameras.

"Iron Eyes, you've ruined a good shot!"

Richard was lying still.

"Richard?" I said, slapping his cheeks. "Richard, you okay? Get the doc, somebody get the doc. He's knocked out."

I grabbed him under those massive shoulders of his and picked him up. Then Sandy shoved his knee into Richard's back—I guess to help bring him around.

"Oh-h-h-h-h."

"How you doing there, old boy?"

"Iron Eyes, get your damn knee out of my back!"

He was okay.

"It's not my knee. It's Sandy's. He's here to help you."

"Hi, Sandy," he said quietly.

"How do you feel, Richard?"

"Fine. It's just my nuts. They're killing me."

17

WE WERE BACK in Hollywood doing some interiors for *A Man Called Horse* when one day a photographer showed up on the set. He said he was from a big ad agency in New York and asked if he could take some pictures of me while I worked. Wanted to show them to his boss.

"We're doing an ad campaign for the environment," he explained. "You'd be perfect for it in that outfit."

"That right? I'm very busy these days. Take your pictures, but I can't promise you anything."

After photographing me he pulled out some sketches, preliminary ideas for the ad. One of them showed an Indian in a small canoe in what looked like the middle of an ocean.

"What's that?

"That's you, if you agree to do the ad."

"Like hell it's me. If you folks had done your homework you'd have known I can't swim."

"Oh? Well . . . what shall I say back in New York?"

"Tell them I know plenty of Indian actors who'd more than welcome the chance to be in a campaign like this."

"Yeah, but—"

"You'll have to excuse me now. I've gotta get back to work. Let me know how you make out."

I didn't hear from this guy for almost a year. After we finished with *Horse,* I was off for Spain to do *El Condor* with Jim Brown and Lee Van Cleef. When I got back, I started a comedy called *Cockeyed Cowboy from Calico County* with Mickey Rooney, Dan Blocker, and a whole bunch of oldtimers. The ad agency man stopped by the set again. He said his people would settle on no one but me for the ad campaign since *A Man Called Horse* had just been released.

"Will you please just stop by Columbia studios and have a chat with the director, Elliot Charles? I think they're in a mood to give you anything you need to make it safe for you. It's going to be a fine ad, Iron Eyes, our environment is going all to hell. What do you say?"

What *could* I say? You have to understand that whenever you attain any kind of celebrity—however humble, like me—you're going to have people constantly asking for favors. Friends, charitable organizations, hospitals, schools, you name it. I could spend the rest of my life doing nothing but benefit projects, which isn't a bad idea only it doesn't pay the rent. And I already spent every spare minute I had with Indian causes. I always wanted to do something for conservationists, though, and it was explained the ad had something to do with an organization called Keep America Beautiful, Inc. that Lady Bird Johnson was involved with. The Johnsons were both good friends of mine and I'd already appeared on local TV in Texas for a few cleanup campaigns Mrs. Johnson had started. I agreed to see the director at Columbia.

Elliot Charles is a nice looking man with a long, flowing black beard and long hair. He looks, in fact, exactly like my notion of Jesus Christ. I immediately agreed to do the ad. You have to trust a man who looks like that.

"What can we do to make you feel comfortable in the water with that canoe, Iron Eyes?"

"Simple. Get a helicopter and have it hover overhead while we're shooting. Just in case I tip over."

We began filming in the San Francisco Bay, where I spent hours canoeing among the ships and along the shoreline. Six days later, we had the "crying Indian" public service message in the can. The tear you see trickling down my cheek in the end—in response to the defiling of our sacred land—was at first my own. I can cry for the cameras, and help it along with an old trick: looking directly at the sun for a few seconds. But studying the dailies, we thought it wasn't strong enough. My expression looked a little more like I'd been on an all-night binge than deep concern for the environment. We spent an entire day reshooting the tear scene, with me both crying naturally and using a drop of eyewash. Thanks largely to Elliot's directing and editing genius the final result was better than anybody expected. In fact, some people who had been working on the project were moved to tears just reviewing the edited version. It was apparent we had something of a sixty-second work of art on our hands.

The effect it had on the public was amazing, overwhelming. In its second year of worldwide distribution, it tallied up some $30 million in donated air time—something of a record. (Smokey the Bear came in a close second.) I like to believe it made a significant contribution to the environmental awareness of the seventies, going far beyond the original idea of involving people in "beautification." I also became an instant "facial" celebrity. If only the movie buffs knew me before—and Western movie buffs at that— everybody now knew the face with the tear for the environment. Everywhere I went, throughout the United States, Germany, France, Japan, it was always the same: people swarming over me, asking for my autograph, touching my beads. It certainly is funny how things work out. Here I'd struggled in the movie business all my life, trying to carve out a name for myself, and just as I get into the big time with major roles I become recognized as the Indian who cries in a TV ad. The Great Spirit moves in mysterious ways.

I also got tons of fan mail, literally hundreds of letters daily. One day I was flipping through this pile with Birdie when she picked up one and said, "This is from the mayor."

"Oh, yeah? He must want something."

She read it out loud. It said the Emperor of Japan was visiting the United States on such and such date, requesting my presence for a formal reception, and so on. Joining us would be John Wayne, Charlton Heston, and Peter Falk.

Actually I thought this was some kind of joke, as Mayor Bradley is a good friend of mine and not averse to a good laugh. I called up Duke, who was recovering from his second bout with cancer on his ranch in northern Arizona. He thought it was a joke, too.

"What the hell does the Emperor of Japan want with four bum actors like us," he grumbled. We checked with the Mayor's office. It was no joke.

I showed up at the Los Angeles Music Center first, decked out in my dress buckskins and double-trailer war bonnet. There to greet me at the door was an FBI man, my old friend from the war years. "Hello, Iron Eyes."

"Well, what the hell are you doing here?"

"Protecting the Emperor of Japan from you guys, what else?"

"You gonna search me?"

"Nah, go ahead."

That was good. They probably would have taken my camera off me. An FBI guy will know you all your life and yet not trust you with a thing like a camera.

Practically every Los Angeles city official started showing up, including some women from the library board I knew. I walked over and started chatting with them and in walked Duke.

"Where's the bar?" he bellowed. "Iron Eyes, let's have us a drink."

We were standing at the bar having a drink, and Duke noticed all the women staring at him.

"Whad're they gawkin' at, anyway? Ain't they ever seen a cowboy and Indian drink together before?"

"Listen, Duke, could you do something for me?" I pulled from my leather pouch an antique, hand-woven Indian basket that the Southwest Museum had given me to present to the Emperor. "Would you hand this basket to the Emperor while I take a picture?"

"What, do I look like the basket case here?"

"C'mon, I want the picture to send back to the museum. They'd really appreciate it."

He snatched the basket, grumbling assent. Chuck Heston then showed up with his wife. For some reason Peter Falk never made it. We all lined up to shake hands with His Highness as he entered.

Emperor Hirohito arrived with a train of official-looking Japanese, all wearing blue suits. Beside him was a Black bodyguard who must have been six-foot-six. I was the first in line, probably owing to the ceremonial nature of my garb.

"You cry man, cry man," he said, pumping my hand way up and down, up and down like a pump handle. I thought any minute my mouth would start spewing water. We exchanged polite small talk, and he said he'd seen me in "very many" movies. Then he moved on to Chuck Heston.

"Oh, you Moses. No beard now, hah hah." He shook hands with him the same way for about five minutes.

Then he got to Duke and said with a grin, "Hah, you very big cowboy!"

"That's right, your Highness," Duke said, dropping the basket in the Emperor's extended hand. "Now whadya say we just kiss."

When Duke was in his final days, I went to see him in the hospital. He was much thinner, but he was still the Duke, never giving up.

"I exercise every day, Iron, walk up and down the stairs. The docs won't let me go, so one of these days I'm gonna sneak out of this joint. Just keep walkin' when they aren't lookin'."

We talked about the old days, and all the good times we had. He was in pain, but never complained except to make a joke of it. Before I left, he took my hand and said to say hello to all our friends. I nodded, and couldn't say anything.

Soon, no one was allowed to visit him. He was getting too frail looking, and he wouldn't have his friends seeing him like that. But he fought for his life right to the end. His daughter told me later that, up to three days before he died, Duke Wayne was still struggling up and down those steps.

I kept busy through the late seventies with both TV and movies, and one day I got a call from Charlie Pierce.

Charlie's one of the few truly independent film makers in Hollywood. His new movie idea, *Grey Eagle*, was based on a Cheyenne legend about a mountain man who lived among the Human Beings (the Cheyenne, and other tribes, thought of themselves as the only true "people") in the early 19th century. Ben Johnson was playing the hero, Colter, and I was to be his Indian friend Standing Bear. We met with Charlie to discuss the script, and things went along smoothly till we got to the juicy parts.

"Okay, in this scene here, Iron Eyes, you get to sleep with a big, fat woman—"

"Whoa, wait a minute. Whaddya mean, a 'big, fat woman?' I suppose we're gonna call her a squaw, too?"

There was silence for a minute as we all contemplated that prospect.

"I don't care if it is part of the legend," I said finally. "I'm getting too old for . . . that. Suppose we leave out the fat woman and I move in with Colter. That's in the legend, too, but I notice in this version I get to live in the hut next door."

We made a slight alteration in the story, I live with Colter, and I don't have to go through any hair-plucking rituals.

Near the end of the script we came to a blank section.

"What's this?"

"That? That's secret."

"Secret? Since when is something on a movie script secret?"

"It's a surprise, I don't want any press leaks till we're ready for release."

"Yeah? What do you have me doing in it? Scalping somebody's genitals? Using bad language: an Indian, folks, for the first time on the screen saying dirty things."

"Hail," drawled Ben. "Don't worry about that. I used dirty language and got an Academy Award for it [*The Last Picture Show*]. I'll swear on the screen, but I'll be a sonavabitch if I'll appear naked."

If you didn't see the movie, I don't want you to get the idea it was X-rated. It was, in fact, relatively "clean," the sort of thing you can take your kids to and not squirm in your seat. At least today's kids. Moreover, it was as authentic as *A Man Called Horse*.

We filmed *Grey Eagle* for several months up in Montana, and when it came time for the "secret" part, Jack Elam was called in. Charlie's secret weapon was reserved for him, not me. It was the old Cheyenne "trial by ordeal," and it had never been filmed. A defendant had one end of a rope tied around his neck, the other to a stake pounded in the ground. Cheyenne warriors would form a circle, just beyond the radius created by the rope. All the participants were armed with knives, and one by one the warriors would engage the man tied to the rope. If he managed to kill a warrior before they could jump back in the circle, or before he got killed, he was innocent. If not, it was considered a strong indication of his guilt, and they bumped him off with a clean knife throw.

"All right," said Jack, "what the hell's this rope doing around my neck?"

Poor Jack patiently stood there with his neck in a noose while Charlie explained his secret. You might remember Jack Elam as a fine character actor with wandering, bug eyes who usually played the heavy. I first met him on the set of *Sitting Bull*. He was an accountant, constantly badgering W.R. Frank to give him a part. As a mountain man friend of Colter in this picture, he was a good guy for a change, a character much closer to his actual personality. You'll never meet a more cooperative and professional performer than Jack. He wasn't any youngster now, but he was going to do this rope scene and do it right.

"Now let's see how this feels on you, Jack," said Charlie. He grabbed the rope in the middle and yanked him down. I thought he'd broken his neck. "How's the neck? Burn you?"

"Yeah," mumbled Jack, getting himself up slowly. "I'd better wear a high collar."

"Now here's my secret, fellas," Charlie went on. "Jack, see that sapling over there? We'll attach the rope to it, and you're gonna run like hell. It'll bend, see. Won't hurt you, and we'll have a hellava scene where you jump at the Indians and are held back by the rope."

Jack did exactly as he was told. He ran, the "sapling" stood rigid like an oak tree, he went flying into the air and flopped in the dust. That time I think it *did* break his neck.

"Oh my *God!*" he moaned, lying on his back.

"See?" cried Charlie, excitedly. "Didn't hurt a bit, right? That was *beautiful!*"

Just as we finished up the location shooting for *Grey Eagle*, I received notification of being honored by the state of Nebraska for humanitarian services. A whole week of wining and dining was planned in North Platte, with the governor presiding. The award has something to do with Buffalo Bill, who as you may have gathered isn't exactly my favorite American hero, but what the hell. I was in need of a vacation, and I really do enjoy these home-spun activities away from Hollywood. Birdie and I flew out there and settled ourselves into a Holiday Inn, probably the same place that Tim McCoy, Chuck Heston, and Ben Johnson stayed when they received the same award.

I didn't notice anything wrong on the flight out, or through the week, but at the final dinner banquet Birdie didn't look good at all.

She also didn't eat anything. I put my hand on her knee and spoke to her gently.

"What's the matter, Birdie? You look pale. And you haven't touched your food?"

"It's nothing. Probably just the pork rinds we had for breakfast with the ladies' auxiliary."

"Sure?"

"Of course," she said, unconvincingly. "Stop making a fuss."

That night back in the hotel room Birdie looked worse. She even seemed to be having trouble breathing.

"That does it, I'm calling the doctor."

"*No!* No doctors. Just take me home, Iron Eyes. It's my . . . gall bladder. I'll be all right if we're home."

"*Gall* bladder? Since when do you have gall bladder problems, Birdie? You're seeing a doctor first thing."

When we arrived home I hustled Birdie into bed. She still refused to see a doctor, so I called mine on the sly. He came over immediately.

"There's nothing *wrong* with me. This is ridiculous, doctor, you've wasted a trip."

"Suppose you let me be the judge of that, Birdie," he said gently, taking her pulse. "Okay, now let's just open up here a bit. . . . Birdie, just open your blouse up, please."

She clung to the top of her dress.

"Tell Iron Eyes he has to leave the room."

The doctor gave me a "what now?" look.

"It's all right," I said, closing the door. "I'm used to this."

Ten minutes later he emerged and broke the news. While I was away, Birdie had suffered a massive heart attack. She had to be taken to the hospital immediately. He would come along and see we got admitted okay.

"So, what are we waiting for?"

"She's getting ready. Said she wants to look her best. Frankly, Iron Eyes, it's a miracle she's alive, and here she is putting on a party dress."

We finally got Birdie admitted at the Hollywood Presbyterian Hospital for a series of tests. I stayed with her till visiting hours were over, then went home and got on the phone to Germany. I knew a heart specialist there who was supposed to be one of the best in the world and I offered him $10,000 if he'd fly over and have a look at Birdie. He agreed to come for nothing.

"Just get me a decent hotel room," he said.

My German friend worked with the other doctors at the hospital and came up with the same prognosis. Birdie had at best six months to live unless she had immediate open heart surgery. I guess I expected it, but Birdie refused to go under the knife.

"Six months? That's not so bad," she said in that matter-of-fact way of hers. She straightened her shoulders like a soldier as she sat up in bed. "I don't need that much time."

"Birdie, what are you talking about? The doctors said if the operation is successful you could live a normal life for years."

"Doctors!" she scoffed. "What do they know? If the operation isn't successful, then what? I refuse to die on an operating table, all cut up like that."

"But, Birdie—"

"Now, now. Don't argue, I've made up my mind. I want to go home, Iron Eyes." I knew it was no use arguing.

"Birdie, how long have you known your heart is bad?"

"Oh, not too long."

"You've known for years, haven't you?"

"Nonsense," she said, but didn't look me in the eye.

Birdie lost weight rapidly at home. I looked after her every spare moment I had—in fact, I was only at the studio a few hours a day. But after two months it became apparent she needed hospitalization. I got her one of the private "chalets" the hospital provides for convalescents—only after promising she could wear her grandmother's dress and beads.

"I'm not going out wearing one of those silly gowns," she said, her voice still strong when she insisted on something.

When she was readmitted, the doctors gave her a week to live. Two weeks, three, a month passed. I stayed by her every day and on into the night, only going home to sleep. Then one evening as I watched her rest peacefully, she said my name without opening her eyes.

"I'm here, Birdie."

"Give me your hand."

I did, and she smiled slightly. Her eyes were still shut.

"You know, all the years we've been together you've never told me you loved me?"

"I've been a fool, Birdie. I do love you. It's just . . . difficult for me."

"I know. And you've been a good husband—off and on. Who's going to look after you now?" she said, sighing.

"You will, Birdie. Always."

"My secretary, Sandy Redhawk. You know her?"

"Sure."

"She's a good woman, Iron Eyes. And she's warm, too, not like me."

"Birdie, please, not now."

"Promise me you'll give her a chance. I'll feel better knowing—"

"Birdie, it's you I want."

"You'll need looking after, Iron Eyes. *Promise* me you'll talk to her."

"Sure. Anything."

"Run along, now, Iron Eyes. You wear me out."

I kissed her on the forehead.

"What time are you coming tomorrow," she said, through her sleep.

"Same as always, Birdie. Eight in the morning."

"Good . . ."

And I left her. In the middle of the night I got a call from the hospital. I didn't know the voice. It said Birdie had passed away at four A.M.

I could not think of anything but going to work the next day. I was numb, and nothing had sunk in yet. Birdie's loss was so great for me—only now did I realize what a treasure she was. How I relied on her strength! But something in my mind, something protecting it, kept me from feeling anything. We were doing some additional studio interiors for *Grey Eagle* and nobody knew what had happened, but I couldn't remember any lines. Finally I gave up, went home, and started drinking. It was the only thing I could do to get through the funeral preparations, and the condolences from well-meaning friends and, when the word got out, the endless phone calls, the press, flowers, visitors. I thought I was going nuts, and maybe I was. At the funeral, with Birdie's friends and mine, and many Hollywood people, it exploded. I wept. I ranted and cursed, saying something about Birdie not wanting anybody at her funeral, and threw everybody out except our son, Arthur. Robert was up in Oregon in a hospital with a broken leg he received in an accident. Birdie had insisted on a closed casket because her long, beautiful hair had been shorn. But at the crypt I had the caretaker open it.

"She looks so young and beautiful," said Arthur.

"Does that surprise you?"

"No, it's just that I . . . never noticed it before, how beautiful she was."

Indians have a tradition of a loved one placing an eagle feather in the hands of the dead, to guide them in the flight to the Happy Hunting Ground. I whispered goodbye to Birdie, gently lifted her fingers, and placed the feather. The casket top was shut.

I went on a drunk for a week or so, maybe longer. It all seems to slide into one soggy blur. I wore an ordinary business suit and dark glasses, and went to places where I thought nobody knew me, buying rounds of drinks for hundreds of strangers. I talked with people, mostly about Birdie. I drank all day and on into the night. Finally it got so bad I think I was driving on the wrong side of the street when I got pulled over by a motorcycle cop.

"Hey, aren't you Iron Eyes Cody?"

"So?"

"I'm sorry to hear about your wife."

"Fine. You're sorry."

"You look a little tight, Mr. Cody. Did you know you were on the wrong side of the road?"

"What road?"

"How about if I follow you home, okay?"

He put on his flashing red light, and escorted me home. That cop was a saint, I'll tell you. I could have been canned for reckless and drunken driving and probably half a dozen other charges. And what's more when he left me off all I did was load up the car with beer and pills and camping gear, and roared back out into the street. I had in mind driving up to the sacred hills in Montana and praying to the Great Spirit. Then, because I felt so loathsome and unworthy of life, so lost without Birdie, I was going to do away with myself.

I drove all day and night, seventy, eighty miles an hour. It's a wonder I didn't kill myself in an accident, saving me the trip. I was drinking beer all the time, and slept only one night in a motel. Finally, on the evening of the third day I pulled into Billings, had drinks in a bar with some Indians, then it was off into the hills. Dawn was just breaking as I pulled next to a beautiful lake edged in between the mountains. Geese were honking and making a hell of a racket, diving for fish and fighting with each other. The lake's bank gently sloped down to the edge of the water, and there a big mother goose had nested in some kind of plastic tub some campers had left. She honked in disapproval at my arrival. I stepped out of the car on wobbly legs and breathed in the icy spring air. The snow had just retreated, leaving patches of white glistening here and there. Life in the mountains was awakening from its winter sleep, everything green and fresh.

"It's a good day to die," I muttered.

I stripped off my clothes, spread my arms to the sky, and started saying the Great Spirit prayer.

Oh Great Spirit, whose v-voice in the w-w-winds I-I-I . . .

I was so cold, standing there stark naked in the forty-degree weather and so weak from the drinking and driving, I couldn't continue. I decided to run around the lake to get the blood flowing, get my body accustomed to the temperature. That accomplished, I faced the heavens again and said the Great Spirit Prayer. I prayed and prayed, begging forgiveness, to cleanse my life, to make me worthy to join Birdie in the hereafter. When I started getting cold again, I sat down in the grass, took a handful of sleeping pills, and swallowed them. I lay back and waited. But pills don't work instantly, and the cold started making me shake and convulse. I got up, spread out my sleeping bag, and, leaving the zipper open, climbed into it. I drank a couple of beers. Finally, I dozed off into deep, numb sleep.

Tall, dark figures with knives were standing around me, wailing like sirens. They stabbed at my face, arms, and chest. I screamed and struck back, but my arms were bound. I heard a voice and saw a bright point of light, but couldn't move. Shouts echoed in my brain, like I was in a deep, dark cave. This must be it, I remember thinking dimly. I've made it to the beyond. But it wasn't very interesting. Where's all the game and the endless herds of buffalo? I felt strong hands under my arms. A great light was in my eyes, more voices. I was being dragged, then coverd up with something that I couldn't feel because my body was detached.

I knew that something was wrong, though, that I probably wasn't dead. I couldn't make out what was going on, but I was alive, that much I knew. Then everything was dark and quiet again. I still couldn't move. Some time passed. Suddenly, the sound of car doors slamming, more voices, points of light. Oh, they were flashlights, I could make that out through one eye. The other was swollen shut for some reason. I was lifted into the back of a van and whisked away. Bump, bump, bump along a road. We stopped and I was carried into some kind of clinic. A needle was stuck in my arm. Lying on a table under the glare of lights, I came around. A doctor was examining my face, the swollen eye, my arms, my foot.

"Hello," he said, smiling. "You've had quite a time of it, you know. You're lucky you've got an eye left at all. Those mother geese can be pretty mean when they're hatching young."

"Geese?"

It was explained I had rolled down the slope after falling asleep and landed on the nest of that goddamned mother goose! As I lay half in, half out of the icy lake, she pecked at my eyes and face for about two hours till a ranger heard my yelling and dragged me out. This was the same ranger who was peering over the doctor's shoulder, together with two assistants, while I was worked over and rubbed with a greasy disinfectant. Then I was put into some kind of plastic tent—why or what, I didn't bother to ask—and fell asleep. It was nine in the evening when I'd been rescued. I'd been knocked out for over thirteen hours.

When I woke it was early morning. The swelling around my face had gone down some but my foot was killing me. One of the assistants said they were getting ready to take me to a hospital, that my foot had frozen and "three or four toes might have to come off."

It may have been a good day to die, but the weather didn't seem too favorable at all for having my toes lopped off! I decided at that instant to live. The Great Spirit was giving me a chance to redeem myself.

"Three or four toes, you say?"

I swung off my cot, tied the hospital gown around me, and, right there in the clinic, started war dancing. I did some fast stepping, just like when I was a kid in Oklahoma, and was glad to see I hadn't lost my touch over the decades. I whooped and yelled and danced for twenty, thirty minutes or so. The staff stood there, watching, their mouths agape. I stomped my bad foot on the floor every third beat or so, stomped it and stomped it, and soon I could feel it tingle with more than a dull, frozen ache. Life was coming back to my toes!

Later, I was taken back to my car after another examination by the doc, who said it "was a miracle those toes were still working." I dressed and began the long drive back to Hollywood.

Beginning a new life after living through a personal catastrophe is no easy matter, as anybody who has gone through that kind of hell will tell you. If I might offer some advice: Keep your mind off yourself and do things for other people. It worked for me.

For years, Paul McWilliams and I had been visiting disabled children in hospitals. I've never found anything more moving and heartening for me than getting a smile out of these brave little people. While some are terribly disfigured, missing facial features or arms and legs, their reaction of pure joy sure can't be mistaken. Paul, who has a handicapped child himself, and who's as rough and tough a stunt man and double as any of them, has tears just rolling down his cheeks when we visit these kids. I always come decked out in my finest Indian regalia, and they reach out for me, often with stainless steel hooks for arms, wanting only to be hugged a little. And, boy, we give it to them. You can spend the whole day just going around hugging these love-starved children, turn around and make the rounds again and not have enough for them. When I got back from my trip to the mountains and decided to give life another chance, I stepped up my visits to the kids. Paul and I teamed up with Henry Winkler, the "Fonz" from "Happy Days," another man who really loves kids. Lots of energy, that Fonz has.

[281]

He also has enough love to brighten the lives of a thousand crippled children.

Most of these kids recognize me as the Indian who sheds a tear in the ad for the environment. Even when they can't talk, they'll gesture their greeting by pretending to cry or running their fingers along their cheeks. One day a little boy who couldn't speak greeted me by pretending to grab his hair, as though protecting himself from a scalping. It was especially poignant because the poor kid was completely bald from some cancer drug therapy. Here he was, unable to talk and living in half a body, but he'd watched enough television to believe that the first thing Indians do when they meet you is pull out the scalping knife.

For a long time after Birdie's death I didn't make any movies at all. I quit my agent for a while. For the last ten years or so I hadn't appeared in any movies which showed scalping in excess, or gratuitous violence or sex. But now that wasn't enough; I was through with the damned business altogether. I spent my time among fifteen Indian reservations, giving talks on the importance of unity and the dangers of alcoholism. I put together fund-raising shows with other entertainers and hit up some of my business friends for money to spend on education and housing. I sold posters and lithographs and donated the proceeds to the children of an Assidon Sioux reservation in Montana called the Hope Ranch. Once we loaded up twenty airplanes with wheelchairs and medical supplies and flew all around the country donating these goods to needy reservation folks. I became involved (and still am involved) with the Don Drowty Youth Foundation, which also helps the Indians on reservations.

I'm not trying to sound like a saint, mind you. I had a kind of selfish motive, namely climbing out of my misery and loneliness by helping others.

I also changed in another major department. I swore off the ladies altogether. I just didn't give a damn about it anymore, or thought I didn't. I don't think I mentioned I've a black belt in karate. Well, I picked that up again, even though I've always considered myself lousy at it. It's a good way to work off some steam, if nothing else. Anyway, after several months of poking sandboxes with my fingers and getting flipped over people's backs I thought I was safely on my way to a life of permanent celibacy when into the gym walked a gorgeous blonde karate instructor. Her name was Mary. She started flirting with me but I held fast to my new ways. In fact I told her outright what was on my mind—or wasn't on my mind these days.

"Oh," she said, "that's fine. A lot of people aren't into sex. You certainly look like you could use a good massage, though. You're all tensed up."

"That's what I'm trying to work out here. The conventional way."

"A massage is just the thing, believe me. I'm an expert."

"Well . . . sure. Just a massage."

This karate place is a private home, incidentally, lived in by all martial arts people. She took me upstairs to what I guess was her apartment and into a room filled from wall to wall with a giant waterbed.

"Now, wait a minute. You're not gonna get me into one of those things. I get seasick very easy."

"Relax, relax, Iron Eyes. You're all uptight. Just sit down here, that's it."

To make a long story short, she managed to strip me half naked, did the same to herself, and had me stretched out on that damn piece of undulating plastic as she pounded, kneaded, and rubbed out the wrinkles in my muscles and nervous system. I must admit, it was the best massage I'd ever received. I'm also proud to say I didn't attempt to advance the situation to any other physical exercises. Not interested is all, like I said.

So there we were, lying on her water bed half naked like that when I'll be damned if her husband didn't walk in!

"Good God!" I said, starting.

"Hi there," he said, walking through to the kitchen. "Hope I didn't interrupt anything."

He rummaged around for a beer, and then left.

"See ya," he said, closing the door behind him.

I was dumbfounded. "That's your husband, you say?"

"Sure."

"Doesn't he . . . care?"

"Of course he cares. He's very understanding. We have a very close, open relationship."

So this was an example of the "new" relationships I heard so much of. Well, maybe he thought nothing was going on, as was the case.

"You're serious about not wanting to sleep with me, aren't you?"

"That's right. Serious."

"That's cool. I respect that."

"Great. I respect you, too."

"I'd like you to meet a friend of mine I think you'll like."

"Yeah? Does she give massages like you?"

"She's a beautiful Apache girl and a karate black belt, too. Her name's Sandy Redhawk. If you'd like to stick around a while, she'll be showing up here."

Actually I didn't place the name at first and didn't realize this was the same Sandy who had worked for Birdie on occasion as a secretary. Never really paid Sandy any mind before (for one thing, she's only 23) and couldn't understand why Birdie was intent on my meeting her when she knew she was dying. I went downstairs to work on my karate for a while and Sandy showed up. I'm not going to give you any "love at first sight" corn, but something did hit me about her. Not in a physical way, but . . .

"I do know you," I said, introducing myself.

"Yes, I worked for your wife, Birdie. She was a fine woman."

"She was, indeed. Never met another like her."

We talked, and she told me of the work she did for the police department in helping delinquent kids. She loved children, she said. She also did reservation work. Reservation work, I asked? Maybe you'd like to come along with me sometime. I've been doing a lot of reservation work these days.

And that's how Sandy and I got together. After we visited a Navaho reservation, we knew we had our work cut out for us, so to speak. Everything seemed to fit right, and she said matter-of-factly, "I'm gonna be your girl. Nobody else, right?"

I also got back into movies, but strictly on my own terms. I've had to turn down many a picture I thought wasn't fair to the Indians, or which was too bloody. *Hanta Yo* is one of them. There's some stuff in that book—and the proposed movie script—that is pure nonsense, begging the pardon of all those who think otherwise. Indian women never ate their own placenta, for one thing.

[284]

With Sandy beside me, I feel I'm the luckiest guy in town. Don't deserve anywhere near what I've been blessed with in my life. And I know when I enter the next one, she'll be there to guide me on my way with an eagle feather in my hand.

INDEX